Beautiful Balts

JAYNE PERSIAN is a historian of modern Australia and has a PhD in history from the University of Sydney. Jayne is currently a lecturer in history at the University of Southern Queensland, Toowoomba.

Beautiful Balts

From Displaced Persons to New Australians

JAYNE PERSIAN

NEWSOUTH

A NewSouth book

Published by
NewSouth Publishing
University of New South Wales Press Ltd
University of New South Wales
Sydney NSW 2052
AUSTRALIA
newsouthpublishing.com

© Jayne Persian 2017
First published 2017

10 9 8 7 6 5 4 3 2 1

This book is copyright. Apart from any fair dealing for the purpose of private study, research, criticism or review, as permitted under the *Copyright Act*, no part of this book may be reproduced by any process without written permission. Inquiries should be addressed to the publisher.

National Library of Australia
Cataloguing-in-Publication entry
Creator: Persian, Jayne, author.
Title: Beautiful Balts: From Displaced Persons to New Australians / Jayne Persian.
ISBN: 9781742234854 (paperback)
        9781742242507 (ebook)
        9781742247922 (ePDF)
Notes: Includes index.
Subjects: Immigrants – Australia – History.
 Refugees – Australia – History.
 Reconstruction (1939–1951) – Australia.
 Europeans – Australia – History.

Design Josephine Pajor-Markus
Cover image Kanimbla arrives at Melbourne with the first group of Displaced Persons (December 1947), from where they joined a train bound for Bonegilla Migrant Camp. National Archives of Australia A12111, 1/1947/3/6.

All reasonable efforts were made to obtain permission to use copyright material reproduced in this book, but in some cases copyright could not be traced. The author welcomes information in this regard.

Contents

Introduction 1

CHAPTER 1 Deserving victims 13
CHAPTER 2 'Chifley liked them blond' 50
CHAPTER 3 'A hot Siberia' 76
CHAPTER 4 'New Australians' 112
CHAPTER 5 Inside the Cold War 147
CONCLUSION Memory and multiculturalism 182

Notes 203
Acknowledgments 239
Index 241

In Memory

Libby Roslyn Persian

Introduction

In May 1945, the Drau Valley in Austria was host to a scene from an earlier century. In the immediate aftermath of the Second World War in Europe, 73 000 Cossacks, including several thousand women and children, camped under the stars near Lienz. They had with them about 4000 horses as well as cows and camels. A London *Times* reporter described the scene as 'no different in any major detail from what an artist might have painted in the Napoleonic wars'. The official British Army diary entry described the Cossacks as

> an amazing sight. Their basic uniform was German, but with their fur Cossack caps, their mournful whiskers, their knee-high riding boots and their roughly made horse-drawn carts bearing all their worldly goods and chattels, including wife and family, there could be no mistaking them for anything but Russians.[1]

This group of Cossacks were long-time enemies of the Soviet state. Many had volunteered to fight with the German Army after it invaded the Soviet Union. Some of them had been POWs; others were ranking general officers who saw their chance to see off the Bolsheviks. About half the Cossacks in the Drau Valley had left their homeland in late 1942 and had moved repeatedly since with the retreating German Army following Stalingrad. In the Drau Valley, émigré Cossack forces from all over Europe and 'stragglers' who sympathised with the Cossack cause joined them, including freed forced labourers from the Soviet Union. More of a roving village than a military force, this self-styled *Kazachi Stan* (Cossack nation) of refugees displaced from their homeland was, perhaps, 'the last dying echo of the Revolution'. They hoped to settle permanently in the Drau Valley. Historian Nikolai Tolstoy described their home in the Drau Valley as 'a brief and pathetic resurgence of a way of life that was soon to be destroyed forever'. The Cossacks surrendered to the British and offered to assist the Western powers against the Soviet Union, supposedly a common enemy. Some Cossacks speculated that the British planned to send them to the French Foreign Legion, or to the Middle East.[2]

On 28 May, the British took 1500 Cossack officers to a conference with Field Marshal Harold Alexander to discuss future plans, assuring them they would return to their camp that night. However, at Spittal, near the border of the newly demarcated Soviet zone, they found out that they would be handed over to Soviet authorities the next day. During the night, two officers committed suicide by hanging themselves on lavatory chains. A British Army memorandum noted that the next day the officers were dragged out in twos and threes but difficulties were considerable as they all sat on the ground with linked arms and legs. One Russian officer bit the wrist of a Company Sergeant Major. This not unnaturally caused the CSM and the British troops around him to turn to sterner measures; rifle butts, pick helves and the points of bayonets were freely used with the result that some of the Russian officers were rendered semi-conscious. This show of force had the desired effect and the loading of the remaining officers was quickly completed.

The memo also noted that 'during the journey, two of the Russian officers committed suicide, one by leaping over a precipice and one by cutting his throat'. Reportedly, the Soviets immediately took 31 of the repatriates behind a dockside warehouse and shot them with machine guns.[3]

British officers then informed the Drau Valley camp, now bereft of officers, that a pact in the Yalta Agreement committed the Allies to return all Soviet citizens. They said that British soldiers would come back to put the whole camp – men, women and children – on trains to the Soviet Union. The memo on the evacuation notes that 'the vast majority of the Cossacks were bitterly opposed to return to the Soviet Union', so 'it was considered essential that the fact that they were to be sent to the USSR should be kept from them as long as possible'.

The people, in shock at this betrayal, declared a hunger strike, and hung up black flags and placards to plead against their return. They also wrote a petition, declaring:

'WE PREFER DEATH than to be returned to the Soviet Russia, where we are condemned to a long and systematic annihilation.' The British arrived on the morning of 1 June. The Cossacks, who were holding a mass, formed a protective circle with women and children in the centre, hoping the British would show mercy. What happened next is infamous with allegations of brutality, deaths and suicides. Some people were trampled to death. According to one eyewitness: 'It looked like a battlefield.' Another described how trucks were 'loaded with corpses of men, women and children', while men shot their families before shooting themselves, women threw themselves and their children into the 'cold, raging' Drau River, and others hung themselves from nearby trees.[4]

Watching this chaotic and terrifying scene through binoculars was a small group of Cossacks that included Ivan and his young Ukrainian wife Nastasia, who was about five months' pregnant. Ivan was a Don Cossack from Rostov travelling with his uncles. He claimed the Soviets had shot his brothers in front of him and then sent him to Siberia, to gulag. He had left behind a wife and daughter in Russia.

Ivan met Nastasia in 1943, when she was working as a forced labourer under the Nazis in eastern Ukraine. Ivan was a friend of her father and much older, around 53 years to her 17, but he had offered her an escape if she would marry him and journey across Europe. They left Ukraine on 31 December 1943, travelling with the Cossack Army to Italy via Romania, Poland and Hungary. Their son, Maxim, was born in a shed in Italy during a bomb attack but he died of malnutrition at 14 weeks. From Italy, Nastasia and Ivan

Introduction

journeyed over the mountain ranges, evading Italian partisans, until they reached the apparent safety of the Cossack camp outside Lienz.

After witnessing the merciless repatriation of their camp, Ivan, Nastasia and their small group fled up the snow-covered mountains evading British patrols and surviving for three months by hiding in ravines and killing sheep at night. The British estimate that about 4000 of the original group managed to escape, and 1300 were recaptured the following month. The army memo is chilling: 'The work of the patrols was far from easy. Sometimes it was necessary to resort to bullets.'

After the initial effort, the British treated recaptured Cossacks as 'surrendered personnel' and did not hand them over to the Russians. Apparently, the Russians were satisfied with the numbers and didn't want any more. A sizeable number (perhaps 3000) sent back to the Soviets had been elderly émigrés who, according to the Yalta Agreement, should not have been repatriated. Eventually, Ivan and Nastasia were caught by Austrian police and sent to Kapfenberg displaced persons camp.[5]

Nastasia and Ivan's story is, of course, not typical. In fact, there is no 'typical' story. A displaced person, or DP, has become the generic label for someone resettled by the United Nations' International Refugee Organization (IRO) following the Second World War. In 1945, DPs were predominantly from Central and Eastern Europe and included Jewish concentration camp survivors, voluntary and forced labourers of the Reich, non-German soldiers in military units withdrawing westwards and civilian evacuees fleeing west from the oncoming Russian Army. By 1947, they were joined by refugees from Soviet-occupied countries – Jews escaping anti-Semitism in Poland and Romania, and border-hoppers, usually young, single men from Czechoslovakia and Hungary attempting to outrun the encroaching Iron Curtain. Most were anti-communist and refused to repatriate to Soviet bloc countries. They included Cossacks and other 'collaborators' who specifically feared death, or a sentence of hard labour, if they were sent back to the Soviet Union.

Initially cared for by the United Nations Relief and Rehabilitation Administration (UNRRA), the DPs who could not be repatriated soon became a 'continuing, nagging' problem for the Western Allies. They were eventually categorised by the United Nations as political (rather than economic) refugees from the Soviet system and the IRO started resettling them in any country that would take them.

In 1947, Australia joined countries such as Argentina, Canada and the United States in resettling DPs from Europe. The Australian Government, under the slogan of 'populate or perish', sought to bulk up the population and solve a postwar labour shortage. The DPs represented assimilable 'white' migrants to make up for a disappointing absence of postwar British settlers. It was Australia's first experiment with mass, non-British migration. The new Minister for Immigration, Arthur Calwell, sold the idea to the Australian public by publicising blond, attractive, middle-class Baltic migrants, who of course weren't typical either.

For their part, DPs sometimes concocted false background stories, in order to escape forced repatriation and to seem suitable for resettlement purposes. An entire underground industry grew up to provide false identity papers. So, Ivan and Nastasia's immigration documents are opaque. Middle-aged Ivan chopped some years off his age, and rather than hailing from the Don Cossack region, he claimed Rosonowka, Nastasia's Ukrainian birthplace, as his own. Nastasia, meanwhile, added seven years to her age, in order to make the pair more convincing as a married couple. Ivan told the Australian selection officers that he was an 'old Russian emigrant', stateless since 1920, who had 'escaped from Poland before the Bolsheviks' (he means the Soviet Army), since he had 'an old emigrant fear that they would abduct or imprison him'. He did not talk about fleeing west with the Cossack Army, but instead said he was a labourer in Germany in the last years of the war, and he had the documentation to prove it.[6]

Nastasia and Ivan lived in various DP camps until 1949, when they joined 170 000 other displaced persons migrating to Australia. Ivan had told the IRO that he wanted to go to Venezuela, to join his brother. An uncle, who was with them in the Drau Valley, reportedly ended up in the United Kingdom. Australian migration officials interviewed Ivan and Nastasia in April 1949. They noted that Nastasia was 16 weeks pregnant with her third child, and labelled her fit for the journey. The pair travelled to Australia on the *Anna Salen* in June 1949 with their three-year-old son who had been born in an Austrian DP camp.

In Australia they were processed at the Bathurst reception and training centre. Ivan was required to complete a two-year work contract while Nastasia was sent to Cowra and Scheyville holding camps for dependent women and children. But Ivan absconded from his work contract, leaving Nastasia to pay the holding camp accommodation charges. She was forced to work as a cleaner at the camp, while also caring for her toddler and newborn. It was a harsh introduction to her new country for the young mother.

Meanwhile, Ivan joined the National Cossack Association of Australia, established in November 1950 – his signature appears as one of the founding members. In 1953, a large group of Cossacks, with their Ataman (chief), Lieutenant-General Burlin, attended the consecration of a new Russian Orthodox Church in Cabramatta, Sydney. Cossack associations were also formed in Brisbane, Adelaide, Canberra and Melbourne. In the late 1950s, two burial plots at Melbourne's Fawkner Cemetery were donated for a memorial to those who died at Lienz, or were forcibly repatriated to the Soviet Union.[7]

Ivan later reunited with Nastasia, and they bought a house in the western suburbs of Sydney. They divorced sometime in the early 1960s due to an escalation of domestic violence. Ivan died around ten years later, in 1973. Ivan, a violent alcoholic, once confronted his eldest son with a loaded rifle. His family thought that perhaps 'what he'd suffered in Siberia had got to him and clouded him', that 'his earlier life might have caused his brain to snap'.

And this is where we leave Ivan and Nastasia. Their story highlights particularly well the disparity between the story told by the Australian Government in its pro-immigration propaganda, and the individual backgrounds, war and postwar experiences of the displaced persons themselves. The International Refugee Organization and the Australian migration selectors were not always aware of the real stories, amid the false stories and fake documents. Strategies of accommodation and resistance, of individual and collective agency, worked to transform Russian émigrés and Nazi collaborators into fit workers and New Australians. Instead of passive subjects, Ivan and Nastasia, along with other postwar DPs, traversed complex migration trajectories away from the threat of the Soviet Union and towards an indeterminate resettlement.

Ivan and Nastasia's story was the first DP story I heard. They are my husband's grandparents; their little boy is now my children's beloved 'Grumps', and ninety-one-year-old Nastasia their much loved 'Baba'. I listened to bits and pieces of her story, relayed at her seventy-sixth birthday lunch in 2001, and wondered why I had never heard of the postwar DPs before. My husband's other set of grandparents, also DPs, were from Ukraine – Theodore from the Polish west and Katherina from the Soviet east. They met as teenagers in wartime Germany while working as forced labourers on a farm and married in a rush of postwar euphoria. I listened to their stories and pored over their black and white photographs of prewar Ukraine. After spending a brief period working in a Belgian mine, Theodore, Katherina and their infant daughter made the long journey away from their homes to Australia. Both worked together on the Snowy Mountains Scheme. Neither ever saw their parents again.

As an Australian university undergraduate majoring in history, I was surprised I didn't know that 170 000 displaced persons started arriving in Australia in 1947. My knowledge of postwar immigration began with the Italians and Greeks in the 1950s. Australia's population in 1947 was 7 579 358, and by 1952 the DP cohort made up 2.24 per cent of the population. The perceived success of the scheme paved the way for further assisted migration schemes with non-British Europeans in the 1950s and led to the end of the White Australia Policy in 1973. It also helped to usher in the official policy of multiculturalism.

My interest, sparked by family history, led me to complete a doctoral thesis in 2011 that was centred on memory and commemoration and, particularly, oral history interviews. I dug out existing interviews from various repositories, both recorded and published. I interviewed displaced persons and their children who responded to an advertisement I placed in the *Sydney Morning Herald* in 2007. I also interviewed family friends and personal acquaintances.

I use twenty-two of my own interviews here: thirteen men and nine women, and these interviews encompass the stories of sixteen first-generation DPs and thirteen second generation. The latter were usually children at the end of the war, or not yet born. The (self-identified) national breakdown of the interviewees is a Belorussian–Polish (Wladimir), two Czechoslovakians (Jakub, Michael), two Estonians (Lukas, Edgar), two Hungarians (Marta and her father, Frank), a Latvian (Ralf), a Lithuanian (Julija), three Polish (Adam, Jan) including one Jew (Leo), a Polish–Ukrainian (Robert), a Russian (Kasia), and eight Ukrainians (Andriy, his wife, Nina, Bohdan, Karl, Oksana, Vera, her mother, Katherina, Nastasia, Tanya). The other people talked about in the interviews are Edgar's father, Arved, Kasia's parents, Gustav and

Introduction

Adele, Vera's father and Katherina's husband, Theodore, Nastasia's husband, Ivan (a Russian Cossack) and Tanya's Ukrainian mother, Yelena, and Estonian father, Paul. For privacy reasons, everyone I interviewed has a pseudonym, including Nastasia, Theodore and Katherina; all other details come from what they told me.

Millions of Australians who trace their families from postwar migrations are interested in the movement of their forebears, and their settlement experiences in Australia. This story also connects to contemporary Australian discussions about refugees and asylum seekers. It tells how a heterogeneous grouping of displaced persons became political refugees and then, in an effort to solve the Australian population crisis, potential workers and migrants. When they came to Australia, these same people were disparaged as 'balts' and officially described as New Australians. Concerned social scientists and social welfare groups depicted them as 'people with problems'. Many DPs thought of themselves as part of a 'diaspora' with an 'exile mission'. Most recently, DPs have been upheld as the founding group of multicultural Australia, or an example of past humanitarianism in Australia's refugee policy. All these representations are flawed.

The complex stories of displaced persons journeying from the postwar camps of Europe to a new life in Australia involve prejudice, parochialism and strident anti-communism. It's a two-sided coin with the racial, political and social contexts of the policies and practices that affected DPs on the one hand, and the distinct individual experiences of the DPs themselves on the other. Australia's first postwar intake is made up of many stories: of displacement, migration, assimilation and diaspora; of dramatic demographic change, optimism and welcome.

The book centres on DPs who arrived via the IRO scheme. Mostly from Central and Eastern Europe they were selected by Australian officials from European camps. Not all of them stayed. Many resettled in the United States and Canada for professional reasons, particularly doctors, scientists and academics, whose qualifications weren't recognised in Australia. For others with complex back stories and an ongoing attachment to their homeland, Australia was a pragmatic but unhappy option. Their diasporic thoughts and actions complicate the usual focus on emigration and immigration as a simple narration about moving from one place to another. What happens when circumstances force people to move halfway across the world?

CHAPTER 1

Deserving victims

Several human silhouettes emerge on the corner of each street. They begin to shout with joy. Then, men and women, as if responding to a signal, spring forth from all over the place. Poles, Russians, Czechs, and French as well, all welcome us in their own language, greeting us after the fashion of their homeland. We thought we were entering an enemy town, but it is Babel that receives us as liberators. This war is rich in paradoxes.

– JD Couquet, *Nous sommes les occupants*, 1945,
on the French liberation of a German town[1]

*Ten million displaced persons in Europe
are stateless, homeless, and hopeless.*

– YMCA, 1946.[2]

Ivan and Nastasia, as part of the ragtag Cossack Army, were technically British prisoners. But after evading repatriation to the Soviet Union, they were transferred to a DP camp where they transitioned to political refugees and became potential migrant settlers to countries including Australia.

Displaced persons include disparate people (and stories): Ukrainian forced labourer Katherina, was taken by the Nazis at the age of 18 to work on a German farm; Russian–Estonian merchant banker Arved who moved his young family to Germany during the war because he feared the Soviets; Hungarian lawyer-turned-soldier Frank, was part of a defeated force that surrendered in Austria; and Jewish socialist Leo, was deported from Poland into the Soviet Union during the war and fled Soviet-controlled Poland in 1947. Jan, a (non-Jewish) Pole, was taken from his middle-class family at the age of 14 to work as a 'slave labourer' in a box factory in Germany; his older brother died in Auschwitz. Jan says: 'I was stubborn, I wanted to live.' In contrast, Hungarian student Joseph chose to leave Hungary in 1945 because: 'I didn't see myself fitting into the Communist system, so I packed up and left.' He initially saw the journey as an 'adventure: the world was sort of wide open'.[3]

The term 'displaced persons' is now a generic name for everyone resettled by the International Refugee Organization after the Second World War. How did such a varied grouping – politically, culturally and socially – become, in contemporary representations, an 'anonymous mass', their individual stories erased in Cold War posturing. How did the displaced escape repatriation to become political refugees and then end up in such faraway places as Canada and Australia?[4]

Displaced persons

The term 'displaced persons' entered international parlance in 1944 via the Supreme Headquarters, Allied Expeditionary Force (SHAEF), commanded by the United States general, Dwight D Eisenhower. SHAEF sought to categorise people displaced by the war, while avoiding the term 'refugee', which could imply a permanent rather than a temporary state. So Operation Overlord, the SHAEF Plan for the Allied invasion of Western Europe, separated displaced persons from refugees. Displaced persons specifically referred to people outside their national boundaries (refugees were displaced within their country) and who were either 'desirous' but 'unable to return to their home [...] without assistance' or who were to be returned to 'enemy or ex-enemy territory'. Displaced persons included 'evacuees, war or political fugitives, political prisoners, forced or voluntary workers, Todt workers [forced labourers], and former members of forces under German command, deportees, intruded persons, extruded persons, civilian internees, ex-prisoners of war, and stateless persons'.[5]

The definition of displaced persons that emerged before the war ended predominantly related to people in Germany and Austria. They included concentration camp inmates, forced agricultural and factory workers, (non-German) soldiers in military units withdrawing westwards and civilian evacuees fleeing west from the oncoming Soviet Army. Voluntary workers and university students living in the Reich at the end of the war could also claim DP status. These disparate groups, both Jewish and non-Jewish, included Poles,

Ukrainians, Russians, Belarusians, Balts (Estonians, Latvians and Lithuanians), Hungarians, Yugoslavs, and nationals of Romania, Bulgaria and Albania. Displaced ethnic Germans outside their state borders were the only group not included in the official category of displaced persons; they were collectively excluded from the group of deserving victims.[6]

Notwithstanding the exclusion of ethnic Germans, the official numbers of displaced persons were staggering. In August 1944 there were 7.6 million foreign civilian labourers and prisoners-of-war working in Germany itself, comprising around 29 per cent of the Reich's industrial labour force and 20 per cent of its total labour force. Towards the end of the war an estimated 13.5 million foreigners worked in the German economy. At least 12 million were forced labourers; around 11 million survived the war (Germany's population in mid-1946 was around 66 million). In addition several hundred thousand foreigners had been imported into German-controlled territories and the Todt Organisation (a Third Reich civil and military engineering group) had more than a million forced labourers constructing coastal fortifications throughout Northern Europe and Southern France. In May 1945 up to 10 per cent of the 7.8 million troops wearing German uniforms were not in fact German.

In all, there were approximately 12 million displaced persons at the conclusion of the war in Europe in May 1945. Experiences were varied: survivors of death camps were counted in with so-called 'collaborators'. People who moved voluntarily to the Reich – for employment or to study at German universities – were added to forced labourers, who had been deported from their homes and subjected to grim conditions.[7] Everyone was lumped together with the expectation they would all soon return home.

The displaced were a burden on the land, and on the economy. Some DPs, particularly forced labourers from the Soviet Union, were involved in acts of retribution towards the Germans. With agriculture disrupted, these former enemies, 'angry and hungry', let loose in a landscape of destruction taking farm machinery and livestock, perhaps seeing these as 'slave severance pay'. Representations of DPs in this immediate postwar period were uniformly negative. To the Germans who, in a continuation of National Socialist racial ideology, 'couldn't be bothered to try to accurately ascertain the nationalities of DPs', they were known as *schlechte Ausländern* (bad or dirty foreigners) and 'held in the greatest contempt'. They were 'adventurers and do-nothings, who are running the black market'. To Allied military authorities, they were 'surplus population' and 'a nuisance': *kriegies* (prisoners-of-war), 'goddam DPs' and 'lousy Poles'. Jewish displaced persons (and soon all Jewish survivors were officially categorised as DPs), who made up 20 per cent of the immediate postwar refugee population, were infamously described by US General George S Patton Jr in 1945 as 'lower than animals' and 'locusts'. The Allied authorities were responsible for all of them.[8]

After SHAEF ceased functioning in July 1945, DPs came under the protection and control of American, British and French military authorities who, together with the Soviet Union, had divided Germany into four occupation zones for administrative purposes. Two international organisations were involved on the periphery. The Office of the League of Nations High Commissioner, a merged entity incorporating the Office of the High Commissioner for Refugees Coming from Germany and the Nansen International Office, provided legal protection and material aid to refugees from 1938 to 1946. The Intergovernmental Committee on Refugees, set up following the 1938 Evian Conference to assist Jewish migration from Germany and Austria, also cared for refugees after 1943. The main international body, however, was the United Nations Relief and Rehabilitation Administration (UNRRA), formed in late 1943 to prepare and arrange 'for the return of prisoners and exiles to their homes'.[9]

UNRRA was a successor of sorts to earlier refugee relief organisations, such as the American Relief Administration (1919–1923) and various offices under the auspices of the League of Nations. However, instead of relying on charitable and philanthropic bodies, it established an American-led international relief operation. In November 1943 the 44-nation signatories of UNRRA agreed not only to care for the displaced persons, but also to provide relief to war victims at the request of national governments in countries such as China, Poland and Italy that were unable to do this themselves. UNRRA would provide basic necessities, with a goal towards rehabilitation. UNRRA always operated under military jurisdiction and was largely dependent on military supplies. Their 'first and most urgent' task, however, was to organise the displaced persons. UNRRA's ideological basis for this task was to 'bind up the world's wounds' by, in the words of Frank Boudreau of the League of Nations Health Organization, 'destroy[ing] the seeds of a new war which could otherwise find fertile soil in the terrible living conditions in countries torn and devastated by the war'. UNRRA also wished to propagate an American-led 'new growth of confidence' in international administration which was seen as 'indispensable for the future system of general security'. This sort of American ideal was tempered with the experience of imperial rule, which perhaps provided a practical model to follow, particularly for French and British authorities.[10]

UNRRA's main aim regarding displaced persons was to assist repatriation. Liaison officers were appointed by national governments to expedite the repatriation of their nationals. However, UNRRA needed to provide rehabilitation and material support until the return home became possible. In effect, this meant providing all displaced persons with food and clothing rations initially sourced within Germany and supplemented by Red Cross parcels, and housing millions of the homeless displaced in around 900 (mostly nationality-specific) camps across Germany, Austria and Italy. According to a description provided by the 21 Army Group of the British Army, this 'gigantic' task involved:

> Controlling and transporting [...] men, women and children; the setting up or adaptation of camps for them; disinfestations and organisation of hygiene and sanitation measures [...] feeding, watering and clothing; checking and documentation; the provision of medical attention and supplies, the control of disease, and in the case of those who were not to be speedily repatriated, the initiation of rehabilitation, education and entertainment.[11]

DPs camps were hastily requisitioned. Often they were former concentration or forced labour camps. Julija, ten years old in 1945, had fled with her family from Lithuania, ahead of the Soviet Army, the previous year. They ended up at a German DP camp, an overflow camp from a concentration camp at nearby Lingen. She describes the barracks as 'just wood, rotten wood': 'It was just like a big narrow hall which when all the families arrived were divided into little rooms; first it used to be separated by blankets or whatever, then we built ourselves flimsy walls just to separate one from the other.' Conditions did not always improve much. Australian UNRRA worker Helen Ferber described visiting a Latvian DP camp housed in bombed-out buildings in 1947 as her 'first big DP shock':

> Herded as many as seventeen to a room (and one hundred to each latrine), they have to cook and do everything, three and four families together, on one small stove per room. Half of them have only boarded-up or papered-over windows. The partitions within the room, made of papers or threadbare old rugs strung over ropes, provide only scant privacy. In summer they suffocate; in winter they must nearly freeze. They keep their hovels spotless, but a stench of latrines and humanity hits you as you enter the door. Their rations, about 2000 calories a day, are sufficient on paper but … cheerless.

Czech novelist Vladímir Ležák-Borin described the DP camp as a 'soul-killing vacuum in the midway-to-nowhere'.[12]

Historian Daniel Cohen says the DP camp system functioned 'as an alternative welfare state for stateless people'. Displaced persons received special benefits in postwar Germany, and were placed outside German jurisdiction. Many were employed by the Allied military authorities. Everyone in the American zone received rations of American cigarettes to use as black market currency. This welfare reliance soon resulted in a new characterisation. UNRRA worker Kathryn Hulme talked about the 'professional DP ... sitting pretty under the protection of UNRRA'. Joyce Horner, a fellow UNRRA worker from New Zealand, thought that 'having worked as slave labourers for years, reaction has set in and the majority are unwilling to do anything at all'.[13]

UNRRA's motto, however, seemed to be 'helping others to help themselves', or perhaps helping others *until* they could help themselves. UNRRA was internationalist in the sense that it had support and workers from many nations. However, it believed that nation states were the fundamental units of a peaceful, postwar society. Its work was temporary and paternalistic: providing a helping hand until the displaced could return to their homelands.[14]

Displaced persons were expected to return home as quickly as they could, and most did. Many from Eastern Europe reportedly had 'great enthusiasm about going home'. The Allied military authorities repatriated about seven million people in less than six months after the end of the war, and UNRRA another million over the following 18 months. But not everyone felt the pull of home. UNRRA soon came up against DPs who felt they had nowhere to return: some who refused repatriation, citing persecution, (old and new)

Soviet citizens who refused to return to communist rule in their homeland, and all Jews, who had been classified *en masse* as stateless. Others who were initially repatriated attempted to readmit themselves back into the DP camps and were classed as uncatalogued refugees. They were no longer official DPs but 'free-livers' outside the DP camp system.[15]

Soviet non-returners

It was generally agreed that displaced persons from areas incorporated into the Soviet Union since September 1939 were to be neither repatriated nor treated as Soviet citizens 'unless they affirmatively claim Soviet citizenship'. This included displaced persons from Estonia, Latvia, Lithuania and parts of Poland and Ukraine. However, the Allies had definitively promised to assist with the return of everyone else at the 1945 Yalta Conference. This was later clarified to mean any citizen of the Soviet Union on 1 September 1939. Many Soviet citizens had no wish to return home, so Allied military authorities at times carried out forcible repatriation 'regardless of [the DP's] personal wishes'. Like the Cossacks in Drau Valley, Soviet DPs actively resisted repatriation and generally met forced repatriations with 'crying and screaming'. Hunger strikes were common, and several thousand killed themselves in protest, and in fear. An American soldier's description of the forced repatriation of Soviet displaced persons from a camp at Dachau in 1946 is haunting:

When we finally entered the huts we did not encounter human beings, but animals. Most of those who had hanged themselves were cut down by our GIs. Those who were still conscious cried in Russian, pointed at our guns and then at themselves, imploring us to shoot them.[16]

In order to escape forced repatriation, DPs concocted false background stories, and an entire underground industry grew up to provide false identity papers for 'Poles from the Urals' (that is, Soviet citizens attempting to pass as citizens of pre-1939 Poland, who were not subject to repatriation). A British officer noted the difficulties of identification and classification for Allied military authorities, and for UNRRA:

Was [the 'displaced person'] a Jugoslav? Then he might be a Serbian Chetnik who had fought against Tito, but professed undying love for England. Or he might be a Tito Partisan, captured by the Germans but now escaped and trying to make his way back to Jugoslavia. Or again he might be a member of Pavelich's infamous Ustachi, who would no doubt attempt to conceal his identity. Was he a Russian? Then he could be a runaway Cossack, or an escaped Red Army prisoner, or a Latvian who left Latvia before it became part of the Soviet Union, or a displaced Soviet citizen who just did not want to go back home.[17]

Individual entrepreneurs, priests and political groups all contributed to an underground industry for false documents for Soviet citizens in hiding. The Tolstoy Foundation, for example, set up in 1939 in New York by Alexandra Tolstaya, the youngest daughter of the Russian writer Leo Tolstoy, mediated between those who needed to obscure the truth in order to become DPs, and the International Refugee Organization. German authorities and, on occasion, sympathetic Allied officials, as well as DP employees of UNRRA and the IRO, were also involved.[18]

Historian Anne Kuhlmann-Smirnov notes that for many displaced persons who had lived in the Soviet Union, these practices were not new or unique. Under communism many had been forced to conceal their past or manipulate and reinterpret certain phases of their lives. Sheila Fitzpatrick has described the widespread creation of reliable 'file-selves' in interwar Soviet Union, a skill which continued to be important in the 'general identity chaos' of postwar Europe. This fluidity of identity was helped by the fact that Ukraine had been divided in the interwar period between Poland and the Soviet Union; Russians and Eastern Ukrainians could thus claim to be Poles and Western Ukrainians.[19]

Russian teenager Walter later recounted his family's desperate attempts to hide their Soviet origins: 'During father's stint in Siberia he changed his name and his surname and this was done to some extent to protect the families.' After the treaty with Stalin, the family ended up in a Polish camp and

> acquired a Polish life story. I had to learn things like what school I went to, which tram we used to get to school, who my friends were, where was the cinema

in that particular town, because there were interviews called screenings and that is the sort of questions that were asked and if you didn't pass the screening, well then you weren't a Pole. The fact that we couldn't speak very good Polish or very good Ukrainian didn't matter because we could always pass either for Ukrainian Poles or Polish Ukrainians … I even made myself a German life story as to where I came from and I could speak a dialect of the Rhineland so I could hide myself.[20]

Nazi collaborators were concurrently doing the same thing, or changing certain biographical details, in order to be classified as DPs. There are numerous examples. The immigration details of a Hungarian collaborator wanted for war crimes in Hungary were painstakingly reconstructed by historian Ruth Balint. Károly Zentai's original IRO documents state that he and his wife arrived in Germany in April 1945 and that his son was born in 1946 in Germany; subsequent IRO documents claim he arrived in March 1949, after fleeing 'from the Communist Party', and place his son's birth in Hungary. These discrepancies were not picked up at the time.[21]

Other groups not subject to forcible repatriation were expected to repatriate voluntarily. These included former citizens of Estonia, Latvia and Lithuania, many of whom fled west when their countries were incorporated into the Soviet Union in 1944. Poles from east of the Bug River, including Western Ukrainians, were affected by border changes after half of Poland was ceded to the Soviet Union at Yalta. They were also stubbornly resistant to the idea of going 'home'.

The increasingly frustrated Allied forces, operating under instructions to repatriate all displaced persons, were initially at a loss to explain the desperate refusal to 'go home'. Harold Hall, an Australian Deputy Director of a UNRRA camp, reported in October 1945 hearing 'too many similar stories' of a 'black and terrible hatred' of the Soviet Union. He confessed: 'The problem that I cannot solve is the reason for the absolute fear these people have of the Russians.' The head of UNRRA, American Fiorello La Guardia, also exhibited confusion. He did not understand why displaced persons did not want to return home just because they disagreed with communism. He said that while he often disagreed with his government's policies, this was no reason for him not to return to the United States.[22]

For DPs, however, the reasons against return were obvious. Writing in 1947, in English, Ukrainian Ivan Bahryany explained why so many 'Soviet citizens' refused to repatriate:

> I am a Ukrainian, 35 years old, born in the region of Poltava of laboring parents and now I am living with no fixed residence, in constant want, wandering like a homeless cur around Europe – hiding from the repatriation committees of the USSR, who want to send me 'home'. I do not want to go 'home'. There are hundreds of thousands of us who do not want to. They can come for us with loaded rifles, but we will put up a desperate resistance – for we prefer to die in a foreign land rather than go back to that 'home'. I put that word in quotation marks, for it is filled with horror, for it shows the unparalleled cynicism of the Soviet

propaganda directed against us: the Bolsheviks have made for 100 nationalities one 'Soviet home' and by that term they are building the terrible 'prison of peoples', the so-called USSR.

Another displaced person insisted that 'there would be no DP problem if Russia were liberated [from Soviet rule]. We'd walk home on our flat feet.'[23] Many had an existing antipathy towards Soviet rule. Some groups, like Ivan and Nastasia's Cossack Army, were long-time enemies of the Soviet Union and included those who held the Nansen passports that were issued by the League of Nations to stateless (Russian) persons in the interwar period. Their anti-Soviet views were shared by other émigré Russians and nationalist Ukrainians. Katherina's Ukrainian Cossack father had died of starvation in the *Holodomor* (literally 'hunger-extermination', the Soviet-made Ukrainian famine, in 1932–33). Others had more recent experiences. In 1940 hundreds of thousands of Poles were deported to gulag in the Soviet Union; many of these Poles, released in 1941 to join Polish forces against Nazi Germany, found themselves in DP camps at the end of the war. In June 1941 mass deportations were also carried out in Estonia, Latvia and Lithuania. Ralf's father, a wealthy Latvian farmer, had been shot by the Soviets before the family fled by boat to Germany in 1944. Wladimir, the son of a Belarusian clergyman, recalls a palpable sense of 'stress and terror' due to the probability of his family's deportation before their 'dangerous flight' to the west. Others witnessed the bad conduct of the Soviet Army as they swept through Eastern Europe, including mass rapes and looting. Many also had concerns about the low quality of life in the Soviet Union. Laszlo, a Hungarian who had spent time in Russia, observed: 'No freedom, property was taken away, very low wages, health service was not very good, backward country.' Polish displaced person Stanislaw stated succinctly: 'Being in Russia is like being in hell.'[24]

These anti-Soviet feelings were exacerbated by rumours that the Soviets persecuted returnees. Since Stalin had decreed that 'there will be no deserters in the Red Army', DPs generally believed the Soviets would view all returnees – particularly prisoners-of-war but even forced labourers – as Nazi collaborators, and therefore traitors. A Soviet radio broadcast warned that displaced persons who delayed their return until after November 1945 would 'be arrested and sent on the road to the police'. There were reports that local people attacked convoys of returnees at the border and many DPs received letters from family members warning them not to travel home. Jan's Polish father, a mining engineer transported to Siberia in 1939, ended up in a DP camp in British East Africa. He received a letter smuggled out by his cousin saying: 'Whatever you do, don't come back.' Nastasia received a 'surprise', a letter from her father in Ukraine. He wrote: 'Don't come home'; her mother, a forced labourer in Germany, had been repatriated and sent to Siberia.[25]

The Soviets, while acknowledging the taint of collaboration, argued that the fear of repression was exaggerated. Soviet officials suggested that the safe and comfortable camp environment, where people 'do not work hard and they are set in a special atmosphere which is not normal' softened their loyalty to their homeland. The Soviets even alleged that the DPs were 'nourished' in the camps as 'tools of aggression for foreign powers'. Recalcitrant displaced persons were 'contaminated' by the West, and made up of 'an undemocratic/criminal/undesirable element'; they were labelled 'idlers', 'Nazis', 'war criminals' and 'fascists'.[26]

Soviet authorities made concerted efforts to persuade the displaced persons to repatriate, in order to replenish population losses from the war, thwart the rise of an anti-Soviet movement in the West, and prevent international loss of face as the Cold War began. The Allies refused to listen to offers from the Cossack, Anders (Polish) and Vlasov (Russian Liberation) armies to join forces against the Soviet Union, and made little effort to exploit the anti-Soviet attitudes of the non-returners. But Moscow took the remnants of collaborator units more seriously. Soviet Deputy Commissar of Foreign Affairs, Andrei Vyshinsky, told the United Nations General Assembly in 1946:

> It is no secret that refugee camps, situated in the western zones of Germany, Austria and certain other countries of Western Europe, are springboards and centres for the formation of military reserves of hirelings, which constitute an organised military force in the hands of this or that foreign power.[27]

Soviet liaison officers visited camps, pleading with the inhabitants to return, and disseminated propaganda in various languages. A Soviet radio broadcast to displaced persons appealed: 'The fascist animals drove you by force into German slavery, they treated you cruelly and with ridicule, starved you and tortured you. Your motherland awaits you.' Russian interpreters in Nastasia's camp asked: 'Poor people, aren't you sick of this life, moving, hiding? Your country waits for you, your relatives miss you.' However, Soviet delegations who arrived in camps to survey the inhabitants and implore displaced persons to return home often met violence. Ale observed DPs throwing rotten tomatoes at Russian officers, while Anatolij Mirosznyk recalled that in a Ukrainian DP camp, 'when the Soviet officer started to speak, they whistled, shouted, and interrupted his speech. Suddenly, somebody set fire to one of the Soviet cars and then to a second one.' In other camps cars were overturned and Soviet representatives beaten and knifed. Allied military authorities ceased forced repatriations around the end of 1945 as it became apparent that large numbers of returnees met with violence, were deported to gulag or executed as soon as they crossed the border.[28]

Nationalist camp communities

The UNRRA camps were important sites of individual and collective agency and resistance. Camps, and camp zones, were run as semi-autonomous municipalities, or 'camp republics'. DPs were given increasing responsibility; they elected a camp commander and other representatives, formulated camp statutes and provided a camp police force. An informal DP court could impose punishments for crimes not serious enough to go before an Allied military court. Displaced persons were also formally employed in the camps, or by the military authorities, as interpreters, administrators, doctors and mechanics. In fact, some DPs gained enormous power from such positions. Patricia Meehan, a British UN worker, described the camp system as 'government by interpreter'. DPs also set up schools and universities, published community newspapers, magazines and books and developed a vibrant cultural life. All sorts of political groups and committees abounded. Indeed, Ukrainian DP Ihor V Zielyk wryly noted that the 'initial enthusiasm and the availability of free time combined to yield a crop of formal groupings that an outsider might have diagnosed as over-organisation'.[29]

DPs also quickly sorted themselves into nationality-specific camps, albeit with some fluidity. Soviets joined Polish camps for instance, usually to evade repatriation. Ukrainian forced labourer Michael and his Russian girlfriend Tamara stayed in a variety of camps: Polish, Russian and Ukrainian. Victoria's father, a Bulgarian priest, was sent to a Yugoslav camp because the camp wanted a priest. She recalled: 'The recruiting officer suggested that if my great-grandfather was born in Macedonia, so that made us Yugoslavs. Bulgarians were not eligible [for displaced persons status] at the time.' UNRRA reported that 'Polish, Yugoslav, Russian DPs tended to support each other in opposition to screening by [Soviet] liaison officers regardless of past differences'. UNRRA did its utmost to encourage national separations, partly for administrative reasons and partly for ideological ones, although its workers found that some camps showed a worrying apathy towards a national sensibility.[30] Camp Director Harold Hall rebuked the Ukrainian displaced persons at his camp in Esslingen, in southern Germany:

> I have been amazed at the lack of Nationalism displayed by the people of this camp ... I feel that it is the duty of the officials of UNRRA and the bounden duty of your National Leaders to inculcate into your younger people a fierce pride of Nationalism, a pride in the fact that you are citizens of Ukraine, even though you are separated from its boundaries, and temporarily resident in another country.

Hall's motives were hardly disinterested. UNRRA fostered nationalism in the camps in a somewhat misguided bid towards encouraging repatriation. Hall ordered singing the national anthem at all public assemblies, and reiterated that the Ukrainians would soon be 'going HOME'.[31]

Many displaced persons, though, did attempt to keep national sensibilities alive, and established a sense of 'reactive' diaspora and exile mission. UNRRA encouraged a form of self-sufficiency, usually in nationality-specific camps or 'DP Municipalities'. Julija describes her camp as 'Lithuanian. There was segregation, and we wanted it that way.' Nationalist elites wanted to keep a chauvinistic national sensibility alive through schools, cultural activities, national celebrations and commemoration days. Historian Marian J Rubchak has described the DP camps as 'a matrix for cultural preservation, and even further development, in a relatively isolated environment'. Nostalgia, trauma and grief were mixed with a purposeful nationalism, based on interwar and wartime discourses of national self-determination. The camps became training grounds for leaders of groups such as the Ukrainian-dominated Anti-Bolshevik Bloc of Nations.

DP elites (usually from a high-status pre-war background) mobilised their compatriots against repatriation and modelled a community-building process that was later used in countries of resettlement.[32]

As they reconstructed nationality, the DP camps also provided a *construction* of nationalist sentiment in diaspora. The most obvious example is the state of Israel, which historian Dan Diner points out 'had its beginnings [in the Jewish DP camps] in southern Germany'. These emergent nation-building and/or diasporic identities occurred simultaneously with the ongoing excision of the displaced persons from both the polity and historical memory of Germany and the expanded Soviet Union. Some DP groups were fighting not only for national and cultural preservation (or, arguably, creation), but also for their own identity, purpose and agency as 'nationalists' and 'exiles' rather than 'refugees'.[33]

It seems that most DPs did not actively participate in political organisations in the postwar period. However, the constant dissemination of nationalistic propaganda solidified their stubborn refusal to repatriate to lands under Soviet control. UNRRA suspected that 'among many of these people, the political explanation serves merely as a convenient justification and cover for underlying motives which are essentially personal and economic'. While some camp directors blamed 'present comfort and indolence', these personal and economic motives were more likely to include a desire for a 'fresh start' and a strong 'determination to get on'. Historian Anna Holian argues that the leaders of various displaced communities and particularly political groups – the DP elites – were essential in 'edit[ing] out "merely" personal or economic considerations' to emphasise political persecution and anti-communism. In other words, nationalist DP elites articulated a cohesive narrative by drawing the connection between individual suffering and a 'national' epic of community loss, exile and diaspora.[34]

DPs essentially chose which camps to attach themselves to, among varying scales of expressive, purposeful nationalism and municipal organisation. They also decided whether to live in camps at all. Up to a fifth of all DPs lived independently, working or studying outside the camp system, and only visiting to pick up their rations. Others took spontaneous journeys around Europe. Some DPs, repatriated to homelands they no longer recognised, returned swiftly (and illegally) to the camps.[35]

UNRRA and its workers, however, assumed the DPs lacked agency. Historian Peter Gatrell describes the dominant attitude of relief workers as one of 'personal adventure and self-fulfilment', together with an individualised and collective power (and developing professionalism) involved in overcoming 'the arduous and sometimes hazardous nature' of their work. They were usually reluctant to ascribe much drive to the displaced persons themselves, and made little attempt to consult with displaced persons about their future.[36]

Similarly, sociologists and psychologists described DPs as 'apathetic' and 'neurotic'. In one report commissioned by UNRRA's Welfare Division a summary of 'the psychology of Displaced Persons' described displaced persons as exhibiting '[rude], [crude] behaviour, aggressiveness and touchiness', 'phantasy-ridden and "unreal" thinking', 'jealousy', 'recklessness', 'deep despondencies', 'hypochondrial complaining' and 'mental misery'. Peter Gatrell has argued that pathologising DPs in this way infantilised them, and justified all sorts of external interventions. Indeed, the UNRRA report suggested that the 'tools of repair' were 'simple enough': food, clothing, material help and 'administrative guidance'.[37]

UNRRA assistance was, of course, temporary. In 1946 they discontinued the care and protection of DPs from Belgium, Czechoslovakia, Denmark, France, Greece, Luxembourg, the Netherlands and Norway, and threatened to remove support from the remaining DPs who refused to repatriate. UNRRA reduced rations and relocated DPs from camp to camp, and allowed Soviet representatives undue influence, in their attempts to force them home. In May 1946 the Camp Director at Fritzlar, north of Frankfurt, plaintively begged his charges:

> Are you not 'home-sick'? I can tell you that you will inevitably be home-sick some day and that you will irresistibly want to go home, to see again the country where you were born, to which you belong, to meet your friends, your relatives, to smell the odour of your native land.

Displaced persons resisted these treaties and refused repatriation. In May 1946, an extensive repatriation poll of DPs in the US zone of Germany, for example, found 89 per cent rejected repatriation, and 9 per cent refused to participate. Those who refused repatriation expressed in 'a more or less violent form, disagreements and dissatisfactions with the Soviet regime'. Ukrainians insisted they were 'stateless'.[38]

The situation worsened for UNRRA when hundreds of thousands of Jews and 'border-hoppers' (or 'infiltrees') arrived from the east. More than 160 000 Jews left Poland between 1945 and 1947 due to the considerable danger of pogroms. In 1947, Romanian Jews fled via Hungary and Austria. Border-hoppers, usually non-Jewish young, single males from Czechoslovakia and Hungary, attempted to escape the encroaching Iron Curtain – 'communism-in-the-making' – in what has been termed the phenomenon of 'the Voting Feet'. Jakub, a young Czech, viewed the communist takeover with revulsion; he saw the Soviets as a 'backwards people: we knew what was happening in Russia and I opposed that'. Involved in anti-communist activity, he evaded arrest and fled the country when one compatriot was given the death sentence and another was sentenced to twelve years hard labour. Agnes's father, a Hungarian film distributor, bribed his way out of prison and fled to Austria after refusing to sign his company over to the communist government. Sociologist and DP Jiri Kolaja, a self-described 'participant observer', noted that the Czech cohort had a high proportion of prominent people to 'so-called "average citizens"', including Czech parliamentarians and journalists, as well as members of political parties, religious groups, and Czech and Slovak national groups. Border-hoppers, as opposed to the original DPs, were typically of a high social class.[39]

By this time, the hundreds of DP camps were regarded

as 'sociological and psychological cauldrons' as various groupings battled on ethnic, religious and political grounds. One contemporary described the DPs as an 'incredible, almost comical, melting-pot of peoples and nationalities sizzling dangerously in the very heart of Europe'. Jewish DPs, in particular, were forced to isolate themselves from the majority of the camps, which were characterised by an American reporter as 'camps for collaborators'.[40]

UNRRA began to realise that its primary aim of repatriation was 'sheer wasted effort' when even 'Operation Carrot' – which involved bribing the DPs to go home with a sixty-day ration of food – failed to empty the camps. By 1948 the 'guesstimate' that approximately one million people were either from the 'non-returner' DP group or the incoming refugees from the east was characterised as 'the last million'.[41]

A Cold War solution

The last million dug in. They were becoming, for UNRRA, a problematic 'collective anachronism', an irritating remnant of the Second World War. The growing rivalry between the United States and the Soviet Union, however, greatly assisted the DPs who were reframed as political refugees from the new Cold War.[42]

Initially, the chances for resettlement were slight. General Eisenhower famously warned Latvian DPs to return home in October 1945, saying:

> I do not think that Canada wants immigrants who collaborated with the Germans or who believed

Goebbels' lies about our Allies or were too unpatriotic to rebuild their own country. I do not think that South America wants such people. I am sure that the United States does not.

For the communist nations, DPs who refused repatriation were 'enemies and traitors, not only of their own countries, but of all the United Nations', a situation 'poison[ing] the international atmosphere'. Meanwhile, UNRRA had no wish to keep caring for (and spending money on) Soviet citizens who refused repatriation and the increasing numbers of border-hoppers. Yet it had no authority to initiate resettlement.[43]

In northern America, émigré groups had been advocating for the displaced since the end of the war. The Polish–American Congress (an umbrella organisation of Polish–Americans and their organisations formed in the United States in 1944), and others argued that the United States, and by extension the United Nations, had a moral responsibility to solve the DP problem, as 'their plight is attributable to the Yalta agreement to which America was party'. These arguments gained ground with the increasing discomfort in the United States concerning Soviet wartime territorial gains and its perceived totalitarianism that privileged state authority over individual rights. DP migration trajectories were re-narrated into a new Cold War paradigm. State Department refugee specialist Robert S McCollum observed: 'Each refugee from the Soviet orbit represents a failure of the Communist system' and thereby 'constitutes a challenge to the fundamental concepts of that system'.[44]

In this context of 'extreme [diplomatic] touchiness', political debates took place in 1946 between the United States, the United Kingdom and France, who were administering the DP camps in occupied Germany and Austria on one side, and the countries of origin of most remaining DPs (the Soviet republics of Russia, Ukraine and Belarus, as well as Poland and Yugoslavia) on the other. In April, the International Refugee Organization was a new temporary organisation formed by the United Nations to replace UNRRA. Its primary responsibility was to resettle, rather than repatriate, DPs. This mission was of course vehemently opposed by the Soviet bloc, which refused to support the fledgling organisation.[45]

Nonetheless, the category of displaced persons was broadened to include anyone displaced

> who definitely, in complete freedom and after receiving full knowledge of the facts, including adequate information from the governments of their countries of nationality or residence, are unwilling to return to those countries and are further unwilling to avail themselves of the protection of the governments of those countries.

In other words, unrepatriated Soviet DPs were now bona fide refugees. A DP could become a refugee if he or she demonstrated a 'valid objection' to repatriation when they refused it.[46] War criminals, anybody who had participated in the persecution of civilians of an Allied nation or voluntarily assisted enemy forces, and persons of German ethnic origin remained ineligible for IRO protection.

In December 1946 the IRO's draft constitution, specifying its field of operations and promising to 'find new homes elsewhere' for unrepatriable displaced persons, was adopted by a vote of thirty to five, with eighteen abstentions. The United Nations now had the ultimate responsibility to resettle the burgeoning group of eligible DPs, most of whom were people who refused to return to Soviet bloc homelands.[47]

The IRO's first task was to issue Identity Cards verifying the holder as a 'genuine refugee or displaced person' able to access emigration channels. The IRO Identity Cards certified a politically blameless past, safeguarded the holder from repatriation, guaranteed continued maintenance, and enabled possible resettlement. Obtaining the necessary 'refugee status' involved a complicated bureaucratic structure including a 'Test of Eligibility' in which individuals were interviewed using information from government sources, private agencies, cross-examination and witnesses. There was also a Review Board for appeals, based in Geneva. This work followed on from UNRRA's screening practices, and in fact the IRO launched a massive review of individual cases already evaluated under UNRRA due to widespread 'discrepancies and incoherence'. The screening process, however, was still not particularly stringent, it was even 'superficial and in the eyes of some, "corrupt"'. The Eligibility Manual 'made clear that the IRO was not particularly enthusiastic about screening for war criminals', and that a certain amount of untruthfulness was expected. Historian David Cesarani has noted that UNRRA and IRO screening was 'so weak that, in reality, it was useful only for public relations purposes'.[48]

The IRO concentrated on evaluating individual 'dissidence', paving the way for a broader notion of refugees, which privileged the individual over the state. The ideal refugee was now assumed to have 'genuine' (democratic) political creeds as well as 'genuine' reasons to fear persecution. Aside from Jewish DPs, who were classed as eligible *because* they were Jewish, this postwar change made individuals rather than groups eligible for refugee status, and emphasised proof and persecution. The United Nations attempted to codify an international legal framework for refugees, incorporating a language of protection and individual human rights. The 1951 United Nations Convention Relating to the Status of Refugees defined a refugee as a person who: 'Owing to a well-founded fear of being persecuted for reasons of race, religion, nationality, membership of a particular social group or political opinion, is outside the country of his nationality and is unable or, owing to such fear, is unwilling to avail himself of the protection of that country; or who, not having a nationality and being outside the country of his former habitual residence ... is unable, or owing to such fear, is unwilling to return to it.'[49]

The Convention embodied the historical and geopolitical specificity of the DP experience as it applied to people who became refugees as a result of events prior to 1 January 1951. It was obviously aimed at DPs perceived by the West as victims of communist state persecution. Signatories even had the option of limiting their obligations to European refugees. Gil Loescher, an expert in international refugee policy, notes that 'the definition had the added advantage that it would serve ideological purposes by stigmatising the fledgling Communist regimes as persecutors'.[50]

The IRO began to pressure the displaced to present themselves as individual 'asylum seekers', rather than members of ethnic, religious and political groups. Daniel Cohen identifies that the IRO imposed a 'new theatricality', where the incentive of refugee status encouraged an overemphasised 'presentation of self', such as the open expression of fear. It promoted storytelling that fitted the Western vision and definition of individual political persecution. This 'Cold War myopia' privileged the 'political persecutee', a 'true' refugee, over the false 'economic migrant'. This had the effect of further homogenising DPs, reducing them to their Cold War identities. The IRO's pressure on individuals to present themselves as 'political refugees', arguably masked many age-old economic motives for refusing repatriation and aspiring to resettle in the West. According to one IRO officer, motives of adventure and a tradition of economic migration applied to 'most' of the DPs; others estimated that only 25 per cent of the DPs in August 1948 were 'genuine refugees' as set out by the IRO. But IRO policy was to reject only the few who were 'naïve enough to admit that they are economic migrants'.[51]

Regardless of their motivation or means of escape, by 1948 it was clear that the IRO had to resettle the 'last million' DPs, now rebranded political refugees. There were 636 000 DPs under the care of UNRRA, 60 000 in camps still under military rule, 16 000 under the mandate of the Intergovernmental Committee for Refugees, and around 90 000 refugees who had made their way to the West from the encroaching Soviet Bloc prior to 1951. The solution was to rebrand DPs as workers and migrants. As UNRRA relief worker Francesca Wilson observed in 1947: 'Fortunately, the present manpower shortage in Western countries has revolutionised the outlook for DPs.' The emphasis now was for displaced persons to exchange their IRO Identity Card for an IRO passport.[52]

Refugee migrants

From 1948, the IRO funded migration to any country willing to accept DPs. Some countries, including Turkey and the new state of Israel, accepted DPs from a particular cultural background, and the United States accepted a small number as compassionate cases. However, most countries were looking for workers to regenerate their postwar economies. The first European schemes involved Britain, the Netherlands and Belgium recruiting 'bright-eyed [and] healthy' single persons or childless married couples as short-term workers to fill industry shortages in coal mining and textile manufacturing. In Britain a limited scheme was initiated for young Baltic women (the 'Balt Cygnets') to be used as domestic maids, industrial workers or sanatorium attendants for TB patients for the first three months of their stay. Around 100 000 non-Jewish DPs were renamed 'European Voluntary Workers' and defined primarily as labour migrants. Canada and Argentina were the first countries outside Europe to take advantage of the labour potential, with Canada recruiting workers for two-year 'apprenticeships' in specific industries, including lumbering, mining, agriculture and domestic service. In 1948 the United States finally passed the *Displaced Persons Act* which sidestepped earlier migration quota restrictions. Ultimately the United States admitted 400 000 DPs under a sponsorship system whereby a (private or organisational) sponsor had to guarantee housing and employment.⁵³

These 'muscle-gathering missions' meant that DPs, now bona-fide refugees, had to jump additional hurdles. Kanty Cooper, a British UNRRA worker, said: 'We had to sort out impossible people trying to go on schemes for which they were completely unsuitable.' Hurdles usually concerned health and occupation, sometimes race, and always involved a lot of bureaucratic form filling. The United States, the last hope for many DPs, required not only sponsors and medical clearance, but birth and marriage certificates, good-conduct statements from the police, work-testing records, and a certificate from the German authorities stating that the DP had not been charged with begging while in Germany.⁵⁴

The displaced persons were coerced into presenting themselves to fit recruiters' labour requirements. Yugoslav Gordana, a young linguist, recalled:

> the first thing people told us was, 'For goodness' sake, don't say you're a teacher or had an education', because all they wanted was manual workers … My husband used to cut wood every day, for months, just to get tough hands … Other people did the same … My brother said he had been a shepherd because in Canada that's what they wanted. But he didn't look like one. He had glasses and his hands were very, very soft. So they just made fun of him, asked him how many teeth a sheep has and questions like that.⁵⁵

An emphasis on manual work skills was accompanied by a strong racial component. The United Nations reported that 'without openly declaring their unwillingness to accept Jewish immigrants, the various recruiting missions invariably reject all the Jewish candidates'. Non-Jewish, particularly Baltic DPs, were specifically recruited for British work schemes to counter the postwar influx of non-white Commonwealth migrants, due to the racist belief that European DPs were 'of good human stock'. In the hierarchy of race (and class), all recruiting countries saw middle-class Balts as the 'elite of the refugee problem': 'unmistakeably intelligent, conscientious, industrious, energetic, and show[ing] every sign of coming from good stock and good breeding', and relatively wealthy. The Grand Duchy of Luxembourg recruited single workers with no dependants, and preferred Balts. In the United States, almost a quarter of all visas were reserved for Balts. Australia's first shipments were made up exclusively of the so-called 'Beautiful Balts' – blond, blue-eyed migrants who would slip into a white Australian demographic.[56]

Some DP groups were complicit in these representations. Historian Laura Hilton notes that Poles and Balts depicted themselves to potential settlement countries as 'strong, handsome, hardworking, God-fearing lovers of democracy'. In one DP camp publication, Latvians 'somewhat eerily emphasised that 60% of the population had fair hair and blue eyes', and were physically healthy. They also emphasised their anti-communism. Harry Daumont, a Lithuanian who described himself as 'something of a cross-breed between an evacuee and a lately officially recognised displaced person', wrote to the Commonwealth Office of Education in Australia, assuring them that Lithuanians were 'disciplined, obedient, intelligent, sober, industrious, unassuming and of an appearance to match the English–Australian'.[57]

In effect, then, the IRO, 'hat in hand' and desperate to be rid of DPs, presided over and administered a 'labour-recruitment program on an international scale'. The Soviets alleged that 'a real slave trade' was flourishing, with the IRO the 'main purveyor of cheap labour for the capitalist countries', and *The Times* (London) was inclined to agree: 'There is a whiff of the slave market in the invitations to DPs to enter most countries.' Some IRO leaders attacked this 'skimming of the cream' and 'embargo on brains' as ruinous, a denial of the organisation's humanitarian aims. However, recruiting countries saw refugees as 'immense pools of manpower representing every known skill'. The IRO was soon dubbed by the press the 'largest travel agency in human history'.[58]

The IRO's occasional discomfort with facilitating the recruitment of mass labour was ameliorated by a perception that labour would have a moralising and rehabilitative effect on the DPs, that negated the 'evil and anti-social consequences of continued idleness'. This was particularly the case in the French zone, where DPs were required to work and could lose access to food and accommodation if they refused. In January 1947 the British zone also made paid employment compulsory. Such work was considered 'therapeutic' and emancipatory. In practice, Allied employment policies attempted to turn DPs from 'slaves of the Nazi regime' to 'labourers suitable for democracies'. DP 'apathy' was contrasted with state and agency 'action' in a 'grand vision of reconstruction and replacement'.[59]

To emigrate, individual DPs applied to the IRO. The IRO then selected applicants through a process of medical, professional and biographical reviews. The recruiting countries often chose from these successful applicants using their own criteria, entailing a second review process. Recruiting countries rejected the ill, the infirm, the old, and those who stayed to care for them, as 'sub-standard', as well as intellectuals, those with too many dependants and single mothers. The 'minus' or 'hard core' that 'passed through the sieves of nations' were left to fend for themselves. Contemporaries noted that they were the 'most truly forgotten human flotsam of the war': 'despair was the footnote'. In 1949 there were 20 000 seriously handicapped persons, 30 000 of their dependants, and approximately 10 000 others with limited opportunities for resettlement. The IRO initiated and administered retraining schemes trying to resettle these DPs with minimal success. Some were accepted by Norway in 'goodwill' transports. The rest somehow had to integrate into hostile German and Austrian societies as 'homeless foreigners'. The last operative camp, a Jewish DP camp near Munich, was dissolved in February 1957; the others had closed by 1952. World Refugee Year was ascribed in 1959–60 in order to highlight DPs who had still not found a home.[60]

Despite the failure to find homes for the hard core, and the latent issues of nationalism and agency, the IRO scheme was largely viewed as a political and humanitarian success. The immediate postwar DPs were recategorised and joined by political refugees. The thorny issue of repatriation to the

Soviet Union was tackled head on by forming the IRO, and more than one million DPs, now known as workers and migrants, were resettled by the end of 1951.[61]

For the DPs themselves though, resettlement was not an easy answer to their displacement. Some thought that military conflict between the West and the Soviet Union was unavoidable, and any resettlement temporary. Jakub later recalled: 'We all believed that [peace] wouldn't last for more than two years. Or twelve months'. For George, a Polish former forced labourer: 'It was a question of trying, at least temporarily, to go to a country where one could breathe a different type of air. I certainly, coming to Australia, did not expect to stay here all my life.' Egon Kunz, a young Hungarian, reasoned: 'In two or three years time one can learn English and return to Hungary as a man, what we considered to be double proof: one had resisted the Germans and the Russians. On top of that, we were now speaking fluent English and have learned the ways of the West. So this was the idea, roughly. So even on the ship, when I came here, I didn't think of settling in Australia.' Others, though, were 'quite sure that there would never be an end to communism', and thought they would never see their native lands again.[62]

The decision of where to resettle, insofar as there was a choice, was fraught with anxiety. Helen compared the displaced persons predicament to a Ukrainian joke that is translated as: 'The cockroach under the sieve can see so many holes but cannot fit through any of them.' The fate of families could turn on one episode. Bohdan's Ukrainian family was headed for the United States, until his father 'met a couple of [US servicemen] cowboys who wanted to steal his watch'; this turned his father against the States, and the family ended up in Australia instead. Olga, a middle-aged Latvian, desired to go to South America; she thought the language might be easier to learn than English, and the pace less frenetic than in the United States. When she was sponsored to the States, she was apprehensive in letters to her son: 'O-o-o! So much fear!!! ... I don't know why I am going to America. Yet I'm doing it. Without inner conviction.' Stanislaw, a Pole, spent the long ship voyage to Australia:

> Lying on my bunk and staring at the mesh-wire bottom of the berth above me. I contemplated the lonely, desolate and almost unreal state of my existence and silently pondered over all those cherished memories which were an insepar-able part of me – my home, my family, and my country – which by some cruel whim of history had now vanished like the lost continent of Atlantis. Everything that I cherished had vanished, as if crushed to dust by the devastating tide of war.[63]

Over 170 000 displaced persons journeyed to Australia, the country's first mass intake of non-British refugees. What prompted the government to bring them here and how did they sell the new migrants to a suspicious Australian public? For their part, displaced persons came to Australia and were forced to spend time in migrant camps, work off a two-year indentured labour contract, endure family separation and cope with policies of assimilation. How did they respond to these experiences? Did their journey to Australia mark the end of their engagement with Europe, and with politics?

CHAPTER 2

'Chifley liked them blond'

> *There had been some doubt about the quality of these DPs who had the blood of a number of races in their veins. Many were red-headed and blue-eyed. There was also a number of natural platinum blondes of both sexes. The men were handsome and the women beautiful. It was not hard to sell immigration to the Australian people once the press published photographs of that group.*
>
> – Arthur Calwell, Minister for Immigration.[1]

In 1949, the Australian Department of Immigration commissioned the bestselling author Frank Clune to write a book on the refugee camps in Europe and how displaced persons were 'recruited and transported' to Australia. Clune was enthusiastic, reporting that these potential 'New Australians' – a phrase earlier coined by the immigration minister Arthur Calwell – were of 'Slavonic racial stock': 'all had good eyes, beautiful natural teeth, and clear, fresh complexions'. They were 'young, healthy, and able to work', and, wrote Clune, of a 'heroic type': 'Despite Bolshevik blandishments, they refused to return and submit to Russian regimentation, with its crazy one-sided ideas of forced labour, Stalin-idolatry, bogus "trials", and low standards of living.' Clune thus reassured the Australian public that the DPs were racially and politically acceptable: white European (not Jewish or Asian) anti-communists who valued freedom.[2]

Populate or perish

Australia's decision to take displaced persons had its genesis with the shock of war in the Pacific. The experience fostered the postwar reconstruction effort that historian Stuart Macintyre has called 'Australia's greatest experiment' and 'an ethos of national endeavour', which included a government imperative to dramatically increase the population. In 1943, when postwar planning had already begun, a British memo to the Australian Government recognising the need to increase migration for defence and national development, suggested that Australia look to Europe if there was a postwar shortfall in migrants from the United Kingdom. That year also saw a new interdepartmental committee to investigate and report specifically on immigration; a year later its sub-committee recommended that the 'Commonwealth should be prepared to accept *any white aliens* who can be assimilated and contribute satisfactorily to economic development and against whom there are no objections' (my emphasis). It warned that 'Australia's need for population is so great that it cannot afford to be too exclusive as to categories to be regarded as eligible for admission'.[3]

The idea that the Labor government could and should plan a radical new immigration program became an essential element of postwar reconstruction, bolstered by the unifying experience of war. This was particularly the case after the white paper *Full Employment in Australia* in May 1945 advocated entering a new phase of industrialisation to take the country beyond its reliance on rural exports to Britain. A large-scale immigration program had bipartisan support, and was also backed by social scientists such as influential demographer WD Borrie. When the new Department of Immigration was established in July 1945, Labor politician Arthur Calwell (already Minister for Information) lobbied to become the first Minister for Immigration. Calwell took a phrase that had been coined in the 1920s, that Australia must 'populate or perish', and made it his own.[4]

Calwell was a visionary who sought to remake Australia in America's (demographic) image; and he was the architect of Australia's postwar migration program. He set out his views in a personal manifesto published in 1945 (initially prepared for distribution at the Sydney Royal Easter Show), *How Many Australians Tomorrow?*, which argued that Australia's population 'is our number one problem'. While admitting that immigration from Central, Eastern and Southern Europe was a 'controversial question', Calwell suggested pragmatically that 'we must be realistic'.[5]

Calwell's ostensible plan was to increase the population by 1 per cent births and 1 per cent net migration, with an aim of 90 per cent British migration in order to populate a strictly regulated White Australia. There were, however, too few British migrants in the immediate postwar period, partly

'Chifley liked them blond'

due to limited access to shipping and also because they were needed for postwar reconstruction in England. The one million white American migrants optimistically invited into Australia, as well as ideal-type Scandinavian migrants, also failed to materialise.[6]

The Australian Government was of course well aware of the 'last million' displaced persons languishing in Europe. Australia was a signatory and financial contributor to both the United Nations Relief and Rehabilitation Administration and the International Refugee Organization. However, the Australian Labor Party and attendant trade unions were historically wary of non-British immigration. Australia did not have a refugee policy separate from its migration requirements until it reluctantly agreed in theory to accept 15 000 refugees after the 1938 Evian Conference on Jewish refugees. The government had even deported 5000 Asians and Pacific Islanders who had sought refuge in Australia during the war, some of whom had married Australian citizens. Indeed, it was in character for Australia to reject UNRRA's plea in early 1947 to resettle 30 000 DPs. The government made it very clear to the Australian public, that being an IRO signatory did not involve 'commitments to take refugees into the country, our freedom in this regard being unimpaired'.[7]

Machinations in the upper echelons of government told a different story. In late 1945 Calwell commissioned a Commonwealth Immigration Advisory Committee (CIAC), chaired by Labor MP Les Haylen and consisting of parliamentary representatives and delegates from employer and employee bodies, including the Australian Council of Trade Unions (ACTU). After visiting Paris for an International

Labour Office Conference, and investigating immigration prospects in North-Western Europe, CIAC recommended that displaced persons should be recruited and actively assisted to migrate to Australia.[8]

In 1946 Calwell instructed the Australian delegation to the United Nations to secure representation on any association established to handle refugees, as Australia was 'interested from migration angle particularly'. This interest was to be kept secret, to the extent that Australia abstained in the General Assembly vote of 15 December 1946 that conditionally approved the establishment of the IRO. However, by May 1947 Cabinet had agreed to join the IRO (and Calwell later argued that membership conferred a 'definite responsibility for contributing to the situation of the displaced persons problem'). As early as February 1947, the government intimated to the Intergovernmental Committee on Refugees that it might send an Australian delegation to the Occupied Zones to 'draw up a list of skilled workers required in Australia' although 'no decision has yet been reached'.[9]

On 2 June 1947 Calwell instructed an immigration official to prepare a report on the displaced persons available for migration. It seems that by mid-1947, Calwell and Prime Minister Ben Chifley were inclined, in a last-minute, opportunistic 'immigrant grab', to re-examine the prospects among the massive DP population. Historian Andrew Markus has argued that this was a 'closely guarded secret perhaps shared only by Calwell, Chifley and Evatt [the Attorney-General and Minister for External Affairs]'.[10]

Markus describes an atmosphere of 'secrecy and subterfuge'. In the same vein, John Hirst argues that Cabinet 'was not consulted for the very good reason that it would have opposed this move'. CIAC and the Australian Military Mission in Berlin were also kept in the dark. The secrecy could perhaps reflect an 'in-house delegation', which signified the prime minister's fundamental trust in his minister's vision and abilities. Calwell later acknowledged Chifley's support, saying 'Had we had an anti-immigration man as prime minister, or a lukewarm one, we would still be a dull inbred country of predominantly British stock.' Noel Lamidey, Chief Migration Officer at Australia House, later described Chifley as a 'tower of strength' to Calwell.[11]

In fact, the evidence suggests that Chifley had the original vision after a personal conversation with UNRRA's Australian head Robert Jackson. Jackson pleaded for Australia to take 'Balts' and Chifley reportedly said: 'Cabinet won't like it but I will convince Arthur [Calwell]; it will be done'. On 15 June 1947 Chifley broached the subject at the Labor Party Conference, advising that 'every responsible politician or government official preparing immigration schemes knows he cannot be so choosy because there are neither British nor northern, southern or eastern Europeans in sufficient numbers to satisfy the world demand for immigrants'. Specifically, 'at present there is a pool of probably 1 500 000 people in Europe who desperately want to leave the Continent to start a new life'. Chifley warned that 'any country, including Australia, which wants immigrants must try to get them while the European export commodity exists'.[12]

Three days later, Calwell flew to Europe to seek international assistance to obtain shipping and to approach the

IRO about recruiting migrants. Brief newspaper reports of 4 July 1947 noted that Chifley had asked Calwell to inspect European refugee camps to ascertain if there were immigrants suitable for Australia there.[13] Surprisingly, perhaps, although widely reported, this passed with little comment. Newspaper editorial boards were generally in favour and a few letters to the editor also supported it. The RSL and trade union movement, both initially against the plan, were persuaded by Calwell.

In London, Calwell's first meeting was with IRO representatives. His first continental stop was to a large DP camp at Bremerhaven in northern Germany to 'examine conditions firsthand'. He also met with representatives of the Preparatory Commission of the International Refugee Organization (PCIRO), where he was informed that there were 'high-quality' refugees available for resettlement and that the IRO would provide shipping; the Australian Government was asked to pay £10 per head as an *ex gratia* payment because ships had further to travel compared to American destinations and elsewhere. Not only were the potential migrants cheap, but Calwell could stipulate almost any selection criteria. In a press release from Bremen on 9 July, Calwell emphasised that the IRO would 'readily concede' 'complete selection rights' of the DPs, described by Calwell as 'chiefly Poles, Polish–Ukrainians, White Russians and Peterite [monarchist] Jugoslavs'.[14]

Calwell telegrammed Chifley:

> Other countries are keen competitors for best migrant types and unless we act quickly we may lose our

opportunity of securing migrants on selection basis. I am sending 2 officers to make preliminary selection in DP camps of those classes of workers who can best assist our manpower shortages. We would select types specially suitable for rural work, nursing and domestic work in hospitals, labour for our reconstruction programme and developmental projects. Selection will be on general suitability for work to be performed, after IRO and British security have satisfied our medical and security requirements ... Consider this by far most speedy and economical method of securing best types of migrants required for Australia's economic rehabilitation from non-British sources in shortest possible time.[15]

Subsequent events suggested that although the 'best migrant types' according to Calwell's selection criteria soon became relatively scarce, there were still more than enough displaced persons to meet general requirements. As one immigration official pointed out, the PCIRO representatives were selling to a very eager buyer. Calwell had sensed a 'Target of Opportunity'.[16]

Calwell was not motivated by humanitarian considerations. He was interested in the DPs' contribution to Australia's 'population, specifically workforce' deficit. The Hobart *Mercury* later reported: 'Advice received in Canberra reveals that the irrepressible Arthur has decided that the risk of abuse about more refugees is less than the risk of failure of the works programme and admission of complete immigration deadlock.' Calwell confirmed this in 1971:

Primarily what I was interested in was the defence of Australia and its development, so that the people who had made this country and the descendants of those could be assured that they could live in peace and security. I was interested in – it would be wrong to say I was primarily interested in seeing that we gave a haven to oppressed peoples anywhere because we could have given a haven to all the displaced and distressed people in the world. We had an opportunity because of the desire of the Americans to remove displaced persons, that is people who were born in the Baltic states – Estonians, Latvians and Lithuanians – we wanted to help them to get a new country and the Americans [the International Refugee Organization] were paying for it all and so it didn't cost us that very much.[17]

Calwell's pragmatic plan received swift approval from Chifley: 'Thanks for your telegram … I agree with action suggested … and approve you proceeding to Geneva to sign agreement.' Calwell sent out a press release from Paris on 15 July advising that the Australian Government would sign an agreement with the IRO to take 'mostly … people from the Baltic countries', who would be 'selected individually'. The agreement to implement mass non-British immigration, a radical departure in Australian immigration policy, was signed with the PCIRO on 21 July 1947.[18]

'Chifley liked them blond'

Recruitment and selection

Australia initially agreed to resettle 4000 displaced persons in 1947 and then 12 000 per year over three years 'provided the Australian Government can select the DPs *individually* and provided the IRO can provide shipping'. The program's success led to an increase in November 1947 to 20 000 per year, and in July 1948 Calwell announced that Australia would accept up to 200 000 people 'as rapidly as possibly', subject to the availability of shipping. The DPs were to come under a two-year indentured labour program, the men as 'labourers' and the women as 'domestics', with a view towards permanent settlement. The IRO's press release explicitly stated that Australia wanted 'principally "horny-handed sons of toil"'.[19]

The new Immigration Department sent its own officers and medical staff to the camps to work with IRO camp officers to recruit migrants for Australia. Australia was sold as a welcoming, exciting destination, and migrant workers were 'invited to share our life in the best country in the world'. A preliminary advisory committee recommended: 'We can capture their imagination by full employment and vast ventures needing men and women for the development of the country.'[20]

The IRO noted that Australia's Information Department was 'the most active of any with which we have come in contact'; it worked hard to fill its increasing immigration quotas since Australia was rarely the first desired destination. Australian film director Ron Maslyn, on location in Germany, said DPs saw Australia as 'a gambler's shot when attempts to get to America have failed'. Maslyn reported that 'one intelligent DP put it to me "It is Australia or Siberia or starvation"'. For many DPs, Australia's biggest selling point was its distance from 'the red-coloured creep of Soviet Russia'.[21]

To improve the perception of Australia among the displaced persons, and to sell a country of 'industry and sunshine', the Department of Information produced booklets, films and radio plays in English and German (including the film, *The Overlanders*, a bush adventure starring Chips Rafferty). It also produced coloured posters and photographs, and lectures on the Australian 'way of life'. Len Barsdell, Information Attaché to the Australian Military Mission in Germany, reported that 'the DPs like attractively coloured booklets and posters, and they must be simple and easy to read'. In 1947 a poster 'Australia – Land of Tomorrow' was produced: 'a charming design which should, with its sheer novelty and exuberant colour content, capture plenty of attention when distributed overseas'. Instead of 'the inevitable koala bear and kangaroo', the poster showed a 'man astride a cavorting steer'.[22]

Australian officers competed with other settlement countries including, by 1948, the United States, and wanted to skim the 'cream'. The most important category for Australia was race. Specifically, the government needed to uphold White Australia immigration policies to prevent domestic 'political repercussions'. However, White Australia was an anachronism in the context of a new international discourse promoted by the United Nations of racial equality and universal human rights. The Australian Government had to tread a thin line between (populist) national and (liberal) international condemnation. It attempted to do this by selecting 'racial' and cultural types that would assimilate into Australia. In other words, if Australia could not attract enough British migrants, then the government could fulfil its economic and population aims, as well as neatly fitting into an ostensibly humanitarian international program by taking 'white' migrants who could potentially assimilate.[23]

Mirroring the prejudices of other settlement countries, the displaced persons were graded on a quasi-official hierarchy, with 'Balts' at the top and 'Jews' at the bottom. As historian Glenda Sluga has noted, Eastern Europeans had not yet been definitively 'racially' categorised, and it was therefore easier to blur the lines of their identity. For Clune, in contrast, the Soviet Government (rather than its people) epitomised the worst Asian stereotypes. He characterised it as a regime of 'cruel Asiatic brutalities'.[24]

Representations of race were also important in presenting the DP scheme to the Australian public. Egon Kunz has posited that one factor determining the government's earlier rejection of DPs may have been an impression that they were predominantly Jewish. The government had no intention of accepting large numbers of Jewish refugees believing they would not 'assimilate'. Calwell told IRO representatives: 'We are not anti-Semitic but we will have to handle this matter carefully.' There were (necessarily feeble) protests from the IRO, from Jewish organisations and within the DP camps themselves, but they had no effect. Australian officials argued that Australia had had some trouble with Jews, and preferred Balts 'because they are people who are easily assimilated'. After protestations from the Executive Council of Australian Jewry that 'not a single Jew' was included in the first IRO shipments, Calwell assured the Council that in the overall IRO migration scheme, 15 to 16 per cent of DPs selected would be Jewish, which reflected the percentage of Jews among the DP population. This did not eventuate – the ultimate figure was approximately 2.3 per cent, or around 500 Jews.[25]

As well as anti-Semitic prejudice, displaced persons were ranked by nationality for 'assimilation' purposes. A memo from the Head of Australian Military Mission in Germany in June 1947 encapsulates the advice regarding the 'very good types' available at that time: 'Balts' were the 'best material'; Poles would need to be carefully selected to obtain 'assimilable types'; while 'Yugoslavs' would 'no doubt be worth some consideration'.[26]

The IRO insisted on a proviso in the agreement Calwell signed that the displaced persons would be selected 'without discrimination as to race and religion' or marital status. Calwell publicly declared: 'Our policy has no race prejudice. All we ask of DPs is that they be of good faith, good character and willing to work.' However, Helen Ferber, an Australian who worked as a public information officer for the Displaced Persons Headquarters of UNRRA in Paris, talked to Calwell in July 1947 and recorded that he preferred certain racial characteristics. 'He said Australia wanted Latvians': 'It came out in later conversation that he had seen some nice blond Latvians at Bremen, and well, they were blond and Chifley liked them blond.' Calwell stated publicly that 'the Baltic people will have preference over other

'Chifley liked them blond'

nationals' as he assured Australians that 'while in Europe, I was impressed by the bearing, the physique and the general industry of the Balts'.[27]

The Australian medical officers working in Europe seemed overly concerned with noting 'racial' characteristics. Clune reported one of the selectors saying this was because: 'We have to live alongside these people when we go back to Aussie.' One noted that Baltic 'men are often blonde and tanned and would on appearance do justice to a Manly Surf Team'. He thought, however, that some with a 'less than average intellectual standard', particularly Ukrainian women, would be only 'good hewers of wood and drawers of water'. Another medical officer wrote in 1949: 'We are still getting a fair quota of Balts and they are probably the best too. I am seeing quite a lot of Ukrainians now also – they seem pretty dumb, but I dare say that they will make good workers.'[28]

It was clear to observers that Australian officials, in the words of historian Mark Wyman, 'moved cautiously among the camp inhabitants, picking blue-eyed, blond DPs less likely to offend native-born Australians'. Calwell instructed them to 'hand-pick' a 'choice sample' for the first shipments in order to 'dress the window': young, single, healthy, educated 'ideal types', and preferably male. The 'clear ethnic picking order' was deliberate. Selection officer George Kiddle, an ex-RAAF serviceman who became one of the first migration officers, later recalled:

> Our instructions were to take displaced persons from the Baltic states only for the first ship. That is Estonia, Lithuania and Latvia … We tried to pick … good,

decent-looking people ... appearance very much so ... We've got to make sure they look very impressive ... we've got to pick people that look attractive to the Australian population ... we tried to make the first ship particularly impressive.[29]

As a result, early selections were made only from young, single Baltic, Ukrainian, Yugoslavian and Czech displaced persons, 'based on personal appearance and favourable impressions'. An IRO doctor, Dr Ergas, described a group he accompanied to Australia on the ship *General Black*:

Most of this group consisted of young men and women with very few children. They were well dressed ... made a fine appearance, and looked bright and intelligent. Most of them were from the Baltic countries ... The women in general were very good looking. Some had beautiful, dark, long hair; others were platinum blonde with blue eyes, light complexions and very tall. The men were fine looking too ... It was indeed a very select group of young people. They all appeared to be energetic, ambitious, and full of life.

Calwell told the press: 'Aged and queerly cut clothes and European styles of haircut could not disguise the quality of human material.'[30]

This rigorous first selection acted as a 'Trojan horse' for the scheme. The strict racial criteria were soon relaxed in the race to populate Australia cheaply and individual national groups were progressively permitted: Slovenes, Ukrainians,

'Chifley liked them blond'

Yugoslavs, Czechs, single Poles, Hungarians, White Russians, Poles with families, Albanians, Romanians, Bulgarians. In May 1949, it was widened ostensibly to everyone categorised by the IRO as 'displaced persons'. These also included Poles, Yugoslavs and Soviet-origin refugees who found themselves in East Africa, Greece, Lebanon, Egypt and the Philippines. Approximately 5000 German and Austrian-born DP wives were also permitted to migrate to Australia as, according to German law, they assumed the nationality of their husbands when they married.[31]

Relaxation of 'racial' criteria did not, however, extend to Jews. In April 1948 Brigadier FG Galleghan, head of the Australian Military Mission in Berlin, suggested recruiting Poles as other groups diminished. THE Heyes, the Secretary of the Department of Immigration, approved the suggestion with the confidential proviso that 'Polish Jews should not be recruited unless they are exceptionally good cases and then in limited numbers'. In July 1948, when Hungarians were admitted into the scheme, the same stipulation was made. Official feeling was succinctly expressed by one Australian immigration official: 'We have never wanted these people and we still don't want them.'[32]

The policy was made clear in an instruction to Berlin in June 1949: 'The term refers to race and not to religion and the fact that some DPs who are Jewish by race have become Christian by religion is not relevant.' Interestingly, 'race' was also more important than 'religion' for the few Russian and Romanian Muslims who were part of the DP cohort in Australia. One member of the Australian selection team noted that: 'Hitler could not have done better.'[33]

Policy was strict but individual selection officers varied in upholding it. Czech DP Leo, a young Jewish socialist, remembered there were two Australian consuls in his camp,

> a young one and an old one. The old one wouldn't let any Jew through. The secretary was a refugee, so you could go in with a carton of cigarettes, American cigarettes, you would give it to the secretary and she would say: 'Don't say a word, you want to go to the young consul', she knew it.

Race and politics

In Australia, as in other settlement countries, the issue of race tied in neatly with politics. As Suzanne Rutland has noted, the preferred Baltic racial type also happened to be the preferred anti-communist political type. This led to a laxity in political screening. Nazi collaborators and fascist sympathisers, as well as members of right-wing groups such as the Serbian Chetniks and Croatian Ustashi, migrated to Australia under the same conditions of 'Cold War myopia' operating in other Western countries. Other DPs were members of far-right groups such as the Anti-Bolshevik Bloc of Nations, which was anti-Soviet, anti-Semitic, and dominated by radical nationalists, including ex-Nazis. At the same time, many DPs who were anti-Soviet were not necessarily anti-communist. There were also allegations that Soviet agents entered Australia by posing as DPs.[34]

The Australian selection teams – and indeed the Australian Government – were inexperienced in European

'Chifley liked them blond'

languages and geopolitics. After meeting with Calwell's party in July 1947, Helen Ferber wrote: 'Nobody knew anything about the DPs and nobody had planned for them to meet anyone that knew anything about DPs. They just goggled when I started to explain to them some of the problems and pitfalls. Talk about innocents abroad!' A member of the Australian selection team in Germany similarly wrote to a friend:

> The Australian mission is a complete shambles run by incompetent idiots. There is no rhyme or reason in the way a selection officer gets his job. The majority of them haven't got an inkling of the political background of Europe ... They have no prior briefing as to their duties and ... many are the wrong types to be in a job like this.[35]

The selection teams were dependent on interpreters and 'cursory' or flawed intelligence from the IRO and foreign sources. Selection officer George Kiddle later recalled that sometimes they worked with a 'double interpreter – one for that into German, one into English'. Regarding identity documents, he naively commented: 'Whether they were all genuine or not, I don't know, but they all looked pretty crumpled and so on, as if they'd been keeping those very carefully.' Kiddle added that for the first ship, *General Heintzelman*: 'There were no [security] rejections to us in the American zone. Although I think one or two came a bit later when the *Heintzelman* was en route to Australia. We were too busy in Germany, [with] other things to worry about ...' According to Polish DP George Klim, 'it was just a rudimentary sort of few questions and looking at the documentation and that was it. There was no political assessment; nobody was asked about their political affiliations in any way, nobody.'[36]

The teams operated with minimal instruction from Canberra regarding politics in the selection process. The criteria listed acceptable nationalities and the restrictions on Jews, but there was no formal policy excluding Nazi collaborators from Eastern Europe and no information about the various institutions of collaboration. In fact, Jews were discriminated against twice – firstly because of their 'race' and then because of allegations that many were 'Communist Agents'. Likewise, the mainly left-wing Spanish refugees from Franco were ruled out of the Australian scheme perhaps due to both race and politics.[37]

Although Calwell had specifically recommended as 'absolutely essential' the appointment of an Australian Military Officer to carry out political security checks, security was soon sidelined. Two Australian Military Intelligence officers, clutching 'elementary German phrasebooks', did not arrive in Europe until 1949. In practice, and even after the arrival of the Intelligence officers, Australian officials simply assumed that the IRO had screened all displaced persons effectively, and they relied on officials from the United States and Britain for intelligence information. George Kiddle described performing around 138 interviews one morning – 'so it was pretty perfunctory, wasn't it'.[38] IRO sources, however, were generally unreliable, with Nazi collaborators allegedly infiltrating the screening process. In fact, Mark Aarons has convincingly shown that 'many in Western intelligence came to regard yesterday's Nazi war criminals and collaborators as today's potential freedom fighters'. In some cases British officials actively concealed intelligence from Australia so that anti-communist war criminals could migrate under the IRO scheme. Further, any evidence of war crimes presented by communist states was ignored, as was any subsequent information reported in Australia. In other cases, the decision to reject a migrant with a suspect background was overruled by Canberra.[39]

When the Jewish Council brought concerns about alleged Nazi collaborators within the DP scheme, Chifley is reported to have responded: 'When these Baltic women get into bed with Australians they'll forget all that.' Calwell further ignored his own security service, dismissing their evidence regarding the SS origins of some DPs as a 'farrago of nonsense'. Publicly, he warned that if Balts were stopped from migrating under the DP scheme, then so too would Jews.[40]

The ideal 'racial', age and gender types were far more important than political affiliation to a parochial White Australia suffering from a labour shortage. An involvement in wartime atrocities mattered less than a general perception of assimilability, and an ability to labour. Hungarian Károly Zentai, who was accused of war crimes by the Budapest People's Court in 1948, migrated to Australia with 'fit worker' handwritten across his selection documents. Ivan, a Russian Cossack who had travelled with the Cossack Army to Italy and evaded capture by the British in Austria, passed the Australian security questions with a story that he had been forcibly evacuated by the German Army and an entirely imaginary work history in Poland, Germany and Austria. He was pronounced 'fit', with suggested employment in Australia: 'Labourer'.[41]

The Australian selection teams were primarily interested in recruiting young, strong, healthy, male labourers for industrial and agricultural work. The average age of the first shipload of 'beautiful Balts' was twenty-three. The age and gender-specific policy was enabled by initial regulations that did not permit family groups with dependants (particularly aged dependants), single men or married couples over forty-five with children, or single women or childless married couples over the age of forty. The Australian Government aimed to import a workforce, not to give succour to refugee dependants. Selection teams were instructed to recruit sixty or seventy workers for every hundred migrants. In some cases, men with wives and children presented themselves as 'single men', hoping that migration selection criteria would relax. A proportion of these men ended up refashioning a new life, ignoring their responsibilities to their European families and eventually remarrying in Australia.[42]

An ability to labour was the most important criterion after race. White-collar professionals and intellectuals were not wanted, despite some mixed messages in this regard. The Australian mission attempted in 1949 to recruit twenty-four medical doctors to act as ships' doctors. Head of Mission Galleghan expressed confidence 'that they would be employed during their assigned period in hospitals as ward masters' or similar work, and that 'during this period of employment' they should be able to be re-examined in order to begin practising as physicians in Australia. Many doctors who volunteered for this scheme withdrew. According to Chief Medical Officer JN Wheatley this was because:

> Apparently their hands were examined and they were told that they would be required to sign an undertaking to do 'heavy manual work' for two years. It is not understood how 'during this period of employment, doctors should be able to satisfy the Australian Medical Authorities of their skill and make arrangements for the necessary examinations and get themselves placed on the register as practising physicians'.

The reply was that 'no guarantees' could be made to this effect.[43]

Of all adult male displaced persons, around 6 per cent were university graduates, 4 per cent were university students, and 11 per cent were high-school graduates, with the better educated usually from the Baltic States, Czechoslovakia and Hungary. However, from the beginning, the government was 'remarkably consistent' about ignoring any professional qualifications. Dr JS Smythe, leader of the Australian medical mission to Germany, acknowledged in 1947 that 'Australia was interested only in industrial and agricultural workers'. DPs were viewed and presented to the Australian public as 'technologically illiterate'. Polish DP Stanislav Gotowicz recalled that the Australians would say that 'they wanted people with calluses on their hands and muscles'; an Australian selection officer remarked: 'What a pity [we can't see] the calluses on their brains.'

The Australian selection officer interviewing Hungarian

DP Egon Kunz in 1949, recorded that Kunz 'tells a pretty big story [that he is] 1) a member of one of greatest families in Hungary; 2) the real leader of the students' opposition ... 3) a great writer, who could be recognised easily for his extraordinary writings (he says himself) and his style'. Kunz was in fact born into a wealthy family and had a doctorate in Hungarian language, literature and social history. None of this impressed the Australian officials who marked his documents 'Labourer'.[44]

Ukrainian pianist and composer Anatolij Mirosznyk later recalled that he 'had heard that Australia had very developed agriculture, so just in case, I obtained a tractor driver's license'. Officially, the first ship, *General Heintzelman*, carried only labourers, farmers, domestics, waitresses, housemaids and typists, while actually carrying doctors, accountants, policemen, soldiers, scientists, bank officers and teachers.[45]

To make sure that displaced persons were suitable for manual work, they had to be perfectly healthy, both physically and mentally. Calwell wanted 'the best that is in the field'. Medical officers were warned to look out for 'impersonation methods', including 'switching of x-rays and personal substitution', as well as 'bribes and threats'. In his DP novel, *The Uprooted Survive* (1959), Czech Vladímir Ležák-Borin characterised this as 'a serious affair, because not even Poles from the Underground army could falsify lungs'.[46]

Doctors were instructed to reject even people with minor complaints such as varicose veins and tinea, who might be able to 'utilise these disabilities to claim unfitness for work in particular localities or particular jobs'. Gordana described the medical examinations held by a recruiting mission from Australia: 'They looked at you like you were on the market. You had to show your teeth. They also looked at your muscles and you had to walk up and down.' Lithuanian Ale's father said, 'You would think they were looking for pedigree stallions! Oh, it was so embarrassing!' Medical tests also searched for sexually transmitted diseases, and officers were instructed that 'women of child-bearing age should be capable of bearing children'. Ale recalled that 'young women had to parade naked in front of Australian officials'. Chifley later lauded the 'virility' of the young DPs, a selling point in the 'populate or perish' argument.[47]

By late 1948 these strict policies became unworkable as '"bodies" had to be found' to fill ships and the principle of 'net gain' became attractive. As well as 'good and willing workers', Australia needed 'prospective breeders'. Thus, larger family groups were permitted to come, and in February 1949, so were 'widows, deserted wives and unmarried mothers with children'. After several years of pressure both from within Australia and from the IRO, some sick parents or close relatives labelled 'sub-standard' medically (part of the DP 'hard-core') were also accepted. In 1949, Andriy and Nina were permitted to bring with them to Australia Andriy's fifty-year-old mother, Tekla, after guaranteeing that they would be responsible for her maintenance.[48]

There wasn't always a happy ending. Historian Ruth Balint has outlined the case of a Czech DP who came to Australia in 1951; his wife was accepted in 1954 as part of a limited family reunion scheme. Their eight-year-old son, however, was refused entry, because his right eye had been removed due to an infection. A Red Cross officer pled their case to the Australian Government: 'His wife naturally refuses to leave the boy and come to Australia by herself. As a result, a severe case of hardship has been created for all parties concerned.' In other cases, 'mentally defective' or 'epileptic' children were placed in institutions so that parents could emigrate.[49]

Even in the last year of the scheme, humanitarian motivations did not determine the decisions made by the Australian selection teams. As one selection officer argued: 'We are getting to the "bottom of the barrel" now, and why should Australia take all those whom other countries would not have?' He did not want to see 'Australia becoming the dumping-ground for undesirables whom no one else would take'.[50]

In all, 170 700 displaced persons arrived in Australia between 1947 and 1952 through the auspices of the IRO. The main national groups were Polish (63 393), 'Baltic' (34 656), Yugoslav (23 543), Ukrainian (14 464), Hungarian (11 919), Czechoslovak (9142) and Russian (officially, 3256). When they arrived, the DPs were sent to reception camps where they were processed, taught English and learned about the 'Australian Way of Life'. They were assigned to placements for a compulsory two-year work contract, with little attempt to match up qualifications or prior experience with job vacancies, and no attempt to keep family groups together. The DPs were sent as unskilled labour, essentially indentured labour, to heavy industry, public utilities including projects such as the Snowy Mountains Scheme, agricultural work, and domestic and hospital work. Clune advised:

'Chifley liked them blond'

That 'Balt' who is 'working for the Council', chipping weeds on the footpath in front of your house, may have been a Professor of Philosophy in Lithuania, a poet of renown in Poland, a bank-manager in Prague, or a Cabinet Minister in Latvia. He probably speaks seven languages, and now is learning English. Give him a chance, he'll 'come good'.[51]

Ostensibly, Australia rebranded DPs as 'New Australians', a racially and politically acceptable group and a useful source of pliable labour and population growth. But the aims of this labour scheme at the policy level differed markedly from the individual lived experiences of the displaced persons, and the contrast was rarely flattering to Australia.

CHAPTER 3

'A hot Siberia'

This is not democracy. It is Russia.
DP gaoled for refusing to work[1]

Australia resettled more than 170 000 displaced persons from Central and Eastern Europe between 1947 and 1952, just over 2 per cent of the country's population. By the end of 1951, one in about every forty-five people was a former DP. The first task of the Australian Government was to sell the defence and labour benefits of this massive scheme – 'populate or perish' – while alleviating the fears of the local population.[2]

The first displaced persons arrived in late 1947. The country still held memories of mass unemployment in the Great Depression and was cherished as a white 'working man's paradise'. While the government's plans of an unparalleled postwar reconstruction involved national development and full employment, the risk was that the migrant intake scheme would backfire, exacerbating the housing crisis and causing nationwide unemployment. Calwell tackled the two main issues written into the IRO agreement – to ensure 'regular' employment and sufficient accommodation for the DPs – in a spirit of optimism, and in the context of an acute shortage of labour and the infinite 'postwar possibilities' of an expanding capitalist economy.[3]

Calwell decided to provide directed employment on similar lines to that enforced on Italian prisoners-of-war. Polish ex-servicemen, who were granted free passage from the United Kingdom to Australia by the British Government, were also put to work until they qualified for naturalisation (usually after 12 months). Another prototype was the wartime manpower scheme, which directed the workforce to essential industries. The War Workers Housing Trust had erected hostels and temporary 'wartime cottages', as well as utilising makeshift accommodation. All displaced persons between the ages of 16 and 50, except for mothers with young children, were assigned work placements; upon arrival, men were categorised as 'labourers' and women as 'domestics'. Accommodation was arranged by gender; after the initial stay in a reception and training centre, breadwinners were housed in workers' hostels, concrete barracks and tents, while mothers and children moved to dependants' holding centres, often with great distances between them.[4]

Camp life

When the first DP ship arrived in 1947, Calwell outlined the plans to house DPs initially in a former military camp at Bonegilla, near Wodonga in Victoria. He explained: 'The decision to accommodate these migrants on arrival in a well organised reception and training centre is an entirely new departure from previous immigration plans. It is, in fact, revolutionary, and is the first experiment of its kind to be undertaken in this country.' Australian Council of Trade Union (ACTU) officials were invited to visit Bonegilla to assuage trade union fears about the country's capacity to house large numbers of migrants.[5]

Far from being well organised, however, this was a last-minute decision which caused a mad rush for senior members of the Department of Immigration. They trucked sheets and blankets to Bonegilla and worked late into the night to make up beds before the displaced persons arrived the next day. The postwar housing crisis that forced the use of army camps to house DPs also kept the migrants away from urban population centres, restricting contact with the general population for at least the first few weeks. DPs were sent predominantly to non-metropolitan areas to work because of rural labour shortages and urban housing difficulties; there is also an implication that the government was anxious to keep them out of sight for as long as possible.[6]

Bonegilla was the largest, and longest-running, migrant camp. Its central location, equidistant between Sydney and Melbourne, allowed it to serve as a labour distribution point to several states. The other camps used were in Bathurst, New South Wales, Woodside, South Australia and Northam, Western Australia. Greta, near Newcastle, primarily channelled refugees to Queensland. Other camps included Benalla, Mildura, Rushworth, West Sale and Somers in Victoria; Cowra, Parkes, Scheyville and Uranquinty in New South Wales; Cairns, Enoggera, Stuart and

'A hot Siberia'

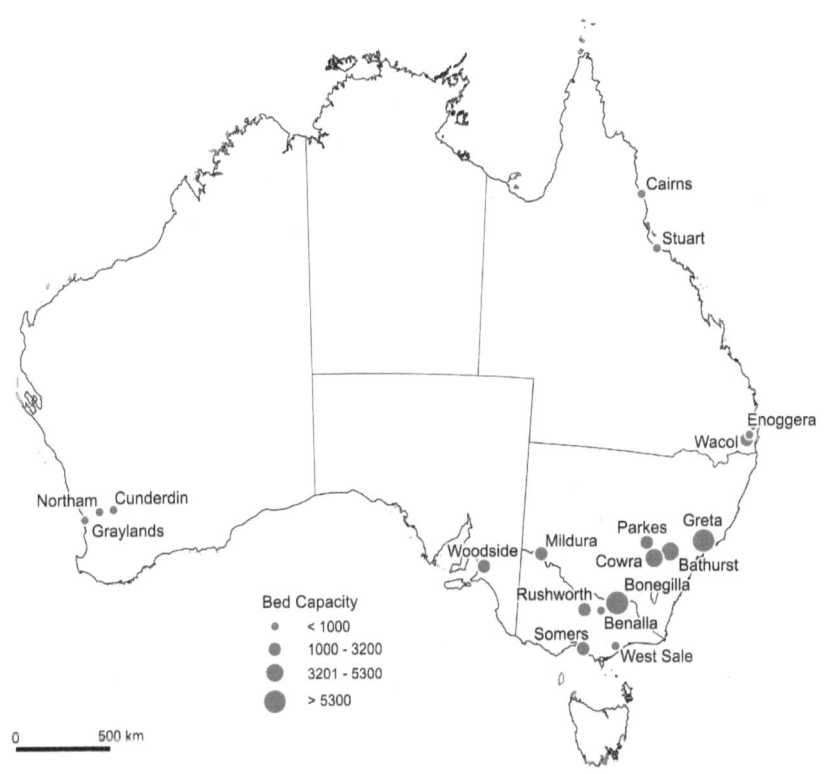

Migrant reception centres were in every state and the ACT. Bonegilla on the Victorian–New South Wales border, the largest and longest-running centre, was equidistant between Sydney and Melbourne and well placed to distribute migrants to their new jobs.

SOURCE Author, drawn by Olivier Rey Lescure.

Wacol in Queensland; Finsbury, Glenelg and Mallala in South Australia; Brighton and Burnie in Tasmania; Cunderin and Graylands in Western Australia; and Hillside in the Australian Capital Territory (see map).

Labor MP and Chair of the Commonwealth Immigration Advisory Committee, Les Haylen, admitted that the displaced persons 'are housed under conditions which the average Australian would not willingly accept. They live in camps, military camps for the most part, which are adequate to shelter them from the wind and storm but not much more.' Australian novelist TAG Hungerford, who worked at a migrant camp in Canberra, characterised the camps as 'real hellholes ... quite rough joints'. Gustav, an ex–Soviet Army surgeon, described the ex-army men in charge as 'paramilitary thugs'. At Bonegilla, the huts were unlined, furniture was basic army issue, and initially men and women were separated into twenty-person huts. Eating, washing and recreation facilities were communal. Each person was allocated an army bed, mattress, pillow, locker and chair, as well as army blankets and sheets, cutlery and army issue clothing, if needed. Food was ample, but meals seemed to consist largely of fatty mutton. As historian Bruce Pennay has noted, the basic accommodation and plain food was a win for publicists who could assure Australians that the migrants were not living in luxury. DP reception and settlement processes were efficient, effective and cheap.[7]

The first meeting with the camp commanders stood out to many displaced persons. The commanders were ex-army types who delivered a standard 'inspirational address' to new arrivals regarding 'camp discipline and hygiene, the way of Australian life, the Australian people, the advantages offered by the Government and above all the freedom of democracy in the country which they have accepted for their future'. Henry Brian Meggett Murphy, an ex-UNRRA and IRO employee, travelled with DPs on one ship from Europe. In Australia, he listened to a camp commandant telling a group containing two doctors, a veterinarian and several lawyers 'that it was no use their showing diplomas to [potential] employers, because everyone [in Australia] knew that they had been bought on the black market in Europe'. One Yugoslav DP, who was directed to work in the northern Queensland cane fields, later said that the first time he realised he had not come out for free was when the terms of the contract were spelt out after he arrived at Bonegilla. In Australia, the DPs were not seen as individuals but as a homogeneous mass of unskilled labour.[8]

The standard four-week reception, orientation and work placement included further medical examinations, a clothing allocation and lectures in 'utilitarian English and the Australian way of life'. This continued the experience of the voyage, where displaced persons had time for leisure and to prepare for their new country. One DP described the reception at Bonegilla as a liminal space, 'a border between one life and another, one way of knowing and another – a geographical, social and spiritual transition to a new realm'. Yugoslav DP Gordana described Bonegilla, situated near the popular swimming spot of Hume Weir, as 'a real heaven for us'.[9]

At the same time, camp life continued the impermanent, controlled nature of DPs' lives: 'It was another transit camp, everything was temporary.' For some, this brought about a mood of 'fear and resentment', the hope of a new life once again delayed. Historian Glenda Sluga later characterised Bonegilla as 'a place of no hope'. Leopoldine Mimovich, an Austrian married to a Serbian DP, remembered ten women in her unlined hut in the depths of winter, trying to sleep under an army blanket each: 'We were shivering all night. We couldn't sleep because we were so cold and you just heard sobbing in the hut'. Lithuanian Eugenia Bakaitis's description is stark:

> Bonegilla was in the middle of nowhere. There was not a tree, not a flower, just an empty army barracks in an empty, hot, dusty place. There was barbed wire all around it like a German concentration camp. And the heat. The supervisor used to tell us to bring bucket after bucket of cold water and pour it on the floor and then we would all sit in it. We felt this enormous sense of deepening isolation. We didn't know where we were, we just knew that there was no way back.[10]

Reception and training centres were temporary accommodations until migrants could be directed to a workplace, but some DPs stayed for longer, particularly during times of industrial unrest or temporary unemployment. Some even became employees of the camp system; Hungarian DP Laszlo Makay stayed working at Bonegilla for over two decades. However, for most DPs, life at a reception and training centre was a brief introduction to Australia where they were processed, before being directed to a worksite. The new Commonwealth Employment Service (CES) officers were instructed: 'Even at the cost of separation, displaced persons must be placed quickly from the Reception and Training Centres: they cannot be left in avoidable idleness and be allowed to bank up.' CES policy was to place husbands and wives in separate employment if necessary. In practice, this could mean sending them to work in different states, even while acknowledging 'the [well-known] undesirability of splitting family units'.[11]

In the early years of the scheme, a working husband sometimes left his family behind in Europe until he could arrange suitable accommodation in Australia. This was not easy while he was working under government direction in a country with a massive housing shortage. After families could enter the scheme, wives and children were placed in dependants' holding centres until the breadwinner could find suitable accommodation. Men could be sent interstate; in one instance, forty displaced persons were sent to work as timber cutters near Adelaide in 1950, while their dependants stayed in a holding camp in Western Australia.[12]

Visits back to holding camps were time-consuming and expensive. They provided little privacy for reunited couples. Halina, a young married Polish woman, later described how at Wacol husbands (illegally) visiting on weekends would 'climb on their wives on Friday night and never went down until Monday'. Sex was 'public because of the design of the rooms and the lack of ceilings. Every whisper was heard rooms away, let alone the moans and groans when you wanted to have a bit of fun'.[13]

Finding and paying for family accommodation near a worksite meant the separated breadwinner had to pay two lots of accommodation fees – for himself near his workplace and up to £3 per week for his wife and children. This situation caused great hardship when some men took advantage of the distance and refused to pay for their dependants. Nastasia's husband, Ivan, was sent to work for the army at

Manly and stopped sending money. Nastasia was forced to work as a cleaner, while caring for her two infant sons, in order to pay the accommodation charges at Scheyville, in Sydney. Some women incurred substantial debts to the government in this way.

The holding centre policies were not clearly communicated to the displaced persons before they arrived in Australia. In a 1950 article headed 'Married Migrants are unhappy living hundreds of miles apart – migrants are in despair', a journalist described his observation of DP men who lived and worked in Sydney while their wives and families were held at Greta and Cowra holding camps: 'In the hostels, after work, I watched the men. None smiled. Yet I had seen many of them when they arrived at Bathurst from the IRO ships, eager, cheerful, full of great expectations for the future.' Michael Cigler, a Czech DP, described the family separations as 'one of the most cruel things … Imagine! In a new country where you need the support of each other, you are suddenly dislodged as a family unit.' A Lithuanian expression was coined to describe victims of the family separation policy: *prievartinis gyvanašliavimas*, or one 'forced to exist as a living widow or widower'.[14]

Women felt as though they were 'held as hostages' for the breadwinner's 'parole'. Irma, a Latvian DP who was housed with her child at Uranquinty, New South Wales, while her husband was sent to work in Melbourne, later explained that 'the difficulty was that we were not together with a family – with husbands. For us, it was as long as we are together, and we are not.' Ukrainian DP Katja, with a toddler in tow and feeling 'full of doubt' about the decision to resettle in Australia, said that this 'was a very difficult time, feeling homesick and missing my husband'. Tanya's Ukrainian mother, Yelena, was stuck at Cowra holding centre with a sick, crying toddler; it 'rained constantly' and she 'got very depressed'.[15]

There were no facilities for childbirth in the centres, and women were taken to the closest hospital. Upon going into labour with her second child, and with no interpreter available, Yelena 'was in such a state' that her husband Paul was 'put in a taxi' at Port Kembla and taken to Penrith Hospital, about two hours drive away, 'to reassure her that everything was fine'. Antoni, a Polish DP, hearing that his wife was in hospital and his two-year-old daughter had been left in the barracks of the holding camp alone, gathered his luggage and gave an ultimatum to his employer, BHP – 'Fix job, money, or back to Europe!' He was called a 'smart-alec' and put in the hardest manual job of the steelworks.[16]

Migrant reception and holding centres were not ideal places to begin or continue family life. In September 1949 19 recently arrived children died, 13 of them at Bonegilla. An inquiry found that children suffering from gastroenteritis had been on a shipboard diet of boiled water for a prolonged time. An estimated 40 children died in 1949, either in transit to Australia, or in migrant camps in Australia, many of them from malnutrition. The IRO suspended the movement of children under the age of one for several months and from December 1949, began flying infants to Australia. Medical facilities at Bonegilla were also improved and blocks with heated rooms, bassinettes and hotplates were set aside for family accommodation. Camp kitchens were supplied with eggs and milk for young children, and parents were given access to refrigerators. Other changes included opening infant feeding rooms, creches and kindergartens, and installing outdoor play equipment. These measures were, however, always too few for requirements.[17]

Marriages also suffered and jealousy was rife. Anxious husbands worried their wives might have affairs with the maintenance workers at the holding centres. Polish DP Halina, who worked as a nurses' aide at Wacol in Brisbane, recalled a highly educated Baltic DP 'quite openly prostituting herself for money'. Social workers identified the main issue facing the DP cohort as 'marital problems' due to family separation. Hungarian DP Edith Tórókfalvy wrote to her husband from a holding centre in Mildura, Victoria: 'It is dreadful what is going on here. Every second couple wants to be divorced.' Adam, a child at the time, remembers 'it was on for young and old' after a domestic stabbing at Greta, New South Wales with 'screaming and shouting, blood everywhere'. Indeed, Australian church leaders condemned official policy for causing widespread separation and divorce.[18]

One local community was moved to help, organising transport once a month for the men working at State Rivers in Springvale, Victoria to travel to the holding centre at Somers, a two-hour drive. According to Ukrainian DP Snowy, they 'felt that it was pretty barbaric that on arrival in a new country they were immediately separated; the feeling was that they should be kept together'. Ukrainian DP Katherina managed to find work with her husband (and toddler) on the Snowy Mountains Scheme, which meant living in a tent and spending long hours cleaning and washing clothes for six engineers, using water from a creek or melted snow. Some women who couldn't find work close by, defiantly, and under threat of deportation, 'squatted' at their husband's work camps with children in tow. In Tasmania, wives and children were forcibly removed from such work camps, and some women threatened suicide during this process.[19]

So many husbands wrote to the Department of Immigration asking that their families be moved closer to them that the department told them to stop: 'The Department knows the moves and will make them as soon as possible'. After June 1950, fewer families were separated, and generally for less time. Married women were released from their work contracts when their husband found work and independent accommodation. Limited childcare facilities were also established at the holding centres so mothers could obtain paid employment (including work at the camp hospital, kitchen or laundry) in order to contribute to the family budget.[20]

In other cases, institutions such as the Swan Boys' Home in Perth, run by the Anglican Church, took in children on a temporary basis. Some displaced parents in Brisbane sent their children to board at Catholic schools in the area, at no cost to themselves; this was arranged by a Polish priest at Wacol. For instance, Polish sisters Anna and Zofia boarded at an Ipswich Catholic girls school for two years, while their mother lived at Wacol and their father worked and lived at Amberley Air Base (near Ipswich). They spent the school holidays with their mother, and their parents visited the school on weekends.[21]

Historian Karen Agutter identified a high incidence of child placement and adoption among the 'widows, deserted wives and unmarried mothers with children' accepted into the scheme in February 1949. Some women, particularly those with only one dependent child, were placed in domestic employment. But most were expected to pay weekly rent in a holding centre waiting for suitable employment that never materialised and ran up considerable debts. Lithuanian widow Elena, for example, who arrived at Woodside holding centre in April 1949 with her five children, owed the Department £230 by November 1950 at a time when the average annual female wage was £146. While social workers encouraged these women to marry, other proposed solutions to the 'handicap of children' involved adopting out newborns and moving older children into orphanages. In 1949–50, 67 children were removed from their displaced parents in New South Wales alone, including adoptions. Mothers were charged around £1 per child per week for temporary placements in institutions. Harold Holt, displaying the government's usual sensitivity to migrant families, declared: 'Now that the mothers have been relieved of the responsibility of looking after their children they are free to engage in remunerative employment, in fact they are obliged to do so.'[22]

The average stay in a holding centre was ten months; historians have described them as 'sitting camps' where families were 'waiting for their lives to begin'. While most moved on, and life did begin (again), the protracted postwar housing crisis forced some to return. Longer stays also sometimes occurred for the so-called 'problem cases' of single women and widows who felt unable to leave the protection of the camp. A Yugoslav displaced person and her three children remained at Wacol from 1949 until the death of her husband in 1956. At Benalla, Mrs J Kozolowski was among a group of women who stayed at the holding centre for 16 years, only leaving when the camp closed.[23]

Camp life and the communal living conditions of the holding centres sometimes caused problems. At Uranquinty a riot broke out when camp management insisted on meals being taken in the communal dining room: plates were thrown, the women 'kicked and scratched at police', and one woman was stabbed. At Cowra, about 30 female displaced persons wrote to politicians, conducted a demonstration and ran up a black flag of mutiny to protest against the poor quality of camp food, particularly for children, as well as heating and general living conditions. Some went on a 24-hour hunger strike. At Parkes, the unpopular director and the camp 'police chief' were beaten by the husbands of some of the women. At Benalla, when women argued for power points so they could use electric radiators in the huts, the department worried they would use the radiators for cooking; the camp was supposed to be temporary, 'not a permanent hostel'. The Benalla branch of the Australian Labor Party took up the cause, and the request was eventually granted.[24]

Indentured labour

At first, the period of indentured labour was vague. Initially it was 'for at least a year', which became two years, was reduced to 18 months and finally raised back up to two years. The DPs (and the Australian press) commonly supposed that this contract of indentured labour was a simple exchange because the Australian Government paid for their passage. This belief was based on information given to prospective DP migrants in Europe: 'Selection will be carried out by Australian Selection Officers and those persons accepted will receive free passages to Australia.' Many DPs thought they owed 'the Government the cost of the trip'. Edward Dukas reasoned: 'If the government paid for our passage and so on and our keep for the first couple of weeks ... you can't expect, you know, everything to be given.' In the words of a Ukrainian DP: '[we] were indentured to work to pay off our grim passage to freedom'.[25]

In fact, by March 1950 Australia had contributed £2 862 000 to IRO expenditure, including the £10 passage contribution for each displaced person, while the IRO had spent £25 000 000 forwarding the DPs to Australia. Bulgarian DP Victoria Zabukovec later noted in her autobiographical novel, *The Second Landing*:

> I read an article last weekend, that by June 1950, about 130 000 displaced persons were brought out to Australia. The cost to the Commonwealth Government was £41 sterling per person. This money was recouped by the government after only two to three months employment, out of income tax alone. The economist who wrote the article called the DP scheme 'The best Australian business investment since Federation'. So let's not get too emotional with gratitude.[26]

'A hot Siberia'

The work contract, the defining feature of the DP scheme, was essentially Calwell's whim. He later admitted: 'This was my idea. I thought it was fair because we provided accommodation at Bonegilla, a former army camp, later at Bathurst and then all around Australia.' He faced some political opposition, particularly from Labor MP Kim Beazley Snr, who objected to a 'tied labour' scheme, and Nationalist MP Thomas White, who noted: 'It is surprising that Europeans ... should be brought into the country on that basis, when, in our own territory of New Guinea, we have abolished the system of indentured labour.' Calwell, however, argued that the DPs had 'two years of guaranteed employment and two years of guaranteed accommodation'.[27] Some DPs, and particularly young, single male labourers, agreed with his assessment of the advantages. Ukrainian DP Andriy was sent to work at Port Kembla steelworks and later said: 'We were in Germany for years and no future, no work, nothing, just bludging round there, angry and with no job, and so, we were here to work.'

For the Australian Government, the 'two years of guaranteed', pliable and vulnerable labour secured trade union support for the scheme, by removing the DPs from direct competition with Australian workers. An agreement with trade unions also compelled DPs to join the appropriate union as a condition of employment, which made them eligible to vote in union elections. Despite this, Calwell apparently promised the business community that the DPs would not become involved in trade disputes. He assured working Australians that 'migrants would not be used to worsen prevailing working conditions, nor would they be used in any industrial trouble in the industries in which they were employed'. If any dispute erupted, the DPs would be removed to their camps until the dispute was settled.[28]

DPs were under the authority and protection of the Department of Immigration for the term of their work contract, and sent where the government saw a need. The new CES acted as the department's agent in each reception and training camp, arranging the transfer of DPs from the camps to particular jobs. In January 1948 the Department of Labour and National Service codified the policy and procedural guidelines within a Department of Immigration framework. The guidelines stated that DPs should not displace Australian workers and should only be placed where there was accommodation available and should receive award rates of pay.[29]

The displaced persons were directed to essential industries for the postwar reconstruction effort, including the building industry, government construction projects such as the Snowy Mountains Scheme and public services such as the railways. In 1950 DPs made up a quarter of the workforce in iron- and steel-works; 30 per cent of the workforce in cement works; 10 per cent of the workforce in the timber industry; and 15 per cent of the workforce in the brick and tile industry. By 1952, DPs comprised 20 per cent of BHP employees at Port Kembla and Newcastle. Female DPs primarily provided unskilled labour in manufacturing industries, and also worked in the public service as typists, in country hospitals and domestic situations (to assist families with three or more children, or doctors' households).[30]

Government and business gained most of the advantages of this system – administrative, economic and political. To the DPs, however, fell many disadvantages.

Donkey work

Integral to the DP labour scheme was the requirement that DPs 'should not be placed in employment for which suitable Australian workers are available or under circumstances leading to the displacement of Australian workers'. Zabukovec described the 'mental, physical and emotional shock' the DPs suffered as a result of this policy as 'a second prison sentence'. DPs were not to be free market workers, but government-directed 'language-deficient unskilled labourers', in Australia to 'do the donkey work in the programme of expansion'. A joint memo from the Federated Ironworkers' Association, the Coal Miners Federal Council and the Building Workers Industrial Union to BHP set out a common policy: 'Displaced persons will be engaged on those jobs which are least attractive to Australian workers ... In other words, they [BHP] will give the Australians "the pickings".' Polish DP Bohdan clarified: 'the migrants did the dirty jobs the Australians were not interested in'.[31]

Most displaced persons had not done any hard physical work for years, if ever. András Dezsèry (who had worked as a journalist, press secretary and editor in Hungary) later described the employment selection process: 'Employers used to come to Finsbury [hostel, in South Australia] and pick out who they wanted to work for them, like a slave market. I was tall and skinny so was never picked. Finally ... [I was picked] to be a rubber worker.'³² One North Queensland cane farmer at Ingham railway station, apparently unimpressed by the DPs' physiques, began to squeeze some men's biceps. One of the men shouted: 'Have a look at my teeth too!' and 'growled at him'. Polish–Ukrainian Karl, whose father was sent to work for BHP at Port Kembla, described another dilemma: 'The work was difficult. Our people were basically off the land, so working in heavy industry was a bit of a culture shock.' Oksana's father, a Ukrainian lawyer and amateur pianist, lost the first joint of all four fingers of his right hand in an industrial accident. Industrial accidents were common.³³

Many of these jobs were in rural areas; employment 'outside metropolitan areas' was directed in order to avoid the concentration of displaced persons in any one locality. Polish DP Mr J Birman complained in 1949 to a journalist that 'the foreigner was considered to be a "strange animal", to be sent to the bush to work while the Australians stayed in the cities'. Workers were accommodated in hostels provided by the Department of Labour and National Service, or in accommodation provided by their employer. Ukrainian DP Sandor Berger described his work and accommodation as part of the massive Snowy Mountains Scheme labour force:

> There were no roads at all, only bush and rocks and mud when it rained, and people had to live under quite uncomfortable conditions. I stayed there in the Snowy Mountains for two winters, during which time I was transferred to five different camps, slept in tents in freezing weather, helped to build roads with pick and

shovel, drove tipping trucks amidst snowstorms and along dangerous narrow and winding tracks that were covered with snow or ice at winter time, and with mud reaching to the knee every spring and autumn, and choking dust clouds in summer.[34]

In a factory work camp near Newcastle, DPs complained the accommodation was 'worse than in German displaced persons' camps'. The camp had wooden huts with no lights or refrigeration, cooking was carried out on an open fire and water carted from a nearby town. In Yallourn North, Victoria, DPs shared tents; amenities included stretcher beds, straw mattresses and lanterns. As historian and second-generation Lithuanian DP Josef Sestokas notes, 'the new arrivals thought this was all a bit backward, but were reluctant to complain'.[35]

Some felt their new conditions keenly. One displaced person, working in isolation in forestry in New South Wales, wrote in 1949: 'I am not far from committing suicide. I am working now for five months in the wood. I am sorry to say, but I am getting crazy … I cannot eat, I cannot sleep, my nerves are so bad that it is difficult to control them.' Some South Australian railway worksites were so isolated that if DPs requested a release after working for six months, staff were instructed to reassign them. In 1948 it was announced that DPs working in the sugar industry would be released after completing two seasons in the industry, rather than two calendar years. Such compassion was an exception to the rule and, indeed, this edict was revoked in early 1951.[36]

There were some instances of 'cultured European girls of seventeen or eighteen sent to cook for cane cutting gangs in North Queensland'. Social worker Hazel Dobson alerted the government to the fact that in the cane cutting gangs, 'at least four women are pregnant … the work is very arduous and in the frailer type of woman, could result in the loss of the child'. A CES officer's informal handwritten response on the report stated: 'The CES did not knowingly send pregnant women and can't be responsible for pregnancy. Miss Dobson does not appreciate the problem we had to get enough labour in May.' Pregnant women were usually redirected from their work placement to a holding centre only in the later stages of pregnancy. Young girls were also sent to work at mental hospitals, and Lithuanian DP Ale Liubinas recalls how this experience, as an eighteen-year-old 'without knowledge of the language or any training in how to deal with such patients' led to 'anxiety, anger and depression'.[37]

Professional lockout

The Department of Immigration was not interested in compiling a central database of potential employability, even though this information was freely available. The department never handed over its selection documents to the Department of Labour and National Service, which allocated work to the DPs. Similarly, the IRO's *Professional Medical Register* was described by an Australian official as 'of not much value in Australia'.[38]

If a migrant could prove to the appropriate union that

he possessed a tradesman's skill, such as in the metal trades or carpentry, he could usually be allocated an appropriate workplace. However, professional jobs were seen as 'too good for bloody migrants'. When employers did request displaced persons with particular professional qualifications and skills, the department either refused permission or gave it grudgingly, and retrospectively extracted qualifications and employment details from individual DPs via a form letter. Even after the public service and the private sector began clamouring for professional DP labour in mid-1949, only 400 DPs were employed as professionals, and 350 as semi-professionals, during their indenture period.[39]

In hand with the government's wilful ignorance of any DP's professional skills was the refusal of professional bodies to accord DPs professional status. Around 300 doctors arrived in Australia but their European qualifications and certification by the IRO Medical Boards were consistently ignored by the British Medical Association in Australia (and its successor, the Australian Medical Association). They could not practise on the Australian mainland without requalifying. If they worked as medical orderlies in migrant camps they were not to be addressed as 'doctor'. This was despite a severe shortage of medical graduates in Australia.[40]

Forty displaced doctors subsequently worked in the tropical colonial territory of New Guinea, initiating, among other achievements, its first major health program. In the mid-1950s, Queensland, New South Wales and Tasmania legislated to allow DPs who had completed five years medical work in New Guinea to register as medical practitioners. Around six doctors were also employed on a year-by-year basis by the Department of External Affairs in Antarctica; but they were blocked from practising when they got back to the mainland by the Victorian Medical Board. As the Melbourne *Herald* put it in 1950, when a Lithuanian, Dr Kostas Kalnenas, was reported to have successfully operated on the senior meteorologist at Macquarie Island, 'If European medical men can be entrusted with responsible Federal work, it is not logical to put special barriers around them in the States.' This obstruction nevertheless continued.[41]

Gustav, had worked as a prisoner-of-war surgeon in Austrian hospitals under the Nazis, was sent fruit picking in Australia. Another six years at university in Australia seemed beyond him due to his poor English, and the need to make a living. The rest of his working life was spent in factories, on the production line and then working in factory laboratories. He remained bitter about this abrupt end to his medical career. His wife Adele, an Austrian theatre nurse, worked first as a cleaner, then a nurses' aide, and eventually, with the encouragement of local colleagues, as a theatre nurse attendant.

While the Institution of Engineers stood out as a beacon of helpfulness, other professional associations including dentistry, veterinary science and lawyer institutes all refused to register displaced professionals, not only during the indenture contract but ever afterwards, in some cases. The Musicians' Union requested the government exclude selecting musicians from European DP camps, arguing that Australia had an excess of demand, particularly in the café–restaurant scene. It didn't stop there. In a 1951 letter to Immigration Minister Harold Holt, the Union complained that

> the housing of migrants in camps has encouraged the formation of small groups, ill equipped musically, but well rehearsed as Show men. They provide themselves with an array of instruments, satin shirts, ribbons and Mexican hats. Thus equipped they secure employment, where they intermingle with patrons and exploit their difference of manner and speech.

Holt replied that

> none of the migrants in relation to whom the Commonwealth exercised selection controls were brought to the country because they were musicians. Attainments in the arts have never been the subject of enquiry because the whole basis for selection has been fitness for particular employment. That rule will continue to govern selection in future.

Unable to restrict displaced musicians from entering the country, the Musicians' Union insisted that all musicians playing in orchestras must be naturalised citizens.[42]

As the department noted in 1949: 'In many cases, of course, DPs, in view of their lack of Australian qualifications, e.g. by reason of State legislation, may be employed only as professional assistants.' Calwell later remarked: 'Frustration and unfriendliness have been their common experience at the hands of the Australian professions.'[43] There are many examples of the 'talent and laboriously acquired academic qualifications' of displaced persons going to waste. One story publicised at the time was that of Latvian singer Apalonia

Sapalis, who was placed as a kitchenhand even though a Melbourne opera company expressed interest in employing her. Calwell's response to this publicity was clear (and harsh):

> Australia has a right to expect that these people – no matter what their skills or attributes – will give their services for a period of up to two years in some branch of the Australian economy in which labour is scarce ... When this particular young woman had fulfilled her obligations ... she would be free to exercise her talents ... DP girls are performing more immediate important work functions in Australian society by working as domestics in hospitals than they could ever perform with any grand opera company.[44]

Zabukovec included in her novel a celebrated anecdote, which has been repeated in various guises elsewhere:

> The story went that one of the migrant doctors – no-one seemed to have caught the name – had been questioned sternly by his three examiners about one of the reference books that the migrant doctor had referred to in his examination paper. 'How did you manage to get access to this reference book?' asked the chief examiner, rather miffed. 'It's only available in the specialists' library, to which you have no access.' There was a moment of deep silence, after which the migrant doctor answered in a quiet voice: 'Gentlemen, I wrote that book'.

Zabukovec adds: 'The story became the stock-in-trade of all Europeans who had suffered a humiliation at the hands of certain individuals, in an otherwise cordial and compassionate host society.'[45]

This loss of professional status hit some DPs hard. Wladimir's father, a Ukrainian priest, felt 'insignificant, self-conscious, inferior', while Oksana describes her lawyer father's experiences at work as 'terribly, terribly traumatic', causing him to 'psychologically shut down'. Kasia's father, a Don Cossack who had been the head of a technical college in Russia, felt 'always bitter; like slaves, somebody who had been made use of'.

Young, well-educated Egon Kunz, from one of the wealthiest families in Hungary, spent the early part of his two-year work contract at Adelaide Potteries and Ingot Cotton Mills in Sydney. He later described a 'tremendous amount of breaking down of confidence, intentional and unintentional', as he had trusted a British country to look after his best interests:

> We could never imagine that a gentleman would be employed in any other capacity than a gentleman.
> That was so deeply in us that we just could not believe it ... And I thought, oh well, Australia is supposed to be a very deserted place, there are lots of deserts. So there will be a lot of Ukrainian and Polish peasants building a road and I will count their salaries or something like that.[46]

Professional displaced persons who migrated under private sponsorship, rather than under the IRO agreement, tended to do better. Lukas's father, an Estonian doctor, lived with friends in Wollstonecraft while completing his Australian training at the University of Sydney and set up a private practice within a few years of his arrival. DPs, though, could not get released from their contract to attend university, even with a guarantee of maintenance. TAG Hungerford noted the irony:

> It was the price they paid for freedom – some of them, for life. If in two years hands that curled round picks and shovels forgot the feel of scalpels and bows, it would be unfortunate but not fatal. They were assured of continued work as labourers in a country shorter of doctors than of manual labourers.[47]

The Adelaide *Advertiser* (20 June 1949) reported on propaganda broadcast by Moscow Radio regarding the fate of the displaced persons:

> Twenty thousand displaced persons have been conveyed to Australia from Western Europe. Work and a good life were promised them, but they are coerced by intimidation. Not one of them knew they were doomed to slavery and a hideous life, or that they would be separated from their wives and children. Australia's welcome was a prison. The European displaced persons were put into special camps, where they were given several English lessons ... and then the white slaves

from Europe were dispersed among employers and were used for the heaviest manual labour. Engineers, doctors, and lawyers work as stevedores and stonebreakers, and all women, whatever their professions, are made to work as servants in private homes. They are bereft of all human rights.

The *Sydney Morning Herald* responded to this item sympathetically: 'What becomes of freedom and equality when DPs are directed to the sort of work that Australians reject?' Similarly, Hungerford noted with pity a 'drab fabric of disenfranchisement' blanketing the indentured labourers. Calwell's response to such criticism was shrill and unequivocal:

They have a choice in the DP camps in Germany ... These people were brought to this country at no expense to themselves and are being given the privilege of living in one of the best democracies in the world. It is not too much to ask them ... to give this country something in return for the benefits it is conferring upon them. They cannot expect to walk in here and pick and choose the jobs they like.[48]

As well as being allocated the worst jobs, the system was inherently inflexible. The only control DPs had over the terms of their contract was the opportunity to request a change of employment due to geographical distance from family or friends, urban areas, or professional and social opportunities. Others wanted better working conditions, or shift work so that they could continue to study. A District Employment Officer (DEO) had to agree to any request (and social workers were sometimes involved at this stage). There are numerous examples where the personality of the DEO and the English skills of the petitioner affected the response.[49]

Displaced persons have variously characterised themselves as 'the White Slaves of the twentieth century', 'like black fellows', and as 'transported' members of 'the fifth fleet', working 'convict-like'. Polish DP Halina, after describing the contract as 'slave labour', explained how some former forced labourers felt:

> Those migrants were people with little education, with little worldly experience and with shocking experiences during the war, shocking experiences. And those migrant camps were reminders of those shocking experiences. And they, perhaps not entirely consciously, expected something dreadful to happen to them from the authorities, because this was five years from those terrible experiences, make no mistake about it, they were shocking experiences! So you naturally haven't recovered and you come into circumstances quite different, but on the surface similar, and that's what was so terrible.[50]

Calwell was met years later by a displaced person who told him 'We were your slaves'; he responded: 'It wasn't quite like that, you know.' Later commentators such as academic Donald Horne, writing in 1971, agreed with Calwell's critics:

DPs were bought very cheaply. Most of them were penniless. They had little or no other choice. They were transported to Australia for [almost] nothing, housed in old army huts, even tents, and put to work on construction projects, mainly in the country areas. For two years they were bound to manual labour. After that, it was up to them. From an economic viewpoint they were a godsend.[51]

The contract obviously curtailed individual freedoms and strict insistence on it sometimes gave the impression it was a two-year sentence for people deserving punishment. Indeed, a directive from the Minister for Immigration stated that 'recalcitrant women from the Repatriation Hospital (in Brisbane) were to be placed [for employment] in mental hospitals' as punishment to the individual (for recalcitrance) and as a deterrent to others. Similarly, Yallourn North, a work camp for the State Electricity Commission of Victoria, was described by DP workers as 'cold, wet and miserable' in winter and 'a hot Siberia' in summer. In fact, magistrates in Melbourne on occasion offered criminal defendants two choices when sentencing: six months in prison or work at Yallourn.[52]

Defying the contract

Some displaced persons refused to comply with the terms of the contract. This could include a form of passive resistance, being 'surly' and 'argumentative' to employers, in the hope of discharge. Estonian DP Edith, for example, placed in work at Greenslopes Repatriation Hospital (and probably one of the 'recalcitrant women' referred to on page 105), was described on discharge as 'very arrogant and abrupt in speech to Staff Supervisors – verges as near to rudeness as possible. Work fair (servery never looks clean), but Mrs Sillar finds time to smoke'. The local migration officer noted that Edith was 'well educated and considered to be [the] ring-leader of trouble-makers'. She was also 'no doubt [the] person responsible for [a] statement to [the] press' in a *Sunday Mail* article headlined 'Balts at hospital claim ill-treated'. The article alleged that the DP workers were 'frequently reminded that they were homeless and should be grateful for small mercies'. The hospital supervisor denied the complaints: 'There is one small element who feel that domestic work is not good enough for them, and I could name them.'[53]

Others, often characterised as the 'better educated', used 'tricks and evasions', particularly false medical certificates of incapacity, in order to effect a transfer from hard manual work or to resist relocation. Hungarian DP Frank, a lawyer, was sent to work in the Queensland cane fields. Terrified of snakes, he obtained a doctor's certificate and was then sent to factory work in Orange, New South Wales. Similarly Kati, a Hungarian DP, later admitted how her husband had evaded the work contract:

> Julius was not used to hard physical work ... He could not cope with such a strenuous job and needed to take on other work. He swallowed some chocolate wrapping which showed up on the x-ray as an ulcer. He was advised to take it easy for a while. This is how he got

'A hot Siberia'

out of the contract ... Many of the DPs had a difficult time under the two year contract.[54]

Other displaced persons simply 'started not to follow the rules', finding their own work or leaving employment 'without permission', while some refused to work at all. An unofficial estimate of 5 per cent of the DPs had to be 'reminded of their contract' by being stranded in a reception camp without a work permit or unemployment benefits after refusing particular employment. Others absconded and could not be traced.[55] In one isolated timber mill in Western Australia, almost half of the 149-strong DP workforce had fled within 12 months. At a Queensland brickworks, half of the allocated DP workers 'gave notice, saying the work was too hard, fares and transport unsatisfactory and the pay was too small'. In April 1950, the Newcastle Conference of the Clay Products Association heard that 'the present position in regard to Balt labour was most unsatisfactory'; two-thirds of workers moved on after a few weeks. By 1951, more than a hundred DPs each week were illegally leaving their allocated jobs, with up to 5000 in New South Wales alone having broken their contract.[56]

A migration officer in Queensland argued that a 'drastic' solution to this problem was needed, as 'once a displaced person has left his employment and his case is awaiting some decision' he 'occupies space in a hostel' where 'securing payment for his accommodation' is difficult 'and he becomes a bad influence on others during his idleness'.[57]

Yet, the indentured work scheme was, according to the CES, 'almost impossible to police'. All displaced persons were registered by Alien Registration Teams prior to entering the country, and destination addresses were recorded once a DP was given an initial work placement. After that, though, it was up to the DPs to inform the authorities of their whereabouts. In 1951 the Broken Hill *Barrier Miner* reported that 'the Department of Labour and Immigration Department are finding it difficult to keep track of all migrant workers'. A 1955 report admitted that 'the Department of Immigration possesses no comprehensive lists because migrants often fail to notify the Department of their moves'. According to an officer in the Alien Registration Section, the attempted control of DP workers was 'an absolute waste of time and resources'.[58]

Calwell determined that he was 'not going to allow a magnificent scheme to be wrecked by a few fools and agitators'. Displaced persons were threatened with relocation to worse jobs, and the 'steamroller of deportation' began. The DPs had been admitted to the country on a Certificate of Exemption from the notorious dictation test of the *Immigration Restriction Act* (1901), which could be set in any European language in order to deport anyone the government viewed as racially or politically undesirable. The DPs could technically be deported to Europe at any time (although the IRO disagreed with this reading of the situation). Around 42 had been deported by 1951 because they 'had proved to be unsuitable as migrants'; the reasons included 'refusal to work'. Eugene Suschinsky, for example, an acrobat who had an 'unsatisfactory employment history', was deported on the basis that: 'He had continued to accept stage engagements and has not been in approved work for the past three months.' Calwell threatened that 'the remaining offenders will either mend their ways and return to their allotted employment or else they, too, will be deported as soon as that can be arranged'.[59]

However, the publicity given to these deportations misfired when an increasing number of dissatisfied DPs began demanding deportation to escape from their contract and gain an inexpensive return trip to Europe. Polish DP Jewsygnij Blagi stated categorically: 'I don't intend to work. I am a political migrant.' He told the authorities that he wanted to protest to American President Truman that he had been brought to Australia under false pretences. Another Pole, Stanislaw Pawlowski, gave various reasons for wishing to be deported, as reported by the Secretary of the Department of Immigration, THE Heyes:

> At two interviews he stated that he wished to return
> to Europe ... [because] he had eye trouble which
> he considered incurable in Australia and which was
> augmented by Australian climatic conditions, that he
> did not consider Australia a good place in which to
> begin a new life and that under no circumstances would
> he ever live in a tent, that he had a de facto wife and
> two children starving in Europe to whom he wished to
> return.[60]

Czech DP Rudolf Hrelica not only refused to work and stated his wish to be sent back to Europe, but also attempted to influence other DPs into not submitting to the labour contract. Thus, from the beginning of 1949, CES officers were prohibited from 'threatening' DPs with deportation. So, when a DP working in Tasmania pleaded to be taken 'back to Germany', he was told by officials that this was impossible as it was too expensive. Similarly, Russian displaced person Kuzma Ivanov's German-born wife had been committed to a mental health facility, he himself had walked out on his contracted employment, was under suspicion for writing a letter in Russian to the Queen, and had been diagnosed as 'being of low mentality as well as probably psychotic'. He wrote to the Department of Immigration requesting deportation and received the reply that 'it is regretted that there are no funds available to this Department which could be used to assist you, but there is no objection to you and your family leaving Australia at any time by your own arrangement and at your own expense'. In any case, by mid-1951 the IRO was categorically refusing to facilitate the repatriation of deported DPs.[61]

For refugees still in Europe, Australia did not look like the best option. An officer at Bonegilla warned the Department of Immigration that 'some people who have already come to Australia are writing [to European DP camps] to confirm the facts of slavery'. An American observer confirmed that a sudden fall in recruitment was the direct result of unfavourable reports sent by DPs in Australia to the recruitment centres in Europe. In 1951, groups of DPs met ships coming from Europe shouting: 'It's no good! Go back home again!'[62]

Some DPs chose to migrate to Canada and the United States when they finished their indenture contract in Australia. Sociologist Jean Martin lived with around 200 DPs in a migrant hostel in Goulburn, New South Wales, for her doctoral research into assimilation. 'One of the favourite topics of conversation', she noted, was the possibility of leaving Australia for some other country. By 1958, approximately 2000 Lithuanians, or 20 per cent of the Lithuanian DPs in Australia, had left for the United States. As one DP doctor wrote to the *Age* (Melbourne) in 1950: 'Who would take the blame if there should be only one among the foreign doctors in Australia who could give something to mankind or science and was prevented from doing so? Could he be blamed if, being disappointed, he left Australia?'[63]

Those who stayed found a new beginning and a renewed sense of agency once the two-year indentured labour contract ended. They now had the freedom to choose where they lived and worked. While engaging with the vicissitudes of life in a new country, the displaced persons had five years to evolve from 'migrant workers' to 'New Australians' before being eligible for naturalisation. But the process was dependent on the key concept of assimilation, which was oblivious to their past lives and experiences and this sometimes created significant problems.

CHAPTER 4

'New Australians'

This feeling was very strong in [Australia] in us, you know, that ... it is a brutal life, migration, and particularly refugee migration, [it] knows no pity and bloody hell, we will make it!
– Egon Kunz, Hungarian displaced person.[1]

In a press conference to mark the signing of the International Refugee Organization Agreement, the Minister for Immigration Arthur Calwell stated that Australia 'was a country quick to assimilate new migrants' and hoped that the displaced persons would contribute 'their share of European culture' to Australian society. In May 1949, Prime Minister Ben Chifley acknowledged that initially Australians (and particularly those in the labour movement) 'must have viewed with misgiving, and some with grave fear, the introduction to this country of hundreds of thousands of people from other parts of the world whose customs and manner of living have been different from those Australians have enjoyed'. However, he noted with some sympathy that 'it must be an awe-inspiring task to settle into a new country' and that it was up to the Australian people 'to make them fit in as well as they can'.[2]

Calwell was also the Minister for Information so he was in an ideal position to 'condition' the local population to equate migration with a 'healthy economy'. He disseminated the message that 'the new life blood which will make Australia's national heart beat with the strong and measured pulse of prosperity and security has now begun to flow'. Under the catchphrase of the 'Australian way of life', 'culture' quietly replaced 'race' as the unifying characteristic of White Australia.[3]

When Calwell visited the migrant reception centre at Bonegilla in 1949 he emphasised that displaced persons were part of Australia's effort to 'populate or perish'. The children, he said, were 'the little boys and girls whose courage and valour might in the future be needed with that of the children of native-born Australians to preserve this country if it is ever attacked'. He was also keen to use the media to celebrate the sheer number of migrants. The Australian mission in Germany was instructed to identify 'an attractive female child under ten accompanying parents who are suitable subject for publicity' to be migrant number 50 000. They chose a personable seven-year-old named Maira Kalnins, a blonde Latvian accompanied by her five-year-old brother, mother and engineer father. Calwell spent £1000 diverting the *Fairsea* to Fremantle so that he could kiss the little girl when she arrived in Australia.[4]

More generally, Calwell alleviated the concerns of native-born Australians in two ways. He convinced unions that the displaced persons would '*make* jobs not *take* them' and assured the public that DPs could be successfully absorbed into White Australia. Far from being 'communists' and 'anti-labourites' as some trade unions were alleging, or the 'fascists' that concerned Jewish groups, Calwell described the DPs as 'blameless victims of war'. This resonated with many Australians who knew of relief efforts coordinated by organisations such as the Red Cross and the Guide International Service. Calwell stated: 'Many have breadwinners killed and have a desire to make a fresh start in a new country where they will be remote from the bitterness, tragedy and harshness of their experience during the last few years of war.' Welcoming the first shipload of DPs, Calwell enthused: 'Whatever your memories might be of tragedies in the past, we hope your future in Australia will be only pleasant experiences for you.'[5]

Despite pointing out the 'humanitarian, as well as national, importance' of the scheme, an Australian Immigration Publicity Officer admitted in early 1949:

> It was never our intention to find acceptance for the displaced persons through an appeal to the charity and sympathy of the Australian people. An acceptance born of these sentiments can turn easily to … contempt. The line we took was one of frank reporting of facts. We pulled no punches and we made no apologies. We stated frankly the terms of the agreement under which the displaced persons entered Australia (for two years under Commonwealth direction) … Such a frank line appealed to the Australian people.

In other words, the indentured nature of the agreement became the linchpin for acceptance. This frank admission came around the time a Gallup poll showed the number of people in favour of admitting DPs had doubled since 1947, providing they were 'healthy' specimens of the 'right type'.[6]

The Department of Information under Calwell's direction produced propaganda materials including leaflets, newsreels and films which were sent to media organisations, union and employer groups as well as banks and churches across Australia. The department also took advantage of national celebrations such as the Commonwealth Jubilee Year in 1951 when the Jubilee Train distributed 15 000 copies of the leaflet *Why Migration is Vital to You*, and several films about DPs.[7]

The Department of Information produced a number of films. *Mike and Stefani* (1951) used DP actors to tell the story of a middle-class Ukrainian family of four – Mycola (Mike), an engineer, his wife Stefani, their daughter, and Mycola's younger brother, Ladu. The film portrayed the refugee status of the DPs and highlighted the stringent Australian screening process to the extent that viewers criticised their harsh treatment of DPs. Also, its negative depiction of Germany conflicted with Australia's plan to allow German migration in 1952 so the film was withdrawn shortly after release. *No Strangers Here* (1950) showed a DP family settling into a small country town in Australia. Other films included *Marie* (1950), a 'romance' between DP Marie and the Australian sailor who rescued her; and *Double Trouble* (1951), a slapstick revolving around Australians in a foreign country. The films were designed to arouse the sympathy of the Australian public to the plight of the DPs and encourage tolerance, while simultaneously highlighting the innocent, compliant nature of 'grateful and innocuous' migrants. However, the films were rarely shown publicly because they were too dull. The managing director of Hoyts rejected *No Strangers Here*, a film intended for commercial release, for this reason.[8]

The government constantly reiterated the significant DP contribution to the development of Australia as a modern, industrial nation. The Commonwealth Immigration Planning Council (CIPC) was established in 1949, alongside the Commonwealth Immigration Advisory Council, to advise the government on the economic aspects of the migration scheme. CIPC had 12 members, 13 associate members, and more than 50 consultants. It was responsible for moving DPs into industry and developmental projects, and solving any difficulties connected with their employment and accommodation. Chifley's successor as prime minister, Robert Menzies (1949–1966), continually emphasised the theme of 'migrant' contributions to Australia's economic success, with his optimistic slogan 'Australia Unlimited'.[9]

The twin aims of the government's publicity machine was to justify the intake on economic terms, and to quell the expected 'White Australia' prejudice against the DPs, even as those prejudices had operated in their selection. As noted earlier, Calwell instructed the Australian selection teams in Europe to choose easily assimilable DPs, those who could be presented as 'magnificent human material'. He later enthused that press photographs of the early Balt arrivals, 'blonde-haired and blue-eyed', made it easy to 'sell immigration to the Australian people'. Albury's *Border Morning Mail* concurred with Calwell's appraisal of the first shipment, reporting that the women had 'surprisingly good complexions and figures', with 'splendidly formed teeth' and were 'particularly good types'. Department of Information publicist Hugh Murphy found that the Displaced Persons were 'their own publicity agents' who '"sold themselves" to Australia with their smiles, their willingness to work, their music and their arts'. Historians Stella Lees and June Senyard describe how newspapers portrayed DPs as harmless exotics:

> Every week the *Sun News Pictorial* carried at least one item about an immigrant, and for variation a family reunion, a beauty contest or a wedding might be given special treatment with a photograph to touch the heart. The stories had a fairy-tale quality ... Who could object to the little girl in Estonian national dress, the harassed mother of nine, [or] the strong and earnest young man?[10]

The Department of Immigration asked Gwen Meredith, the writer of *Blue Hills*, a popular radio serial, to remind 'listeners of the importance of immigration to Australia and the obligation upon all Australians to adopt a spirit of tolerance and understanding in their everyday contact with newcomers to this country'. Both Immigration and Information, the departments headed by Calwell, were concerned that people welcomed DPs and offered them practical assistance to assimilate. This sort of superficial representation was not always appreciated by individual DPs. Egon Kunz famously noted the lack of real engagement:

The DPs were to be depicted as intelligent, educated, clean-cut and appreciative, not at all the feared foreigner who threatened to lower Australian trade union, health, housing or mateship standards. These intelligent, accommodating people were to be seen as cheerfully accepting the worst jobs, arriving in endless shiploads to man public utilities, break labour bottle-necks, and generally help the war-tired economy recover. After a week of hard and lowly toil, they were encouraged to dress up at weekends in national costume and enrich their new homeland's culture by performing dances as an expression of their gratitude for being permitted to settle in Australia.[11]

The few single women could assimilate by marrying Australians. The *Australian Women's Weekly* asserted that there was no need for young women to change their unpronounceable surnames, as they might not have them for long. One young displaced person wrote to friends in Europe: 'When reading the various articles on us, one gets the impression that we are the most beautiful and best people in the world. They write about what we eat, how we swim and other such stuff and nonsense.' Australian writers set about 'preaching acceptance', with descriptions of the DPs which were 'more fulsome than accurate'. Lees and Senyard found that 'immigration was the most exciting thing to happen to Australia in decades', and 1950s authors often included colourful migrant characters and plot lines in their narratives.[12]

The most important new DP representation occurred when Calwell coined the term 'New Australians' to replace the derogatory terms 'reffo' (mostly directed towards Jewish refugees) and 'balt' (a general term for non-Jewish DPs) in public life. As one DP complained: 'To call Latvians, Estonians and other immigrants "Balts" is most insulting.' Calwell's response was to: 'appeal to Australians to outlaw these expressions. These people have come from Europe to join their destiny with ours in the development of a country they have willingly adopted ... They were innocent victims of war, displaced from their homes and homelands, and now, as Australia is the land of resettlement for them, they are no longer displaced persons. They are newcomers, new settlers, or, preferably, new Australians.'[13]

As a result, the terms 'Balts', 'displaced persons' and 'DPs' were banned from official communications. Delegates at the first annual Citizenship Convention, organised by the Department of Immigration in 1950, 'decided that the term "New Australian" should be taken to include all immigrants, irrespective of their racial origin'. This decision was, however, amended by the third convention in 1952 so that 'British migrants' were distinguished from 'New Australians' in official communications. Delegates argued that 'New Australians' designated newly arrived *non-British* migrants. Displaced persons were encouraged to abandon their perhaps dubious nationalities in order to become New Australians (homogeneous non-British migrants) in what Ukrainian DP and academic Andrew Lachowicz called a neat binding of 'parochial suspicion and patronising egalitarianism'. In this context, some migrants referred to 'naturalisation' as 'neutralisation'.[14]

The idea was to enact the transformation of displaced

persons into New Australians through a 'high speed assimilation' program under the slogan 'Learning to be Australians'. Australia's assimilation objectives during the 1940s and 1950s did have an 'integration' quality, in allowing that migrants would retain some aspects of their native culture and acknowledging interplay with mainstream culture. However, migrant contributions were generally limited to folk dancing and choral displays rather than anything more meaningful. Croatian DP and philosophy professor Kajica Milanov, writing in 1951 in the *Australian Quarterly*, noted that

> Australians probably get the impression that European migrants are quaint and charming people wearing funny costumes, singing exotic songs and performing their national dances; the migrants, on the other hand, get the false impression that Australians are childish people who are 'intrigued' by their old-fashioned costumes, songs and dances – long forgotten in their own countries in Europe.[15]

The term 'New Australian' exemplified the assimilation goal of the postwar immigration program, which left little room for nationalist political expression. The policy tended towards inclusion, but rendered displaced persons, both individually and as ethno-political groups, increasingly invisible in mainstream Australia. For historian Joy Damousi, a striking aspect of the postwar migration scheme was its lack of recognition of the past experiences of migrants, and of why Europeans migrated to Australia in the first place.[16]

'New Australians'

The government's policy of assimilation aimed for social cohesion. It was accompanied by a celebratory citizenship process for New Australians after five years in the country (in 1949 Australian citizenship was instituted with the *Australian Citizenship Act 1948*; previously, Australians had been British subjects). The displaced persons were expected, in the words of a Department of Immigration spokesman: 'To become part of the nation, to cast away forever their European background and become Australians in the strongest sense of the word.' Immigration Minister, Harold Holt, spelled out the official line in 1952:

> Australia, in accepting a balanced intake of other
> European people as well as British, can still build a truly
> British nation on this side of the world. I feel that if the
> central tradition of a nation is strong this tradition will
> impose itself on [the various] groups of immigrants.

New Australians were welcomed only if they acquiesced to British–Australian norms and values.[17]

Australians were also meant to see that assimilation would deter ethnic groups from forming a potential nucleus in times of war (as, say, fears of German enclaves during both world wars) or a strike-breaking force in industrial strife. In order to prevent foreign-language enclaves, the Department of Immigration directly supervised the foreign language press until 1954. A publication needed permission to publish, and at least a quarter of it had to be in English. However, as historians Andrew Markus and Margaret Taft note, there was 'consistently meagre' funding for 'assimilation activities', including the monitoring of the foreign language press. They argue that assimilation policy in this period comprised 'acts of omission, not commission'. In other words, while there was no special funding to assist the assimilation of DPs into Australian society, there is also little evidence of heavy-handed surveillance or coercion.[18]

The Australian Government regarded assimilation as a relatively straightforward process, with the onus on the displaced persons to adjust to the 'Australian way of life'. This apparently self-explanatory 'way of life' encompassed regular employment, owning (or striving to own) a house and car, and, of course, speaking English. Learning to speak English was obviously a practical start to making a new home in monolingual Australia, yet language also had broader overtones that revealed prejudice and suspicion. One Department of Immigration pamphlet advised DPs that Australians 'are inclined to stare at persons whose speech is different. Speaking in your own language in public will make you conspicuous, and make Australians regard you as a stranger ... [try] to avoid using your hands when speaking because if you do this you will be conspicuous.' While Australians were encouraged to welcome new migrants, the newcomers were expected to blend in.[19]

The government's rebranding efforts continued in a flurry of propaganda aimed at both displaced persons and the general public. In 1948, Immigration established a monthly newsletter for the DPs called *Tomorrow's Australians*, whose name was soon changed to the *New Australian* (1949–1973). Calwell said the newsletter would assist in 'Australianising' the DPs. It contained news items and 'Easy

English' language lessons. A supplementary newsletter, the *Good Neighbour* (1950–1969), encouraged native Australians to welcome and assist migrants. These two newsletters were, according to transcultural psychologist HBM Murphy, an 'energetic attempt by the Australian immigration authorities to explain each group to the other and to bring them closer together'. The government obviously wanted to shore up community support for the pioneering DP scheme. (Sir) Richard Boyer, chairman of the Australian Broadcasting Commission (1945–1961) and influential member of the Good Neighbour Movement, later explained: 'It was rightly felt that the new policy would succeed or fail precisely to the extent to which the Australian community itself would welcome and assist the newcomers in social and industrial life.'[20]

The Good Neighbour Movement emerged from the first bipartisan Australian Citizenship Convention held in January 1950, a meeting with the purpose of 'laying upon the shoulders of the Australian people an obligation to welcome the newcomers as an act of national service'. Prime Minister Robert Menzies, an Anglophile but also a pragmatic nation-builder, argued: 'If we admit migrants to our country, as we must, we must also admit them to the warmth and security of the national family.' Ralph Taylor, President of the New Settlers' League, Orange Branch was more prosaic: 'Whether we like them or not, they are here to stay and we have to do the best we can for them.'[21]

The Good Neighbour Movement coordinated an Australia-wide network of existing non-governmental welfare organisations, including the Returned and Services

League, the Country Women's Association, Rotary, churches and the Young Men's and Young Women's Christian Association. By 1954, 120 associations were organised into Good Neighbour Councils and charged with encouraging goodwill at a community level. JT Massey, the Commonwealth Coordinator of Voluntary Assimilation Activities, described this goodwill as 'friendship, Good Neighbourliness'. The member organisations were the 'brokers of the Australian "way"', using a 'handshake and cup of tea' approach to welcome migrants.[22]

This sort of casual plan had variable results. In some locations there was a real effort to meet the needs of newcomers. Ruth Arndt, a German prewar refugee who had qualified as a social worker in England, reported to the Good Neighbour Council from Canberra in 1955 with suggestions from migrants themselves:

> A very simple Polish migrant who has had hardly any education said to me that contact work would never work because the people who are interested in the migrants are the intellectuals, academics and others, not the sort of people with whom the migrants can really be friends. He said that the only people who could do visiting, etc. successfully were working people whom the migrants would feel they could ask back to their homes.

After receiving this feedback, Arndt had some success organising playgroups with both displaced persons and Australian women 'whose husbands do the same sort of work as most of the migrants'. Canberra also led the nation in providing childcare for women attending English classes during the day, and in advocating for a practice of active empathy: 'Nothing could convince [migrants] of our interest and "caring" more than this effort on our part to learn something of their language and their culture.'[23]

Ruth Arndt and her team were knowledgeable and thoughtful, and most members of the Good Neighbour Movement displayed 'sentiments of civility within their bounds of experience'. However, both contemporaneously and in hindsight the movement as a whole attracted a number of criticisms. There was an element of preaching to the converted about the celebratory nature of its public functions, instead of appealing to the wider Australian public. Further, the movement was a native organisation that extended a welcome rather than one practising an assimilatory culture. It was never meant to include non-British migrant participation at a leadership level, beyond some occasional cultural exhibitions for Australian consumption. Perhaps it ultimately, and unfortunately, emphasised the divide between Australians and New Australians.[24]

Until 1970, Good Neighbour Council representatives met annually at Australian Citizenship Conventions which critics, including the Sydney tabloid *Truth*, described as taxpayer-funded 'gabfests'. Here government representatives would view and respond to the council's resolutions. One such banal recommendation was to encourage migrants to change their names, 'such as spelling [them] phonetically to make them easier for Australians to pronounce'. The political aim of the conventions, it seems, was not to promote practical policy or behavioural changes, but to provide positive proof that a broad consensus supported the mass immigration scheme.[25]

The Good Neighbour Movement had a naivety and arrogance in its dealings with the displaced persons (and later migrants). Massey stated in 1951 that the task of assimilation was to 'create somebodies out of nobodies'. Boyer, although recognising homeland cultures, similarly asserted that displaced persons 'are eager, sometimes pathetically eager, to find in the Australian way of life a set of values, a new centre of pride and patriotism around which a life of dignity may be built'. He argued that 'the task of such interpretation is basic to the Good Neighbour movement'.[26]

Historian Gwenda Tavan argues that presenting the displaced persons as 'pathetic' people 'devoid of history or subjectivity' – Massey's 'nobodies' – shored up the support of the middle-class members of the Good Neighbour Movement, whose appreciation of the cultural displays such as folk dancing confirmed their elite status within the wider community. Instead of engaging with the real problems faced by the DPs – family separations and the non-recognition of professional qualifications for instance – the end point of the Good Neighbour Movement was the citizenship ceremony. Citizenship remade the migrants into 'real' Australians. Widely publicised migrant success stories all led towards a wealthy and assimilated New Australian. And even if citizenship failed to turn DPs into 'real' Australians, their children could be expected to become fully assimilated.[27]

Australia's program of rebranding displaced persons as 'New Australians' was predominantly a marketing exercise, albeit a necessary and groundbreaking one. Its primary purpose was to convince native Australians that non-British, European migrants were necessary for a postwar reconstruction of 'Australia United'. The departments of Immigration and Information under Calwell worked to allay fears that the DPs could form ethnic enclaves or act as strikebreakers. Genuine attempts to welcome and assist the new arrivals were few and far between. Most of the problems faced by the DPs were buried under an avalanche of celebratory propaganda.

Post-contract life

There was never an obvious link between the lived experiences of displaced persons under the indentured labour scheme and the government's stated goal of assimilation. In March 1949, Calwell announced that he would consider early release from the work contract for those who showed that 'they were fitting smoothly into the Australian way of life', but the announcement was promptly forgotten and never acted upon. Perhaps the migrant centre accommodations and subsequent direction to rural work was supposed to act, in the oft-quoted judgement of historians Richard Bosworth and Janis Wilton, as 'a sort of physical and intellectual sheep dip' into Australian bush culture. More practically, the indentured labour scheme effectively quarantined the bulk of displaced persons from the urban Australian population for the period of the work contract – generally two years. Historian John Murphy noted that contemporary commentators generously labelled the labour contract an 'apprenticeship' that worked off the supposed debt of passage and also earned the right of citizenship for DPs. However, the frequent transfers between camps and worksites and the family separations it involved had the effect, as one government official acknowledged, of 'breaking roots that may have been established' and undermining assimilation.[28]

Once the indenture period was completed, the main priorities were to find work and permanent housing. Many displaced persons moved to the cities as a matter of personal preference and to chase more congenial or suitable employment. As Czech DP Leo explained: 'I'm not a country cobber; I'm a city man.' Finding suitable private accommodation was still difficult, however, particularly for families. Julija's family of four was initially housed at the holding centre at Uranquinty, New South Wales, while her father was employed in Hay, some 265 kilometres away. When the family reunited in Sydney, accommodation was so scarce that they ended up sleeping on one bed in a rented closed-in verandah. Many displaced persons worked two jobs and saved every penny in order to afford a deposit on a house, or to be able to buy land on which to erect a garage for the family to live in before building a house. Braybrook Shire Council in Victoria reported in 1950 that landowners were profiteering, selling DPs blocks of lands worth £30 for up to £175 and that 'all sorts of inferior building materials had been foisted on them by suppliers'. Julija's family managed to buy a house four years after their contract ended, using contributions from every family member, and taking in two boarders to make ends meet. Lydia Demchenko's family lived with other DP 'squatters' adjacent to an Aboriginal reserve at La Perouse, Sydney; they stayed in what she later described as a 'shantytown' for six years until they could afford to buy a house at Lidcombe.[29]

Calwell judged the indentured labour scheme an unequivocal success for the displaced persons, reasoning: 'After two years, 80 per cent remained with the same employers, both governmental and otherwise. They were quite happy to stay where they had first been placed. They bought their own houses, established their own families, and brought their relatives to Australia to live with them.' The reality, though, was that many DPs were not happy about their situation. Regardless of education, class or gender, they made up the bottom rung of a 'dual labour market', staying in unskilled and poorly paid jobs. The government, of course, had envisaged this role, reacting to union concerns that migrants would take skilled work from Australian workers. Jean Martin noted that DPs in Goulburn, New South Wales, had by 1962 'merged into the lower strata of the community as a whole'.[30]

Prejudice against displaced professionals also remained, to various degrees. Polish DP Stanislaw Gotowicz was rejected for a non-labouring position as a storeman because he was not 'British'. He complained: 'How well I remember – during the war the Germans called us all sorts of names. I can still hear the obscene epithets that were showered on me. But they were our enemies, and such bouquets of garbage we considered as badges of distinction. It's a different game now. Here we're supposed to be building one happy nation living alongside one another.'[31]

Another man recalled that when he showed his employment and education résumé in a job interview, the official interviewing him said not to bother as 'nobody is really interested in your past'. One displaced person complained: 'For intellectuals, artists, Australia has nothing to give except food, accommodation and a place as a labourer.' Former professionals were cut off from their peers due to their new status as labourers; their 'lives shrank to a very narrow existence full of physical exertion, petty emotional hurts, and feelings of frustration and humiliation'. In return, some were somewhat high-handedly outspoken about finding Australia lacking in 'kultur'.[32]

Learning English was another difficulty in the post-contract years. The government refused to communicate or to encourage employer communication with displaced persons in languages other than English, reasoning that this would be 'impractical'. This policy extended even to the few social workers available to assist the DPs (20 in 1952), who were required to work without interpreters. Calwell was aware of the difficulties involved in assimilating a non-British migrant cohort whose *lingua franca* was German. English lessons were organised in reception and holding centres, as well as continuation classes for post-centre DPs, and radio-broadcast classes. The Adult Migration Education Scheme, which was funded and coordinated by the Department of Immigration, used groundbreaking 'situational English' techniques in its lessons; however, most of the teachers had no training or experience in teaching English as a second language. The classes were not compulsory and were poorly attended; attendance was difficult for shiftworkers and more generally unappealing after a long day at work. A 1953 report from Seymour, Victoria, described DPs working on the railways as having 'lost interest in the classes' as they were 'tired at night'. Attendance was also hard for women with young children, and impossible for people working in isolated areas. Out of around 340 000 non–English-speaking migrants in Australia by November 1951 (including our DPs), only 10 000 attended continuation classes. One male DP said: 'I only remember one word "button" and what does it matter anyway. They want us to do the work, not talk about it!' Most DPs ended up learning English on the job.[33]

Many displaced persons, young and starting families, and particularly those from working-class or peasant backgrounds, pragmatically decided to 'make their life here and make the best of what they had here'. This was particularly the case after the end of the Korean War in 1953, in which there was no outright victor between the purportedly communist and anti-communist forces. Hopes of a third world war ending with a Soviet defeat, and going home, faded. Once the decision was made, it encouraged practical efforts to adjust to a new homeland, and some DPs 'began to thrive'. An Estonian DP later explained: 'I did not like [Australia] at all. Shall we be honest? After being here ... the first couple of years, I cried. I wanted to go back to Europe. In later years we met people who were more like us.' Sociologist and Czech DP Jiri Kolaja described the assimilable DP as 'the functional type': 'realistic, active, and cooperative but concerned purposively with present-day problems and personal issues. He adjusts most easily within the new environment, admitting that he may possibly settle down in the new country.'[34]

The passing of time did help with material acquisition,

and with engendering a sense of belonging to a new land. Karl's Polish–Ukrainian parents had been forced labourers in Germany who managed to build their own house in a beachside suburb six years after arriving in Australia. His father worked at the Port Kembla steelworks until retirement. They were 'over the moon for making the right choice coming to this faraway place'. Ukrainian DP Katherina, whose family had suffered under Stalin's policy of collectivisation, and who had then been forced to labour in Germany under the Nazis, said that 'she didn't need to think about what heaven's like, she had found it here'. Also included in this group were people running from their pasts in Europe, which might be collaborationist activities and war crimes, or unwanted family responsibilities.

For others, the difficulties inherent in displacement continued. They had to adjust to another new habitat with the added expectation of rapid assimilation. In the words of Ukrainian DP Vasyl Onufriienko, New Australian life was overlaid with a feeling that 'someone somewhere is whispering with quiet malice, "Acclimatise!"' Polish DP and poet Zoia Kohut explained the difficulties simply: 'This place for us is a foreign land, and that is a pain in the neck.'[35]

Challenges and traumas

Most displaced persons came to Australia without any extended family. Some used the Red Cross Tracing Service to inquire about family left behind in Europe. Often if their families were in Eastern Europe, inquirers, fearful of Soviet repercussions towards their loved ones, said they 'only want to ascertain if their families are alive'. Historian Ruth Balint recounts some heartbreaking stories. The Red Cross Tracing Service reached a Ukrainian couple who wished to know 'who is the enquirer: they have no relatives abroad and their son Boris was reported missing during the war. They ask: Could it be him? And wait for a quick answer.' Boris was eager to inform them that he was indeed alive and in Australia, 'happily married with a daughter and son'.[36]

As well as family disruption, there were also problems for single men who wished to marry. In 1953 there was only one non-British migrant woman to every three marriageable males; by 1959, the Snowy Mountains Scheme, an employment hub for many displaced persons after the end of the contract period, was characterised as 'The Land of Lonely He-Men'. The *Australian Women's Weekly*'s idea that DP women might marry locals (and lose their unpronounceable surnames), didn't work the other way around. The assumption was that Australian girls would baulk at foreign husbands (which of course was not always true). George Bielski, a Jewish Polish DP and Auschwitz survivor, prepared a report for the Australian Workers' Union on 'Problems of the Migrants', with a whole section devoted to this issue. Bielski, who himself married an Australian woman, nevertheless recommended bringing thousands of single women from Europe to solve this 'acute' problem.[37]

Czech Vladímir Ležák-Borin, a journalist and political maverick, arrived in Australia via the United Kingdom and not through the IRO. An outspoken advocate for displaced persons, he initiated correspondence with government departments and ministers, including Harold Holt, and wrote for the press, pointing out the lack of marriageable women for single DP men. Characterising them as 'Australian bachelors of misery', he described 'excellent, strong and intelligent men' who are 'notorious alcoholics, nuisance to the community, lost people because in spite of all their attempts they failed to marry here, to have family which would give them reason for existence'. He argued that 'tens of thousands of European men are perishing here slowly in this way'. His proposal that the government arrange to bring out 10 000 marriageable women, with transport costs to be paid (somehow, eventually) by 10 000 New Australian men, was ignored.[38]

One of these 'excellent men', still single in 1962, explained: 'You can get a good job here and have all the money you want – but *inside* there is nothing.' The *Advocate* (Tasmania) noted a phenomenon of 'lost weekends', where young single displaced persons would wander aimlessly: migrants may be content enough in their work, but 'not so happy in their leisure'. This loss of family and community exacerbated existing problems. Michael's father was a Czech displaced person who married ten years after his arrival in Australia, when he was in his late thirties. Michael described his father's associates:

> A lot of them were completely stuffed. He was living, when he settled in, he was living in the inner-city, inner-west sort of area, in a boarding house situation with lots of Poles, Latvians, Lithuanians, they were sort of living as a group and most of them would have been there twenty years actually, because a lot of them were that stuffed from the war and what they'd seen that they

were pretty hard living. They drank themselves to death, most of them, they didn't really aspire to anything other than the short-term; they didn't amount to much if you know what I mean ... these people, I think the majority of them were very hard living and that takes a toll on anything. They worked but they were hard living.[39]

Alcoholism was not confined to single men. Karl, the son of a Ukrainian displaced person, later recalled: 'A lot of our blokes are heavy drinkers and I know with my father-in-law the things that he went through and he used to drink and a lot of it was to blot out the things, you know.' Nastasia's husband, Ivan, who had rescued her from German-occupied Ukraine, was a violent drunk: his eldest son thought that perhaps 'what he had suffered in Siberia got to him and clouded him and he became totally aggressive'. Adam's Polish–Ukrainian parents were similarly 'traumatised', 'untrusting' and 'suspicious', 'isolating themselves' from the wider community.

Between 1950 and 1951, eighty-five non-British migrants (most would have been displaced persons) were certified for admission to mental hospitals in New South Wales. The government-funded mental hospitals had 'appalling standards', and made little or no attempt to speak to the DPs in their own language. Hospital officials decided that 'interpreters were not useful'. New Australian DP Statys Bildusas suicided at 28. Dr PC Middleton, who examined him, complained: 'He could not speak English, and I could not understand what he was jabbering about.' Usually people sent to mental hospitals lost all social welfare benefits and any dependants living in a holding centre had to pay full accommodation rates, which was a 'considerable hardship'.⁴⁰

Some newspapers began publishing stories of tragic, somewhat pathological Eastern Europeans. *Truth*, for example, described a group of young, single, Polish displaced persons who led 'rootless, remote, uncommitted lives' which had 'a strong Dostievskian flavor' and seemed to contribute to mental breakdown. Similarly, an article in *Pix* magazine described the tragic plight of 'vagrant migrants … a lost race of despondent, neurotic misfits' who had 'gambled their lives in a new world and lost. Maladjusted, beset by language problems, burdened by horrible memories they just can't forget'. In 1950, the Melbourne *Age* reported that a young displaced person working in a Queensland road-repair gang had been observed 'brooding for weeks about his family, murdered by the Nazis'. One night he grabbed a knife from a table and stabbed his best friend in the back, then ran into the bush yelling, and committed suicide. According to the police, 'his mind suddenly snapped'. Almost sixty years later, journalist Mark Dapin described 'excessive alcohol and drug use' among an 'exotic population of elderly' DP men in outback Coober Pedy.⁴¹

Latvian displaced person Helena Walsh later blamed the death of her husband Visvaldis on the stereotype of DP alcoholism. Tragically, when Visvaldis suffered a subcranial haemorrhage, both his general practitioner and an ambulance officer misdiagnosed the condition, with his GP saying, 'There's nothing wrong with your husband that a few days without alcohol wouldn't cure.' Although they subsequently found a more astute GP who organised treatment, he died at age 37. A 1951 social work report found that 'a number of so-called alcoholics have been found to be definitely suffering from some form of mental illness'. Conversely, drunken displaced persons were on occasion mistakenly carted off to mental hospitals.[42]

Good neighbours

The Good Neighbour Movement was supposed to ease such problems. In reality, the movement was voluntary, and both the follow-up by Australians and the response from the displaced was weak. Jean Martin found that the New Settlers League in Goulburn established in 1951 made only sporadic efforts to connect with new migrants before falling into decline and disappearing by the end of 1953. In 1954, a Queensland member of the New Settlers League admitted: 'In the past, we laughed at them' and congratulated himself and his movement on the fact that 'we now laugh with them'. HBM Murphy, who studied displaced persons *in situ*, was highly critical of the movement, arguing that its 'main effect is to excuse higher officials from the trouble of thinking what the differences in the two communities are and what steps need to be taken to overcome them'. Murphy believed more specific welfare services were needed, and not 'too great a discrepancy between the vague principles put out by [the DPs] prospective country of resettlement and the way in which they are actually treated by it'.[43]

In Australia, DPs found prejudice from people used to living under the protected employment conditions and strict immigration conditions of White Australia. Latvian displaced person Helena Walsh later described the general atmosphere:

> Although the faces around me were always smiling, the press and other media often expressed concern that the influx of European immigrants would endanger the 'Australian way of life'. We were referred to not so much as people with feelings and sensitivities but as a new breed of sheep which could endanger the fragile environment. The reason for our migrant status was never mentioned. Comparing the reports with the enticements to come to Australia, it seemed as if one part of Australian society had no idea what the other part was doing![44]

The recruitment of the displaced persons was done without consulting the general community who were presented with the mass immigration scheme as a fait accompli. The new scheme was not unilaterally opposed, but many thought speedy assimilation was important, and that DPs should speak English in public places. Ann Mihkelson, an Estonian DP who arrived in Australia as a child, later expressed her desire to become 'anonymous': 'I desperately wanted to fit in, to assimilate, to disappear.'[45]

One of the earliest memoirs written by a displaced person, that of Hungarian Cecile Kunrathy in 1963, contains a spirited defence of the displaced persons scheme in Australia and an acceptance of the descriptor 'New Australians'. She said: 'I liked the new name. Within five years we would be naturalised and we would leave the "new" off altogether.' Similarly, Polish–Jewish DP Diane Armstrong's parents 'liked being called New Australians. It made them feel accepted.' However, for Ludmilla Forsyth, a Ukrainian DP who arrived in Australia as a child: 'The shining quality of being a New Australian dulled into a painful realisation that some people thought one was a stupidbloodynewstrain and some children informed me that DP stood for Dirty Person.' One DP complained: 'We are only New Australians now. That is like being a DP, just nothing. If you went to America and said "I am a New Australian", what would that mean?' Martin observed that the DPs 'looked upon naturalisation principally as a matter of expediency and convenience', particularly in relation to securing social security benefits, ignoring the 'ideological and emotional significance' the government invested in the citizenship process.[46]

Within the general community there was some hostility. A Good Neighbour member attributed this to Australians having 'a feeling of enmity against those whom they were fighting during the war. They have longer memories than are desirable and their feelings of bitterness have not died down.' Jean Martin further noted that evidences of working-class animosity were common: 'If the bosses were generally felt to be on the migrants' side, fellow-workers were not.' In 1950, for example, members of the Australian Railways Union went on strike protesting that the displaced persons detailed to assist them had 'only a smattering of English and are of little assistance'. By 1953, one-third of Martin's Goulburn cohort had experienced an unpleasant incident at work. DPs were called 'bloody balts' and 'nuts and balts' as well as the older epithets of 'wogs', 'reffos' and 'dagos'.[47]

Polish displaced person Bernard Pilecki recalled arriving at Fremantle Port to taunts of 'Go back you wogs, we don't want you here!' Lithuanian DPs were abused: 'Get back to where you bloody come from, you bloody wogs, and get off the bloody road so we can drive our bloody car.' The poet Peter Skrzynecki, a second generation DP, recalls an elderly lady who came up to his group of friends in the street when he was a child and threatened to 'put us in a plane, into the ocean and feed us all to the sharks'. In even more extreme outbursts of prejudice, young Australians picked physical fights with the DPs. William Dick, in an autobiographical novel setting out 'bodgie' behaviour in Melbourne in the 1950s, wrote: 'Our boys hated these dagoes and bolts [balts] that were coming out here, trying to take over our country. And we told 'em so, and belted them up.'[48]

Even without experiencing direct forms of antipathy, Martin noted that displaced persons occupied an 'isolated and inferior' position at the edges of the Australian community. She observed that 'it was rare for a displaced person to meet an Australian who genuinely wanted to learn about his experiences and views and with whom he could carry on an easy, informal, and even reciprocal social relationship'. Jewish Hungarian DP Paul Kraus describes the 'detached politeness and correct smiles' from Australians that signalled the newcomers' foreignness. Australians were 'friendly', 'tolerant', but 'coldly aloof'. Hungarian DP Marta says that as the DPs had the 'virtue of looking like everybody else', 'pinpricks' of 'insensitivity rather than prejudice' were the norm.[49]

Social scientist and Hungarian displaced person ML Kovacs, writing in 1955, found that the primary difficulties for DPs in Australia were subjective and involved feelings of dissatisfaction, rejection, unhappiness and homesickness, rather than pathological psychologies, or complaints of concrete defects in the new life. He cited a common DP complaint:

> It can hardly be called a 'life'. There is no connection with Australian society. Australia for the time being can be defined as 'a place where I earn my living'. Society does not make any efforts to accept us. Our own efforts of private contact have been disregarded.[50]

Helena Walsh noted the parochial, insular nature of Australian society in the late 1940s and 1950s: 'Nobody was interested in where we came from but everybody asked us how we liked Australia.' Two displaced persons went on to use this question as the title for their memoirs: Latvian Janis Sakurovs, aka Jimmy Saks in 1989 and Ukrainian Anatolij Mirosznyk in 2009 both wrote books titled, *How Do You Like Australia?*. For Helena, 'the most difficult thing to overcome was indifference. People with different experiences did not understand and did not care. For them the war was over. But emotionally, I was still at war, grieving about the fate of my country and the people who stayed behind.'[51]

Perhaps, as Ukrainian DP Sandor Berger complained, displaced persons were 'newcomers' merely to be 'tolerated and useful robots who are here to be put up with during our own lifetime' or 'at best, for the precious gift of a generation of conformists we leave behind'. This view seemed to be propounded by Harold Holt, Minister of Immigration, who admitted in 1952: 'You get the fully assimilated migrant perhaps in the second generation. You don't expect to get it in the first.' Some DPs obviously took this sort of opinion to heart. Hungarian Laszlo Torok wrote decades later, in response to a sociological questionnaire from a fellow Hungarian DP: 'From Australia's point of view, the first migrant generation is a real dead loss, anyway.'[52]

People with problems

While the displaced persons were commonly depicted by the government as 'assimilable' 'migrant workers', indeed 'New Australians', the experiences of the DPs were more complex. Sympathetic social scientists such as HBM Murphy and Jean Martin described them, in line with their training, as 'people with problems'. This followed the example of European social scientists, such as Estonian psychologist Edward Bakis, himself a DP, who labelled the DPs 'neurotic'. As historian Peter Gatrell has noted, mass displacement was increasingly seen and represented as a 'pathological condition of the modern world', a source of 'trauma' and a 'mountain of misery'.[53]

In 1950, social workers working across the country reported handling 267 cases of 'maladjustment and neurosis'. The social workers believed that mental breakdowns came from 'the strain of adjusting in a strange country, often without relatives or friends to assist' that was often 'superimposed … upon years of personal hardship, fear, malnutrition, and sometimes even torture. In addition, the loss of family and loved ones through death or deportation is not uncommon.'[54]

Writing two years later, Murphy wrote that displaced persons suffered from 'displacement neurosis' and criticised the Australian authorities for accepting them 'with little regard to their individual need for asylum'. He argued that DPs who had an initial positive reaction to the two-year work program were experiencing 'a temporary euphoria'. The 'speedy mass assimilation' that Australia wanted, he feared, would result in 'mental strain and mental breakdowns' with potential social ramifications. Murphy warned: 'Excluding personal unhappiness, higher suicide rate and higher mental disease rate, which may be said to affect only the individual, the social dangers are three-fold: criminal, industrial and political.'[55]

To some extent this 'diagnosis' reflected a psychiatric worldview which relied on assumptions about place and the perceived need for a cultural 'home'. By the late 1970s Murphy had reversed his assessment, stating that 'the former belief that immigrants always suffer from an excess of mental disorder is no longer valid'. In 1950, though, Murphy, and others, identified displaced persons as psychologically vulnerable. This turned the tables on seeing migration purely from the perspective of the receiving country.[56]

Psychiatric studies in the following decades took up Murphy's concerns with regard to mental illness and argued that many former displaced persons suffered from psychological problems. The studies highlighted incidences of paranoid schizophrenia and depressive neurosis due to wartime experiences, the stresses of migration and the loss of social status. According to one study published in 1973, the incidence of schizophrenia among the Australian-born was 21.2 per 100 000 for men and 28.6 per 100 000 for women;

the figures for men and women born in Eastern Europe (Poles, Russians and Ukrainians, including Jewish Holocaust survivors) were 121.9 and 159.9 respectively. Another study demonstrated that people from the Baltic region (Estonia, Latvia and Lithuania) had the highest prevalence of alcoholism among the DPs; although yet another study found that alcoholism was no more prevalent among DPs than among British migrants or the Australian-born population.[57]

Murphy blamed the high-speed assimilation program for some of this mental stress. He argued that the differences between the communities were just too great to allow the displaced persons to recover their mental health effectively with the added pressure of assimilation. Murphy compared the lifestyles of Australians and DPs. Australians had a 'tradition of self-sufficiency and independence of social and communal activity with a very simple and largely defensive social pattern so that their personal contacts are few and their capacity for self-amusement great', he wrote. On the other hand, the DPs 'have a recent history of complex, crowded, communal life and of mental suffering which had made them very dependent on affection and on communal support, with a neurotic fear of being rejected'.[58]

Echoing these depictions of psychological instability, sociologist Jean Martin found, in her 1953 study, an 'insecure' group subject to 'migration stresses'. She described the 200 DPs living in Goulburn as 'unusually anxious and suspicious, and sensitive to signs that they were not wanted or appreciated, but also demanding, unreliable, and casual in their personal relationships, and indifferent to the wishes and feelings of other people'. In fact, Martin argued that even those who presented as 'well assimilated' were exhibiting conformist behaviour symptomatic of 'a disturbed and insecure personality'.[59]

Sociologist Jerzy Zubrzycki was a Polish displaced person who arrived in Australia in the postwar period via the London School of Economics. He also found individuals exhibiting occupational and social adjustment difficulties. One Latvian man was an especially 'sorry, pathetic sight':

> His only hope was in [his] wife and two children. In 1944 he was a partisan in the forests. He returned to find that the Russians had taken his family. Here, in Australia, he still thinks about them, and it is on these occasions that he drinks. He boasts of spending all his money on gambling and drink. He has lost all hope of returning to Europe to find his family. Here he reads cheap literature and leads a degenerate life.[60]

Martin and Zubrzycki advocated for increased government services for non–English-speaking migrants and became heavily involved in directing policy away from assimilation and towards a notion of cultural pluralism. In 1953, in front of an audience which included former Minister for Immigration Arthur Calwell, Martin argued for 'a slower rate of absorption, with the attendant maintenance of immigrant group and family life and a lesser degree of personal disorganisation'. She later stated that assimilation policy in Australia had been necessarily 'framed and perpetuated … to legitimate a policy that the state had to sell to the community'. Assimilation was predominantly a pragmatic public relations exercise, perhaps to the detriment of vulnerable sections of the refugee population.[61]

In the years immediately following the contract period, some displaced persons settled happily in Australia, including people who wanted to disappear from their past. Others struggled to assimilate, prompting social scientists to ponder the very notion of assimilability. A third group identified as a specific national or ethnic group in exile, striving for national and cultural preservation. This vocal minority of DPs refused even to entertain the concept of assimilation. Finally, an anti-communist group was determined to influence Australian society and politics. The unique perspectives of this diasporic minority and anti-communist cohort contributed to the way the Cold War unfolded in Australia.

1 *Above* Harold Hall (centre) was a member of the first UNRRA team to leave Australia in 1945. He worked in the US zone in Germany until 1947. During this time he was Deputy Director of Camp 208 Esslingen, and later Director of Camp 524 Ellwangen.
Harold Rex Hall papers, NLA, 2611706.

2 *Left* UNRRA camp, probably drawn by a Ukrainian DP at Esslingen am Neckar in southern Germany. The text says 'Arrived!!!'
Harold Rex Hall papers, NLA, 2611706.

3 *Top* Arthur Calwell, Minister for Immigration, with his private secretary, RE Armstrong, at Australia House, London in June 1947. The purpose of his trip was to establish the postwar immigration scheme. NAA: A12111, 1/1947/20/1, barcode 7475845.

4 *Above* The first Australian selection team from the new Department of Immigration: Colonel Sellars, Bill Barnswell and George Kiddle (1947). Kiddle later said their instructions were to pick people from the Baltic states for the first ship, people who looked 'attractive to the Australian population'. NAA: A12111, 2/1947/35A/1B, barcode 30654307.

5 *Right* The Commonwealth Department of Information tried to sell Australia as a land of 'industry and sunshine' through booklets, films and posters, such as this poster from 1947. Australia was not generally the destination of choice for displaced persons so the department worked hard to spruik its advantages. NAA: A12111, 1/1947/3/7, barcode 7529171.

6 *Right* The 1947 poster 'Australia – Land of Tomorrow', by artist Joe Greenberg, was expected to capture plenty of attention through its exuberant colour and novelty. Museum Victoria.

7 *Below* The parents of a baby born aboard the *Fairsea* are also about to start a new life as the ship approaches Perth (1949). NAA: A8139, VOLUME 7; barcode 8318170.

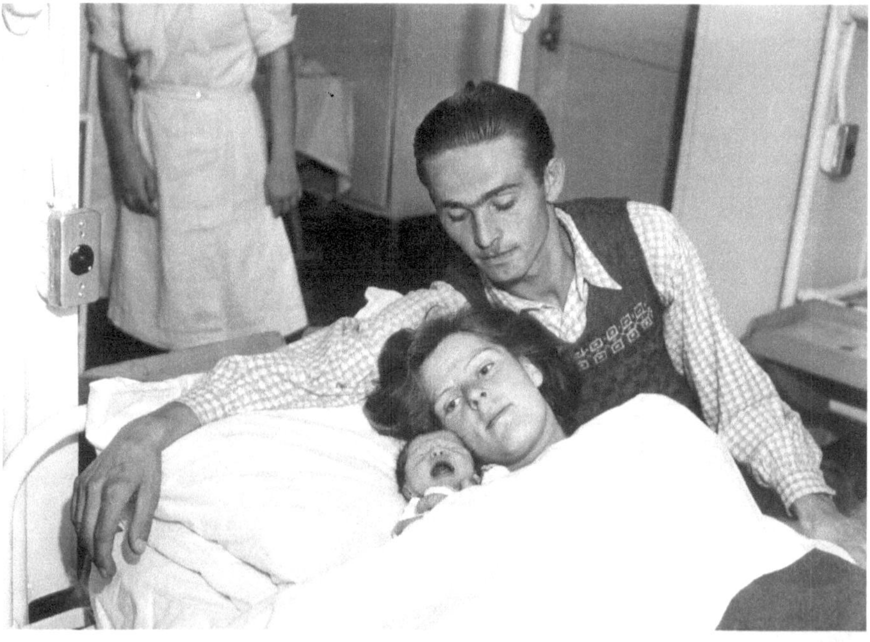

8 *Above* Arthur Calwell with the Kalnins family (1949). Seven-year-old Latvian DP, Maira Kalnins, was carefully selected as the 50 000th New Australian to create a media opportunity for Immigration Minister Arthur Calwell. NAA A8139, VOLUME 7, barcode 8318052.

9 *Below* Children on directors' chairs outside the huts at the Bonegilla Migrant Centre (1949). The basic conditions of the reception centres gave publicists the opportunity to reassure the Australian public that migrants were not living in luxury. NAA: A12111, 1/1949/22/20, barcode 8275061.

10 *Opposite top left* Mealtime in the dining-hall at Bonegilla Migrant Centre. Food was ample but consisted largely of fatty mutton (1949). NAA: A12111, 1/1949/22/8, barcode 7427626.

11 *Opposite top right* Egon Kunz (1949). The Australian selection officer interviewing Kunz in 1949 was not impressed when Kunz said he was from one of Hungary's best families and a great writer. But Kunz was born into a wealthy family and had a doctorate in Hungarian language, literature and social history. NAA: A11939, 110, barcode 31708671.

12 *Opposite middle* Vladimír Ležák-Borin (in 1957), a Czech migrant to Australia was a world traveller and something of an enigma. A British intelligence officer observed that he been in the pay of every important Czech political party, often simultaneously, and, by his own admission, had often worked secretly or openly against many of them. NAA: J25, 1957/10070, barcode 31708670.

13 *Opposite below* From the left is Australian author and journalist Frank Clune with three Immigration officers (Harold Grant, Bill McCoy and Frank Appleton) who were supervising displaced persons embarking on a 2 am train. The DPs were travelling to Italy to join a ship bound for Australia (1950). NAA: A12111, 2/1950/51A/1, barcode 8293649.

14 *Above* Arthur Calwell, Minister for Immigration and a group of children in front of huts at Bonegilla Migrant Centre (1949). Calwell was a vigorous advocate for bringing displaced persons to Australia, making the slogan 'populate or perish' his own. Albury City Bonegilla Collection.

15 *Top* Entry to Bonegilla. Bonegilla now displays a plethora of commemorative artworks and activities acknowledging the migrant experience. Wodonga City Council.

16 *Above left* This silhouette figure of a pregnant woman at Gateway Island Wodonga by artist Ken Raff is part of the new commemorative endeavours which have taken on a life of their own. Bruce Pennay.

17 *Above right* Photo board of Marie Herbst, a language instructor at Bonegilla who married one of her migrant students, Paul Szilsay. This is one of many photographs taken by Szilsay during their courtship. Wodonga City Council, original image Albury Library Museum.

CHAPTER 5

Inside the Cold War

Australia has their bodies. Europe still has their minds.
— Sun-Herald, 1954[1]

Vladímir Ležák-Borin was a postwar enigma, a Czech migrant to Australia who was much more than he seemed. Arriving at the tail end of the postwar DP scheme, contemporaries described Borin as a 'fraud', someone from the 'political underworld'. Borin's somewhat convoluted journeys, both political and geographical, allow us to glimpse into the life of an active displaced person from the political elite.

Borin's life also points to the ambiguities inherent in disrupting grand narratives: in this case, the idea that DPs were politically uncomplicated New Australians. Borin left the Communist Party after a visit to Moscow in 1934, and was possibly a Nazi agent in Paris. In London he provided information to Czech communist agents. Denied British citizenship, he arrived in Australia in 1952 where he wrote the first DP novel and advocated for displaced persons on various issues with federal politicians. He also continued his political activity, associating with the far-right Australian League of Rights, and working with the Democratic Labor Party.

Borin left Australia in the mid-1960s. His journey back to the Soviet Union and his death is a matter of conjecture. Was he invited to return to Prague by the Czech leader Alexander Dubček in 1967 during the Prague Spring, and killed during the Soviet invasion the following year? Or did he die, of natural causes, in Czechoslovakia in 1970? Was he a 'world traveller' and 'complete cosmopolite', a political 'adventurer' or a sleeper agent for the communists?

Before we continue Borin's story, let's look at the milieu of 1950s Australia and the DP diaspora.

Nationalist diasporas

While the Australian Government encouraged the assimilation of individuals, a number of DPs saw themselves as members of specific national and ethnic groups striving for national and cultural preservation in diaspora. Some desperately held on to the past, through language and memory. Others eagerly participated in a growing Cold War discourse of anti-communism, as first-hand witnesses to the evils of the Soviet Union, or as outspoken anti-communist activists.

As in postwar Europe, DPs drew lines on ethnic and nationalist grounds at the first opportunity. Forced together in Australian migrant and work camps, displaced persons quickly formed social and political groups to preserve their marginalised cultural traditions and identity. Such groups aimed to 'build culture within a culture', that is, to continue the nationalist building work begun in European DP camps.²

This occurred through DP organisations such as churches, choirs, theatre and dance groups, discussion groups, libraries, sporting groups and political associations. By 1953, every DP nationality was represented in the 38 nationality-specific groups in Sydney alone. A journalist observed how

> the stronger national groups in Sydney already have established themselves in clubs or societies. They are usually unlicensed clubs, often run in conjunction with a café ... They specialise in musical evenings, dances, socials, chess tournaments, and ear-bashing sessions about national, racial and political problems 12 000 miles away.³

Schools, choirs and dancing groups provided a structural 'framework for the community', and proved to be 'a bright spot on an otherwise dark background of hard daily toil'. Oksana says that her father, previously a highly respected lawyer, involved himself in religious, educational and cultural Ukrainian activities in Australia partly, she feels, to 'block out the reality of life' as an indentured, and later, lowly paid, manual worker. Similarly, Zofia's Polish mother, unhappy because she 'hated the weather' and 'missed her mother and sisters', immersed 'herself in Polish culture in Australia'. According to Polish displaced person George Klim:

Naturally people kept more or less to their own national groups. For just natural reasons. There was no animosity. It wasn't a reason for ... I mean, conflicts were not the reason. It was just simply the fact that you spoke your own language and you had your own traditions.[4]

Another Polish DP, Kazimierz Sosnowski, explained somewhat defensively that Australians had nothing to fear when DPs shared cultural activities with their children: 'Everything we teach them [dancing, singing, history] what is not against this country.'[5]

The displaced persons had of course migrated to Australia as refugees, predominantly to escape the Soviet Union rather than because Australia had any pull factors. Latvian DP Andrejs told Calwell when he arrived in Fremantle in August 1949: 'We came to Australia as a land of freedom as Pilgrim Fathers, escaping persecution in our own country. Not for the flesh pots of Australia.' National, community and personal loss caused wounds that were, according to Polish DP Halina: 'quite raw and big and bleeding'. Community groups helped to assuage those wounds. As the editor of the Polish newspaper *Wiadomosci Polskie* explained the need for Polish clubs and community centres: 'New settlers, relaxing at the weekend, would like to meet their old friends and countrymen.' Ethnic community groups provided for the social needs of ordinary displaced persons and also enabled high-status individuals to maintain their status within their communities, as founders and office-bearers. Jean Martin observed in Goulburn in 1953 that where Australians saw only similarities, the DPs valued their differences, not least those of nationality and class.[6]

Some social clubs provided settlement advice and financial assistance to their members. Snowy explained the origins and benefits of his small Ukrainian DP community in Melbourne:

> We'd been set up in Europe to look after our people who might arrive, it was our future job. We were talking about it in every camp. Nobody knew where he was going but wherever we went we would make sure that we stuck together, remember who we are, keep our traditions. Life in the camps strengthened us. In camp we met people from many hundred kilometres from our villages and developed a liking, respect and trust. Here were seven or eight of us from all over the Ukraine but we were like one family. In Australia we've been living together … without a bad word, caring for each other rather than just for ourselves.

In short, nationality-based communities were substitutes for lost families, villages and towns, encouraging DPs to continue a form of communal life, just as they had done in the European camps.[7]

Displaced persons also founded newspapers to serve the needs of specific communities. The *Australijos Lietuvis* (Australian Lithuanian), for example, was first published in September 1948 at the Migrant Holding Centre in Leigh Creek, South Australia. As DPs moved out of migrant camps and finished their two-year work contract, local bulletins became bigger and more widely dispersed. By 1950 the *Australijos Lietuvis* was printed in Adelaide as a fortnightly tabloid for a national readership. Each of the major national groups started at least one mass circulation newspaper: by 1953, there were 67 newspapers in 22 individual languages and two contained material in several languages. Periodicals were also available from abroad, particularly the United States.[8]

Sonia Mycak studied DP literature in the immediate postwar years and found a lively literary life with distinctive literary cultures, writers' clubs and associations, recitals and festivals, competitions, and the production of periodicals and books. Yet most of this literary output 'remain[ed] hidden within the many diverse ethnic communities' since most DPs did not write in English, and did not draw from themes of life in Australia. The Ukrainian community, for example, perceived that the 'present geographical locale of the community' was 'accidental and temporary', and that 'all experience connected with this location' was 'inauthentic and undeserving of serious treatment'. Similarly, Katarzyna Kwapisz Williams shows that Australia was portrayed as a ghetto, or a transitory space, in the Polish literary community; a 'shelter and temporality while waiting for independent Poland'. The few displaced persons who wrote in English usually had in mind a diasporic audience overseas, not an Australian one. Ukrainian Dmytro Chub (Nytczenko), for instance, was very active in the Ukrainian community in Australia, particularly in the fields of literature and education. He published many books in Ukrainian and English while working at the State Electricity Commission in

Melbourne. His novel, *So this is Australia: the adventures of a Ukrainian migrant in Australia*, contains 'strange reports and adventurous anecdotes' for the entertainment of a diasporic Ukrainian audience. It was written in English specifically for the large Ukrainian–Canadian market.[9]

However, most DPs, perhaps up to 80 per cent, never formally associated with any specific ethnic community group. Michael Cigler, for instance, early on differentiated himself from his compatriots who were involved in Czech associations, because he found the active members of the community 'too nostalgic'. He described the Czech Club in Melbourne in the 1950s:

> They were mainly older people who didn't have a chance to mix as we did, the younger people. When I started to study I realised – I am not a snob – but my interest was different to their interest … I wasn't going to waste my time talking about something which happened ten or fifteen years ago. I'm interested in what's happening now, what's going to happen in the future.

Cigler described the shrinking attendance at national functions and general meetings, as Czech displaced persons integrated into Australian society, while social events such as theatre and dance remained popular. From around one hundred Czech organisations in the early 1950s, there were only 15 left by the mid-1960s. One Hobart correspondent to Czech newspaper *Hlas Domova* in 1957, reported: 'There is nothing here now. Czech life is dormant and I think it will never awaken again.'[10]

For others, the distance from Europe, geographically and culturally, assisted their integration into mainstream Australian society. Latvian displaced person Anug explained: 'We tried in the first years to maintain our festivals and traditions but it just didn't click, it wasn't the right time of the year ... you change, the differences become yours, part of you.' Social status was also a factor. Lukas's parents, medical practitioners who were sponsored migrants rather than part of the IRO scheme, didn't mix with other Estonians from 'crappy suburbs'; instead, they found new Australian friends at their middle-class workplaces. In this regard, Michael's childhood experiences are typical:

> Dad was never religious. Better things to do on a bloody weekend! ... We pretty much did the Aussie sports and things like that, we used to like running and that sort of stuff too ... I like a lot of things about the European culture and things that they get into but just growing up here, it is a pretty good place as well. [My Czech father] didn't really bring us into his background that much, a bit of food really, a bit of the food.[11]

Social scientist and Hungarian DP ML Kovacs argued that even though the 'absolute majority' of DP respondents did not belong to any sort of community group (61 per cent of his sample of 148 respondents in 1954), existing groups still had a positive influence. They served 'as cushions in many cases to absorb part of the shock incidental to the socio-cultural adjustment by recreating a fraction of the familiar milieu'. They also secured 'opportunities for learning more about the receiving society through collating experiences', enabled DPs to receive 'inspiration from the example of the more resourceful individuals', and acted as 'socio-psychic "lightning conductors"' for the 'neutralisation of adjustmental tensions'.[12]

Jean Martin, continuing her research into the displaced persons, published *Community and Identity: Refugee Groups in Adelaide* in 1972. The book examined the formal group organisation in fourteen Eastern European minorities in Adelaide from 1948 to 1967. Martin had observed a rather 'weak and casual' group participation rate among DPs in Goulburn in 1953, but found that for members of the Adelaide ethnic community groups 'there was never any doubt about which minority any particular person or association belonged to, or derived from'.[13]

Rather than being concerned with integrating into a newly pluralistic Australian society, a minority of displaced persons were intent on fighting what Australians thought were 'anachronistic battles'. Polish DP Halina described the holding camp at Wacol, Queensland, where Balts were 'particularly hated because many of the Baltic States' citizens had joined the German army' and had maltreated 'people from different nationalities'. There was also animosity between Ukrainians, Poles and Russians, and towards German women who had married DPs in order to leave Europe. Halina explained that 'there was absolute hate for those women, they had a difficult time there; just as during history the animosities were between different nations, so the same nations [at Wacol] were enemies. They had to live together, but they were enemies actually.'[14]

In December 1949 an Australian teacher at Bonegilla complained about an 'apparent tendency to Fascism among certain groups of students', claiming that a Serbian DP, a block supervisor, was 'using his position of influence to disseminate fascist propaganda among other recently arrived migrants'. The man turned out to be a former senior official in the Nazi puppet government of Serbia, a fact known but ignored by the Department of Immigration. Likewise, Latvian displaced person Konrad Kalejs, who was later charged in the United States with war crimes as head of an SS unit, worked for three years as a documentation and processing clerk at Bonegilla. Journalist Phillip Knightley later said that when visiting Bonegilla he was shown a storeroom of items seized from migrants' luggage. It contained 'Nazi memorabilia – busts and photographs of Nazi leaders Adolf Hitler, Hermann Göring and Heinrich Himmler, SS daggers, Nazi flags, copies of *Mein Kampf*, photographs of officers in SS uniform, Nazi party cards and pamphlets'. In 1951, the Adelaide *News* reported that camp officials seized a 'Hitler statue' with a 'flexible arm which can be raised to give a Nazi salute' along with 'leather cat-o'-nine-tails, German Army bayonets, knives, decorations and swastikas' from DPs. However, reported the *News*, there was 'no direct evidence that any of the migrants was a Nazi'.[15]

In the Bathurst camp, Jewish DPs complained about anti-Semitic persecution. Baltic DPs physically attacked them, while Ukrainian DPs forcibly removed skull caps and threatened: 'If you want to eat with us, you can't wear a skull cap.' At Fairbairn and Eastlake migrant hostels, SS armpit tattoos, and scars where tattoos had been removed, were frequently sighted, and one DP was quite open about having been a volunteer in the Kraków Gestapo in Poland. Anti-Semitic slogans were scrawled on the walls. Jewish DP Moses Berger was told by a Lithuanian: 'Don't forget how it was in Europe, and it will be the same here.'[16] In 1951 a letter writer to the *Sydney Jewish News* alleged:

> Fascist journals are freely circulated in Australia. Reputable New Australians are being threatened and systematically denounced by organised neo-fascist groups. Australian citizens who protest against the mass migration of war criminals are accused of communist sympathies.[17]

The Australian Government, however, claimed that allegations of fascism came only from 'sectional groups' – namely, Jews. The government refused to extradite any DP on charges of war crimes to the USSR or Soviet-backed countries, saying it did not trust their legal systems. When in 1951 Yugoslavia requested the extradition of two alleged war criminals, ASIO's Director-General, Brigadier Charles Spry reported to the government that Milorad Lukic and Mihailo Rajkovic 'are unceasing in their campaign against communism and can and do assist ASIO to the limit of their ability'. In other words, ASIO found the two wanted men were invaluable informants who infiltrated Yugoslav groups and combated communist influence. They were not extradited.[18]

Relations within communities were complex, and party political, class and ethnic differences continued. In the United States, the common bond of anti-communism was rarely strong enough to overcome existing resentments and conflicts among DPs.[19] The small number of politically active Czechs split into factions in Australia: the Republican Party, National Democratic Party, Businessmen's Party, National Socialist Party, Populist Party, Social Democrat Party and the Separatist Party. Russian organisations included the Association of the White Army, Cossack associations, the Monarchist Movement, and the Venerators of the Sacred Memory of Tsar-Martyr Nicholas II. Some Hungarian DPs supported extreme right-wing newspapers such as the fortnightly *Becsulettel*, a 'newspaper of anti-Bolshevist Hungarians', which was printed in Sydney; others supported Melbourne's distinctly liberal *Magyar Elet* (Hungarian Life). According to Ukrainian DP Antin Danyliuk, 'we brought with us to this new land our intransigence and chieftainism'.[20]

Yugoslav DPs were among the few who arrived to find prewar communities of compatriots in Australia. This was somewhat unfortunate, though, because the Yugoslavs already here were predominantly actively pro-communist and pro-Yugoslav and did not welcome the newcomers. Croatian DP Joe described the division between these prewar migrants from Yugoslavia and the separatist and anti-communist DPs: 'We were quite isolated and unpopular; they avoided us … They called us Ustashis, fascists, Nazis, throatcutters, butchers, gangsters, all sorts of things because we wanted to call ourselves Croatian.' In turn, DPs including the alleged war criminals Lukic and Rajkovic began an anti-communist campaign against the prewar Yugoslav Immigrants Association.[21]

Exile mission

The major sources of political energy related to the diaspora and anti-communism. For some DPs, convinced that they 'represented the heart, the living soul, of their people', a sense of exile, rather than a narrative of migration, was paramount: '*They* were now the sovereign nation.' Their national pasts were 'living organisms only flourishing' in the 'memories of their former citizens'. As one Latvian displaced poet expressed it: 'We are the hope and blossom of our native land!' Sociologist and Czech DP Jiri Kolaja described this '"mission" type' of DP as 'the bearer of the group values and the guardian of the group cohesion. Believing strongly in his future return, this refugee considers the present situation as something transitory.'[22]

Language was an important way to focus on the diaspora. As one DP put it, 'Polish scouting was based on the exclusive use of the Polish language as a practical means of preserving Polish culture and tradition.' Ukrainian Suzanna Prushynsky recalled that her family was so involved in the Ukrainian community that the children 'were not allowed to speak English at home'. An article on the Ukrainian Scout Movement in Australia raised a 'problem' for boy scouts, asking 'how to reconcile loyalty to [Australia] with our national consciousness and, especially, how to stand up to the unprincipled pressure towards assimilation'.[23]

Gunta Parups, a noted Western Australian artist, was a staunchly nationalistic Latvian DP. Her daughter Andra said in 1991: 'Gunta rarely paints landscapes: the childhood place is difficult to remember, the lived-in place consciously ignored ... The fact that one day an Australian landscape appeared in her work surprised and annoyed her.' Gunta had always argued: 'I am still a refugee, not an emigrant.' For her, Australia was 'a kind of Siberia for the Latvian soul'. She advocated raising 'Latvian national self-awareness' in order to fight 'Russification in Latvia and assimilation here in Australia'. The family lived the belief: 'We are all here because of the bloody war. We are here in this dry hot land waiting to go back to our real home once the communists are overthrown.' Her children were not allowed to play with 'dirty English-speaking children'. Andra later recalled: 'When I look back, it feels like I was a member of a cult. My life outside school was guided and strictly controlled by my parents and grandparents ... I knew that I had been chosen to play a special role in life – to maintain my "Latvian-ness" come what may. To ensure that "Latvian-ness" outlived and conquered communism and Soviet colonialism ... [T]he past and family were all-important, they were everything.'[24]

This stubborn preservation of cultural identity could also work as a battlefront to protest communist rule in their homelands. Members of many communities and associations had, according to Jan, whose father was heavily involved in various Polish bodies, a definite goal to fight communism. The First Congress of the Federal Council of Polish Associations in Australia, for example, held in January 1950, passed an Ideological Declaration: 'We are members of the Polish nation who, at various times and in different circumstances, managed to choose freedom and thus became the Australian Group of Free Poles.'[25]

Some took on an ambassadorial role as part of this Cold War identity. One Ukrainian community leader explained in 1950: 'If our purpose is to acquaint the Australian people with the Ukrainian problem and to secure Australian sympathies for our liberation struggle, we must be attentive to the paths which lead to this goal. Australians are not interested in politics and react negatively to direct propaganda.' Instead, since Australian officials encouraged folk dances and performing in national costume, they should work this enthusiasm to their advantage: 'Our costumes and dances might well arouse interest and draw attention to the pamphlet, *What Do You Know About Ukraine?*'[26]

As historian John Radzilowski points out, ethnic anti-communism was largely inseparable from émigré nationalism but this was not necessarily a narrow or exclusive form of nationalism. In fact a shared anti-communist nationalism encouraged cooperation between 'enslaved nations' to influence western policy. The former political, military and intellectual elites of Eastern Europe thus formed organisations such as the Baltic Council of Australia and local branches of global exile groups, the headquarters of which were based in Washington and Stockholm.[27]

The National Committee for a Free Europe, established in 1949, was an umbrella organisation financed by the American Central Intelligence Agency (CIA) and the US Department of State, in exchange for strategic information and propaganda. Its primary purpose was ostensibly, in the words of former United States diplomat JC Grew: 'to assist refugees from the six Iron Curtain nations of Eastern Europe [Albania, Bulgaria, Czechoslovakia, Hungary, Poland, Rumania] so they can furnish democratic leadership when these countries regain their freedom'. Its four divisions comprised Radio Free Europe, Free Europe Press, the Exile Relations Division, and the Mid-European Studies Centre. Similarly, the Assembly of Captive European Nations, established in 1954, represented delegations of exiles from Albania, Bulgaria, Czechoslovakia, Estonia, Hungary, Latvia, Lithuania, Poland and Romania. Ukrainian and Byelorussian émigrés were not admitted, in order to avoid giving ammunition to Soviet propaganda, but the Assembly did cooperate with these so-called 'separatist movements'. The exile organisations issued anti-communist statements and reports on conditions and events in their homelands, organised petitions to the United Nations and to Australian authorities, and publicly celebrated and commemorated the anniversaries of national triumphs and tragedies. They labelled these activities 'external affairs'. Exile organisations were dominated by the 'highly nationalistic, often military-oriented and right-wing sections within the member communities' and tended to be 'insular and conspiratorial', representing only a narrow segment of their fellow nationals.[28]

Rather than practising a benign form of identity politics, the leadership of these organisations in Australia was notably fascist. Laszlo Megay, for example, a Hungarian displaced person and president of the Australian branch of the Anti-Bolshevik Bloc of Nations (ABN), had been accused of genocidal war crimes. He was dubbed the 'Mass Murderer of Ungvar', after the town in Hungary where he was the mayor. His successor as ABN President was Constantin Untaru, who had been Treasurer for Romania's Iron Guard national government. The Croatian Liberation Movement, perhaps the most extreme of any of the exile organisations, included a terrorist arm and was headed by former members of the Croatian Ustashi.[29]

For these organisations, the Soviet enemy was always active. Writing in 1972, Jean Martin noted that displaced persons reported a 'long history of Soviet attempts to influence and harass émigrés and their organisations'. DPs received communist literature or letters detailing personal information in the mail, presumably from Soviet authorities. The inaugural Soviet Embassy in Canberra sparked a major alarm in 1948 when they placed an announcement in the *Canberra Times* that Baltic DPs should register with the embassy, and were entitled to Soviet citizenship. Soviet Ambassador Nikolai Lifanov later issued a clarification that registration was not compulsory, but a matter of choice.[30]

The Soviet Embassy was also behind personal approaches to displaced persons in order to persuade them to repatriate. Historian Sheila Fitzpatrick has shown that Soviet diplomat Anatoly Gordeev, who arrived in Australia in December 1951 tasked with repatriating DPs, had trouble identifying and contacting them. However ineffective such repatriation attempts were, the fear of contact with the Soviet Embassy was real. A Ukrainian DP, Olga Noiman, told Gordeev: 'People think if you [visit the Embassy], you don't return but are put in prison and can't be freed because of diplomatic immunity.'[31]

The possibility of Soviet spies hiding within ethnic community organisations was another cause for anxiety. Displaced persons pointed to the anonymous distribution of communist propaganda. Sociologist and Russian DP Anatole Konovets, writing in the mid-1960s, alleged that pro-Soviet elements were active in the Russian DP community, 'acting as undercover Soviet agents' and 'organising campaigns for return to the USSR', directed by an agency in Moscow called 'the Soviet Committee for Cultural Relations with Compatriots Abroad'. By this time, Russians who had arrived in Australia via European camps had been joined by White Russians (that is, anti-Bolsheviks) from China. The pro-Soviet Russian Social Club in Sydney was a hive of espionage activity in this period, including acting as the site where the Polish-born Australian agent Michael Bialogusky met with the Third Secretary of the Soviet Embassy, Vladimir Petrov, in order to persuade him to defect.[32]

George Klim, prominent in the Newcastle Polish community, later explained that in his experience:

> There were none who did it officially. But there were certainly a few people ... A very small group who ... did what the Communist regime instructed them to do, or suggested to them to do. There was a very small group which was financed by the Communist Consul-General here until 1990. They usually formed either sport associations, or Polish–Australian cultural groups, they called themselves. Five, six, a dozen, whatever, twenty ... They were well-known, or reasonably well-known because apart from those, there were people who tried to infiltrate our organisations ... They didn't succeed, or their success was very limited.

Klim admitted that the 'main object' of his community work was political, to counter communist propaganda.[33]

Individuals also feared engaging with the Soviet machine, and rumours regarding the presence of Communist agents were common. One displaced person expressed a fear that 'Communist agents in Australia might "rig" accidents to kill him and his wife'. Lithuanian DPs Stefan and Genovefa Pietroszys hid for decades in a series of bush camps, in 'fear of the Russian KGB secret police'. Others were frightened that residing in Australia would have adverse impacts on relatives at home. After writing to family members in Eastern Europe in 1956, Ukrainian DP Grigory reported receiving a letter from the Soviet Embassy in New Zealand. This letter stated that 'all is forgiven', and encouraged him to return to the Soviet Union.[34]

Displaced persons expressed frustration that 'Australia, [in] general, does not even know what communism means'. To one man communism meant 'a thousand million dirty, uncivilised, hungry reds are on the alert and are only waiting for the signal, to run down first and then liberate the free world from its belongings, its wives, daughters, and everything that is shining'. Slovakian DP Martin Halas explained to the Australian press: 'Often we are told, "Can't you forget now that you are away from the Iron Curtain countries?" But we cannot forget while Communism exists anywhere.' Polish DP Jerzy Bielski, an immigrant organiser for the Australian Workers' Union, noted in a public address for the United Council of Migrants in Canberra: 'We feel it our duty to warn our Australian friends, who know very little about Communism and what it is really like'; if communism gained hold in Australia, 'concentration camps in Central Australia would be no more comfortable than the concentration camps of Siberia'.[35]

The Petrov Affair in 1954 focused Australian attention on Soviet espionage and DP anti-communism. Vladimir Petrov, Third Secretary of the Soviet Embassy in Canberra, defected with alleged documentary evidence of Soviet espionage in Australia. His wife, Evdokia, who hadn't defected, was escorted by the KGB at Sydney Airport to a plane returning to Russia. At the airport they were met with a violent anti-communist demonstration, demanding that the KGB release Evdokia. The Melbourne *Age* reported that a 'furious' demonstrator drew 'his finger across his throat in an age-old gesture of hatred'. Nikolai Harkoff, a Russian DP and the President of the Russian Anti-Communist Centre of Australia, argued that this was a 'spontaneous' demonstration held by 'different sections of the New Australian community'. He told a reporter: 'We knew what would happen to her – we have seen it happen in Russia. We desperately wanted to help her'. Evdokia was offered asylum at the last minute, when the plane refuelled in Darwin. The Petrovs settled in Australia.[36]

Petrov later claimed that his only real success infiltrating anti-Soviet groups in Australia was reactivating former Latvian agent Andrei Fridenbergs, who provided him with information on members of Melbourne's Latvian community. Fridenbergs, a former barrister and Esperanto enthusiast, denied the allegations. But Latvian newspapers in Australia described him as a 'spy' and suggested boycotting him. Arkadi Alexandrovich Morozow, a well-known political activist in the Russian community, later recalled: 'We were pleased that now, at last, Australians had seen for themselves that which forced us to flee the Communists. It was the same in other ethnic communities. Poles, Latvians, Hungarians, and many others, rejoiced in the unmasking of the Soviets.'[37]

Radical local politics

As part of their work contract in Australia, displaced persons had to join the appropriate trade union, to allay union fears that they could become strike-breakers. However, the press reported in 1950 that 'nearly all unions' had to apply 'pressure' when anti-communist DPs initially refused to join what they perceived as left-wing bodies. Some DPs refused to join communist-dominated unions. In return, these unions objected to DPs as right-wing union-busters 'hostile to the aspirations of the Union'. The Victorian Regional Director of the Builders Labourers' Federation expressed concerns that some DPs were escaped war criminals whose pro-Nazi pasts might influence them to act as stormtroopers to break down the unions.[38]

In 1948, the 'Rankin Affair' gained notoriety. A member of the Federated Ironworkers' Association of Australia (FIAA) was brutally attacked at Brown Coal Mine in Yallourn North, Victoria. The FIAA's complaint to the Bendigo Trades Hall Council alleged that several Balts were overheard in the mess 'lauding Fascism and decrying the form of government we have in this country'. When an Australian ex–prisoner-of-war who objected was assaulted, another, Mr Rankin, went to his friend's assistance. Later that night,

Rankin was attacked by DPs armed with knuckledusters; he was in hospital for three weeks. The Council asked for a full inquiry by the employer, the State Electricity Commission of Victoria, and protested against the settlement of such undesirable migrants. They argued that 'many' were only technically displaced 'because the Nazis lost the war'. Calwell, in turn, dismissed the need for an inquiry, saying that only 'Communists and Communist sympathisers' were making these allegations against Baltic migrants.[39]

Behind the bluster, the government was concerned on the one hand that there were communist agents among the displaced persons and, on the other, that Australian communists would woo DPs. Immigration Minister Harold Holt stated in 1951 that the only migrant 'sent back to Europe for political reasons' 'was a Communist organiser'. And while acknowledging that DPs were generally 'more antagonistic to the communists than are any other people in the world', the 1949 Commonwealth Immigration Advisory Council expressed fears that local communist groups might take advantage of their ignorance of the Australian political 'set-up'. The union fears that DPs were overwhelmingly right-wing, however, were more accurate. Many DPs were frustrated that they were not eligible to vote for the 1951 referendum proposing a ban of the Communist Party of Australia. Jewish Hungarian DP Paul Kraus remembers that his father was 'deeply disappointed' when the referendum was defeated.[40]

While Menzies' Liberal Party seemed sufficiently anti-communist for many displaced persons, Australian politicians wasted no time in using (and being used by) ethnic associations and individuals in order to champion a 'noisier' form of anti-communism. The main players were the hard right of the Liberal Party, disparaged as the 'war criminal right' because of their connections with fascist DPs, and the Democratic Labor Party (DLP), created when the Labor Party split in the mid-1950s.[41]

In 1953, the Joint Baltic Committee invited Liberal MPs William Charles Wentworth and Douglas Evelyn Darby to advise the newly formed United Council of Migrants from Behind the Iron Curtain – both were DP organisations. Darby was vehemently anti-communist, arguing that 'Soviet Communist tyranny and its agents worldwide' threatened the 'Free World', and that 'the slaves in the new continent Sovietska outnumber those that were in America'. Similarly, Wentworth was later described as a 'staunch friend of the Captive Nations of East Central Europe'. He shared platforms with members of the Liberal Party's Migrant Advisory Committee, including Laszlo Megay (the Mass Murderer of Ungvar) and Constantin Untaru (the Treasurer of Romania's Iron Guard). The Australian Security Intelligence Organisation (ASIO) observed that Wentworth was consorting with 'Fascist New Australians'. Similarly, Liberal Senator John Gorton spoke at an Anti-Bolshevik Bloc of Nations rally in Melbourne with Jaroslav Stetsko, a leader of the Nazi-affiliated Organisation of Ukrainian Nationalists. It seems a mutual and strident anti-communism was more important to these Australian politicians than the potentially unsavoury past of a displaced person. Like the officials during the migration selection procedures, they were prepared to ignore the past.[42]

The most important attempt to organise the displaced persons for an Australian political cause occurred when the Australian Labor Party (ALP) split in 1954, leading to the formation of the anti-communist Democratic Labor Party (DLP). The split was caused by an ideological rift between the national leadership, led by Dr HV Evatt (who was seen as pro-communist), and the majority of the Victorian branch, who were heavily influenced by anti-communist BA Santamaria and his Catholic Social Studies Movement ('the Movement'). Because the trade unions were affiliated with the ALP, anti-communists then began to gain influential positions in the party itself. The displaced persons were seen as natural allies of a pro-Catholic, anti-communist cause. Importantly, they could vote in union elections, whether they were naturalised or not, and their support was perhaps instrumental in gaining control of the party.

This association with a local political movement for anti-communist and politically minded DPs engendered the first sense of belonging to an Australian cause, in the spirit of a global Cold War battle. Polish and Russian DP newspapers, for example, urged their readers to join a union in order to oppose pro-communist union members. The Polish newspaper *Tygodnik Katolicki* editorialised in May 1955: 'We wish to remind all Polish members of Australian unions that, as Catholics, they are under a moral obligation to combat Communism within their respective unions, in the first place by voting against Communist candidates. We did not come to Australia, after having refused to return to our Communist dominated country, only to fall under the heel of Communist power here.'[43]

In Victoria, the ALP's 'New Australian Council' provided a nucleus for DP involvement in the split. Between 1952 and 1957 they shared a common objective and sense of urgency. One DP, injured by left-wing counter-demonstrators in a protest march, said that as the dentist pulled out pieces of his broken tooth, he felt he really belonged. A couple of prominent DPs were employed by Santamaria's Movement as migrant organisers; they managed around sixty postwar migrants (displaced persons and others), working in 12 languages, who handed out propaganda to other non–English-speaking migrants. One Australian official remembered: 'When the split started, we were running night and day to those migrant people.' Some continued to associate with the DLP as members of its New Australian Council, formed in 1958. In that year, Hungarian DP V Kormos stood at the bottom of the Victorian DLP Senate ticket for 'the struggle to preserve Australia's free and democratic way of life'. The Senate campaign included photographs of 'happy migrants' in national costume, 'enthusiastic in their applause for the DLP policy'. Other displaced persons participated in rallies. For instance, a demonstration of around 5000 people in Richmond, Victoria, supported the 1956 Poznań uprising in Poland. A politically active DP later remembered: 'It wasn't easy, but sometimes it was exciting and it was something to do.'[44]

In 1959, Jerzy Bielski, a Polish displaced person and former immigrant organiser for the Australian Workers' Union, joined with a Greek migrant to form the New Citizens' Council (NCC), a trade union with exclusively migrant membership. Among its aims was to rid the Australian

Labor Party of 'crooks and communists', as well as ensuring that migrants could hold higher office in the trade union movement. Albert Monk, the President of the Australian Council of Trade Unions, spoke out against this 'mischievous propaganda' and promised that he would do 'everything possible to liquidate' the NCC. It was also declared a 'bogus organisation' by the New South Wales State Labour Council. A year later, the NCC withdrew its trade union registration and became a rather unsuccessful political party.[45]

Mainstream trade unions soon lost interest in DPs. Jean Martin found trade unions wooed non–English-speaking migrants as a political resource in the period of 1948–1954. After 1954, DPs became just numbers and the unions maintained a policy of assimilation. The Federated Ironworkers' Association, which had a large migrant base, added a 'New Australian' section to its union journal in 1952 but this was dropped in 1954 'when it was felt there was no continuing need'. Items on migration in the union journal peaked between 1949 and 1952 and then rapidly declined. Perhaps the DPs collectively were less useful to unions once the anti-communist fight was over.[46]

It's harder to ascertain mainstream political participation and voting patterns, once displaced persons were naturalised and eligible to vote in general elections. The Liberal Party and the Labor Party both had New Australian Councils and welcomed migrant votes. Sociologist Jan Pakulski observed that although Hobart's Polish Association was strongly anti-communist, the Polish DP community in that city did not necessarily vote for conservatives. In the pre-election campaign of 1949 the community in general expressed pro-Labor preferences, in allegiance to the sentiments of local workers. On a state level the Poles as a community supported various Labor politicians.[47]

It's time to turn back to Vladimír Ležák-Borin, who moved into this political milieu in 1952 when he came to Australia. Borin was not part of the IRO scheme, but his story ties together a number of the themes outlined above.

Vladimír Ležák-Borin

Borin claimed descent from the royal Hapsburg family of Austria and was, ostensibly, a Czech journalist, novelist and playwright. Born in 1902 as Vladímir Ležák, he later said he served in the Czech partisan army in 1918 against the Germans; in 1920 against the Hungarian Communist Army, and then with the Ukrainian Army against the Russian Bolsheviks; and in 1921 he fought with the French Foreign Legion in Algeria. He joined the Communist Party, apparently adding the Russian name Borin, and wrote for the communist press, until he visited the Soviet Union in 1934. Afterwards, he stated that he was 'shocked' and deeply disillusioned by witnessing 'starving children begging for pennies' in this purported communist utopia. Another story, spread by his detractors, was that he was 'one of the most violent communist agitators' in Czechoslovakia, charged with converting peasant agrarians, but 'bought with hard cash' over to the side of the Agrarian Party, for which the Communist Party expelled him. In any case, he became an outspoken opponent of the USSR, and of the Edvard Beneš government in Czechoslovakia (1933–1938), allying himself with Milan Hodža, former leader of the Agrarian Party and ex-Prime Minister of Czechoslovakia (1935–1938), and a rival of Beneš.[48]

After the Nazi invasion of Czechoslovakia, Borin fled to London in 1940, via Paris (and Hodža), leaving his wife, Marie, and daughter, Vera, in Czechoslovakia. He later said that his 17-year-old son was killed by the Germans. He claimed to be on the run from the Nazis after a spot of pro-Czech espionage activity, and to have worked for the French Police Political Department in Paris against members of the Czech Communist Party. However, the British Government received intelligence that he was an active collaborator in Czechoslovakia and even perhaps a Nazi agent in Paris. The Czech National Committee in London alleged that Borin had edited a National Socialist newspaper and organised a Czech Fascist Group. They also charged him with causing the arrest of a woman in Prague who refused to cooperate with him and work for the Nazis. Borin, in turn, accused committee members of being active in secret communist organisations. One British intelligence agent reported that Borin 'gave a convincing picture of himself as an opponent and victim of the Benes group, who was at the same time a fervent believer in the Czech liberation and supporter of the allied cause'. Another found he was 'unreliable, being everything by starts and nothing long'. A final report observed:

> Lezak has thus at one time or another been in the pay of every important Czech political party (according to some authorities he has generally been in the pay of several at the same time) ... At almost any time during

the last fifteen years he has by his own admission been working secretly or openly against the party to which he most recently belonged ... The Czech authorities consider that Lezak is an extremely dangerous person and should not be left at large, and in view of the facts stated above, MI5 are entirely of the same opinion.[49]

At best, Borin was an 'unreliable person' and 'it was safer to keep him out of possible trouble'. Borin and other prominent Hodža supporters were interned on the Isle of Wight in 1940. During this internment he described himself to supporters as an 'unknown foreigner' and a 'broken statesman'. After his release in 1942, he continued dissident activities against the Czech Government-in-Exile led by Beneš in London. A British intelligence officer reported that 'he is the intellectually unimportant type, but stormy at mass meetings'.[50]

Borin's postwar activities with the Czech National Committee in Britain put him in contact with leading British fascists, and he successfully evaded an extradition attempt by the Czech government on a war criminal charge. He also, however, apparently admitted passing 'unimportant information' to Czech communist agents and receiving 'a large sum of money' as payment. Other allegations included acting as a Russian 'agent-provocateur' in Polish Government circles; he was declared to be 'subtle and clever'. A British intelligence officer observed that at public events Borin 'spoke badly and at length on the menace of Soviet Russia'. Even though much of the intelligence against him was propagated by the Czech Government-in-Exile, which was in permanent conflict with the Czech National Committee to which Borin belonged, there was a strong suspicion in London that he was 'playing a double game', and was in fact a Soviet spy.[51]

Borin was denied British citizenship after he condemned the Anglo-American response to the Soviet takeover of Central and Eastern Europe, and spent time in Germany and Switzerland. In 1950 the CIA echoed London's confusion about the 'adventurer' Borin. They received intelligence from the former Czech Minister of Industry that Borin 'had been a Communist since 1945 and is considered to be a dangerous person'. Noting that he had recently written an anti-Soviet article in the émigré press, the CIA questioned 'whether such is intended as chameleon writing to cover other motives or actual activities'. They concluded they could not answer this question.[52]

In 1952, Borin was back in London and had contacts with the Australian DP community. The 170 000 displaced persons who arrived in Australia between 1947 and 1952 included about 9000 Czechs. A compatriot had set up a timber harvesting concern in Tasmania at the end of his two-year contract, and asked Borin if he knew anyone interested in working with him. Borin suggested the son of his close friend, Dr Locher, a conservative Czech leader in London. Jan Locher migrated to Australia that same year and so did Borin, apparently for the sake of his health (in 1948 he was diagnosed with cardiac degeneration, chronic bronchitis and emphysema). His daughter, Vera, who had apparently spent the war years interned in Bergen-Belsen concentration camp, joined him.[53]

Borin worked as a migrant organiser for the Australian Railways Union, the Ironworkers' Union and the Liberal Party, and then for Santamaria's Movement and the nascent Democratic Labor Party (DLP). During this time, Borin wrote for and edited various Czech émigré newspapers. In one article he claimed that there was a 'communist conspiracy in the Australian unions' and migrants should 'actively combat their moral enemy communism in the trade union movement'. He also described Santamaria's Movement as 'the only people in the Anglo-Saxon world who realise clearly that Communism must be fought in the factories'. According to organisers, though, Borin's DLP work was just a job; at the end of the campaign, he disappeared. One Australian official described Borin as standing 'out like a big building, with the others just trams underneath'. At the same time, fellow Czechs labelled him 'a fraud' and 'of the political underworld'; a Polish displaced person described him as 'a sponge in politics, he soaked everything up'.[54]

In 1954, Borin came to prominence in the Australian press when a Czech Lutheran leader, Dr Josef Hromádka, visited Australia. Hromádka, a socialist and founding member of the World Council of Churches, spoke at a world peace forum in Melbourne. Peace organisations in this period were often encouraged by the Soviet Union to differentiate it from a perceived American attitude of warmongering; they were communist-influenced, and thus attracted anti-communist protest in western countries. In this case, Borin was not only representing the small group of 'Free Czechs' in protest at Hromádka's appearing as an apologist for the communist Czech government; Borin claimed to have known Hromádka personally since 1914. Hostile DP demonstrators chanted 'Let Borin speak!' The press reported that 'New Australians hissed and booed and distributed pamphlets' against Hromádka. Borin may well have published the pamphlets in association with the Australian League of Rights. The *Anglican*, appalled that an 'eminent Christian visitor be howled down', asked: 'Were the mob new or old Australians?'[55]

Borin applied for naturalisation as an Australian citizen in 1957. The Department of Immigration noted that he was 'not highly regarded by Czech nationals and is of definite interest to Australian Security Intelligence Organisation (ASIO)'. He was, however, cleared by both ASIO and the Commonwealth Investigation Service and naturalised in April 1958.[56]

Borin was an outspoken advocate for displaced persons, and secretary of the (migrant-led) Settlers' Association in Tasmania. He corresponded with government departments and ministers, and wrote press articles about the lack of marriageable women for single male displaced persons, and the absence of New Australians in responsible government positions. To a family friend, these efforts were characterised as part of a 'successful career as a ministerial advisor in the federal Liberal Governments of the 1960s'. However, Minister for Immigration Harold Holt did not really consider Borin's letters and complaints seriously. Privately, he labelled Borin as 'one of the more articulate of our European settlers' in a patronising exchange with Alexander Downer Snr, who agreed with Holt that 'Mr Borin has quite a lot to say about a variety of subjects'. As one of Borin's associates noted: 'They are mocking at us.'[57]

Borin's 1959 autobiographical novel, *The Uprooted Survive: A Tale of Two Continents*, follows a group of male Czech DPs in Europe and Australia. The Czech protagonist, Blaha, scathingly characterises the Communist Party as 'Government by the People – for the People – damn the People!' The anti-communist DP in Europe who had managed to escape the communists was, however: 'nobody and nothing; just a human rag'. DPs were 'puppets of destiny'. Blaha migrates to Australia as a DP on behalf of the Czech National Committee in London, in order to shadow a communist agent and to continue the 'fight for freedom' in Australia. In the novel, Borin criticises Australia, outlining the problems that male Czech DPs faced including prejudice from Australians, a lack of single women, alcoholism and mental illness, unemployment, homesickness and language difficulties. He also presents Australia as a 'Never Never Land' where people can break free from their European histories. Nosal, the communist spy, wishes to escape from Moscow's control. Upon his naturalisation he mutters: 'I wish I could really become an Australian.' He ends up a boundary rider in outback Queensland: 'clean-shaven, sun-browned, grey-haired, dressed in horseman's garb with a big hat', denying his Czech heritage with an Australian drawl.[58]

In the early 1960s Borin became interested in the anti-communist plight of Southeast Asia. The USA Council against Communist Aggression and the Alex de Tocqueville Society sponsored him to carry out research at the National Library of Australia. At some point during the 1960s he journeyed back to the United Kingdom expecting to be away for 12 months. He was apparently invited by Czech leader Alexander Dubček to return to Prague in 1967 during the Prague Spring. His friends in Australia heard that he was killed during the 1968 Soviet invasion. Other sources say he died of natural causes while visiting Czechoslovakia in 1970, after living in Scotland and Austria.[59]

Borin was of course something of an outlier, neither a typical DP nor a New Australian of DP origin, but an exemplar of the active political elite. He continued his dubious and somewhat ambiguous political activities in Australia, and beyond. A world traveller, self-described as a 'complete cosmopolite' and 'citizen of the world' his decade in Australia was just one part of a transnational, politically active life.[60]

Just as Borin pursued his political interests by focusing on Southeast Asia and then travelling back to Czechoslovakia, other politically active displaced persons continued their fight against communism. Western countries however were not particularly interested in finding ways to harness this diasporic anti-communism. The activities of most DPs diminished over time with the long duration of the Cold War, the practicalities of settling in a new country and the ageing process.

Jean Martin observed that by the late 1960s an outspoken anti-communism in exile was less common among DP groups and individuals. Anatole Konovets saw this from a pragmatic perspective: 'Even a political émigré is subject to the process of acculturation and gradual assimilation, particularly if his political aspirations are not satisfied for a prolonged period.' In Australia, much of this political energy was redirected into an engagement with ethnic affairs and multicultural policies. Indeed, many community leaders reached new prominence under multiculturalism as ethnic Australian citizens rather than Cold War warriors. How did this refashioning begin, and how did multiculturalism impact on the legacies of displaced persons in Australian society?[61]

CONCLUSION

Memory and multiculturalism

> *[Bonegilla] is an incredibly moving and important site which should be preserved for all Australians, not just those whose family came here. I'm a sixth-generation Australian and I was moved to tears.*
> – Prue V, Bonegilla visitor 7 April 2007.[1]

> *My mum says, 'I hate this place.'*
> – Anonymous, Bonegilla visitor 19 April 2009.[2]

A diverse group of people were categorised as displaced persons in the postwar period. Over time as the Cold War got underway, they were relabelled refugees and political refugees. Then, in an effort to find them homes, they were sold as potential workers and migrants to societies who needed a population (and labour) boost. Those who came to Australia were disparaged as Balts although officially welcomed as Calwell's New Australians. They themselves had distinctive identities, including a vocal minority who thought of themselves as part of an anti-Soviet and anti-communist diaspora, waiting in exile to go home. From the 1950s to the 1970s concerned social workers and academics depicted the DPs as individuals and communities in need of aid. In recent times, in their role as the first mass non-British migrant group to Australia, they have been identified as the founders of a multicultural Australia.

For Australian policymakers the DP scheme was a great success, a boon to labour and postwar reconstruction. DPs were, in the main, easily assimilated and they were the vanguard of migration programs in the 1950s and 1960s. Sociologist James Jupp, writing in 1998, observed that the scheme opened up the possibility of non-British mass migrations 'by showing that Australians would not reject such migration if it presented no threat to working conditions or to the total domination of society by those of British or Irish origins'.[3]

Formal migration agreements, often with assisted passage, were subsequently made with Malta (1948); The Netherlands and Italy (1951); West Germany, Austria and Greece (1952); Spain (1958); Turkey (1968); and Yugoslavia (1970). There were intakes of refugees from Trieste in the mid-1950s, Hungarian and Czech refugees in 1956 and 1968 respectively, from Chile in 1973, from Vietnam in the late 1970s, and from Poland in the early 1980s. The conservative political legacy of displaced persons, buttressed by anti-communism, was not lost on Prime Minister Gough Whitlam, who reportedly complained in mid-1975 about having to accept 'hundreds of fucking Vietnamese Balts' (who would presumably not be voting for the Australian Labor Party).[4]

A kind of pluralism

Approximately one million people have migrated to Australia in each of the six decades since 1950. In the 1950s and 1960s non–English-speaking migrants were particularly concerned with language difficulties and access to government services. Even when there were large numbers of other non-British migrants, the DP influence still underpinned Australia's specific migration and settlement policies. Social scientists, along with professionals such as social workers and teachers, recognised the practical difficulties faced by migrants, and led the way in finding solutions.

Sociologist Jean Martin continued her research into the displaced persons, noting a decline in contact between ethnic and Australian associations, such as those incorporated in the Good Neighbour Movement. By the late 1960s, the novelty had worn off for Australians, while New Australians had a growing suspicion of being patronised and exploited. Martin argued that DP efforts instead went into what they saw as 'potentially pluralist structures' such as churches, sports groups and the scouts. Her interest in pluralism, as sociologist Peter Beilharz notes, established her as a 'major force in defence of the emergent idea of multiculturalism'.[5]

The government attempted to engage with these issues by recognising that non–English-speaking migrants retained their cultural identities. An Integration Section was established within the Department of Immigration in 1964, which provided an extended program of English language courses and grants to community agencies. Yet many felt that the services for recent migrants did not go far enough to make Australia a properly inclusive society. Jean Martin was a particularly vociferous critic, arguing that 'the actual policy changes' between assimilation and integration were less than clear. Integration, in practice, was not an alternative to assimilation but a variant of it. The department's integration section implied that assimilation was a two-stage process that took time. Indeed Martin contended that integration policy reflected a government in 'denial': 'While the Australians have been stubbornly looking in the one direction, a kind of pluralism has been quietly consolidating in the other.' Australian society is not plural 'in the sense that our polity is based on ethnic segments', she pointed out 'but in the more limited sense that ethnicity is a source of formal and informal groupings and of some cultural differentiation'. The postwar non-British migration schemes, beginning with the displaced persons, had changed Australia's cultural landscape. Martin described a model she called 'robust pluralism' (or 'ethnic structural pluralism') as an alternative to assimilation; this is now known in Australia as 'cultural pluralism' or 'multiculturalism'.[6]

Sociologist and Polish DP Jerzy Zubrzycki, who met Martin in 1957, a year after he arrived in Australia, also advocated a broader model of cultural pluralism which

> stands for the retention of ethnic identity and continued participation of individual settlers in minority group activities. [It] implies, therefore, a rejection not only of the attempts to promote an amalgam of cultures but also of any assumptions of Anglo-Saxon superiority and

the necessary conformity to English-oriented cultural patterns.[7]

These opinions began to gain influence during the late 1960s. Social scientists at the Australian National University (ANU) had always had close relations with the Department of Immigration; demographers WD Borrie and Charles Price had been in a 'close working relationship' with the fledgling department since the late 1940s. When ANU sociologist James Jupp published *Arrivals and Departures* (1966), department secretary Peter Heydon (1961–1971) read it avidly. At the time, the government was concerned with the growing rate of migrant return; they did not want migrants to leave. The book comprehensively listed migrant welfare problems and complaints concerning government policy and blamed this dissatisfaction for the increasing return rates. To address the issue, Heydon invited Martin and Zubrzycki to regular informal meetings. Zubrzycki also contributed to weekly seminars attended by departmental officers and politicians. These academic interactions with government encouraged a celebration of 'multi-culture' (a form of ethnocentrism) that contributed to public policy.[8]

The Whitlam Government (1972–1975), while remaining focused on a practical provision of services to non-English-speaking groups, expanded the academic conception of multi-culture. In 1973, Labor Immigration Minister Al Grassby announced a new policy of multiculturalism in a speech that emphasised the immigrant nature of Australia.[9] Grassby spoke of the 'many threads making up the national fabric', envisaging an ethnic pluralism whereby 'each ethnic group desiring it, is permitted to create its own commercial life and preserve its own cultural heritage indefinitely while taking part in the general life of the nation'. Grassby bemoaned the fact that national images contained no space for 'the Maltese process worker, the Finnish carpenter, the Italian concrete layer, the Yugoslav miner or ... the Indian scientist'.[10] This policy of multiculturalism borrowed from Canada's official adoption of a multicultural policy in 1971, and the concept was also influential in the United Kingdom and The Netherlands.

By linking multiculturalism to the issue of national identity, the Whitlam Government transformed the notion of White Australia. Instead of being described as 'workers', 'migrants' and 'New Australians', displaced persons were now valorised as contributing to 'nation-building' and 'cultural diversity'.[11] Australia, by recognising and celebrating diversity, was to become more inclusive: it no longer demanded that migrants assimilate to a notional British monoculture.

Some displaced persons were heavily involved in the multicultural movement. Wadim (Bill) Jegorow, for example, a Russian DP, was a member of the Australian Labor Party and a 'dogged promoter of ethnic services by state and local government'. Jegorow enthusiastically described the founding of the Ethnic Communities' Council of NSW in 1975 as 'an example of democratic mass action enabling representatives of ethnic communities to speak for themselves and make their own decisions for the first time in Australian history'. The policy of multiculturalism thus enabled some DP groups to achieve a form of political representation.[12]

Sharing stories

The advent of multiculturalism brought with it a burgeoning interest in migrant novels and memoirs, as forms of life writing. Displaced persons had arrived in Australia with little documentary evidence of their lives in Europe and had found no encouragement for their stories in a society intent on assimilation. When they were not simply ignored, DP narratives were co-opted to fit into government and media images or they became part of a hidden diasporic literature.

Under the multicultural umbrella, DP writers flourished. Hungarian DP András Dezsėry, for example, founded a number of English-language ethnic journals, anthologies and presses in the 1970s and 1980s directed to an Australian audience, which focused on themes relating to migration and settlement. By the mid-1970s there were 26 so-called ethnic writers (that is, migrants whose mother tongue was not English, or their children), including DPs, published in English in Australia. Most were second-generation migrants.[13]

In 1978, Loló Houbein compiled the first bibliography of migrants who had published in English in Australia. A decade later, Alexandra Karakostas-Sêdá assembled a bibliography on works in languages other than English. Both bibliographies included the work of many displaced persons, along with other non–English-speaking migrants, seeing them as 'ethnic' writers in a 'multicultural' Australia, rather than, say, Hungarian authors who happened to live here. Migrant literature began to enter the Australian canon from the 1980s. Annette Robyn Corkhill, the author of one of the first immigration anthologies, explained in 1985:

'Nowadays it is clear to many people that ethnic Australians are as Australian as those whose roots go back to the First Fleet. Hence, their literature is just as Australian and their cultures are just as valid.' Displaced Persons writing, and migrant writing generally, fed into the political vision of multiculturalism; its authors offering an ethnic viewpoint under the rubric of national narrative(s).[14]

A number of first- and second-generation DPs have subsequently become notable Australian authors. Award-winning poet Peter Skrzynecki is a second-generation Polish–Ukrainian, whose work focused on themes of exile, dispossession, the search for identity and assimilation, has been set on the secondary school curriculum in New South Wales. *Romulus, My Father*, the 1998 memoir of philosopher Raimond Gaita, which tells of his Romanian father's life in Australia, was another award-winning work that was set for study in both New South Wales and Victoria and made into a popular film starring Eric Bana. *The Ghosts Trilogy* (1985–95) by Janis Balodis, a second-generation Latvian DP, looks at the struggles of a group of (Latvian) DPs in postwar Australia. John Hughes' memoir *The Idea of Home: Autobiographical Essays* (2004), which centres on stories told to him by his Ukrainian grandfather, won both the New South Wales Premier's Literary Award for Non-Fiction and the National Biography Award. Writer–Director Sophia Turkiewicz's films, particularly *Silver City* (1984), based on the holding centre at Greta, NSW, and *Once My Mother* (2014), a reimagining of her mother Helen's journey from Poland to Australia through the eyes of her daughter, have further succeeded in bringing displaced person stories to the

Australian mainstream. DP works have been translated for a European audience too – into 'the voices of [their] parents'. In contrast, Bulgarian DP Victoria Zabukovec had difficulty finding a publisher for her comprehensively researched autobiographical novel *The Second Landing*. The University of Queensland Press told her that the work, a sweeping saga of DP experience, was not relevant to Australians because it did not get to Australia until more than halfway through the book. Undeterred, Zabukovec self-published and launched her novel at the Migration Museum of South Australia in 1993.[15]

Sometimes established Australian authors bring extended family memories into a broader Australian literature. Australian poet Les A Murray and novelist Richard Flanagan, for example, both married to second-generation DPs (Hungarian and Slovenian, respectively), have portrayed DP experiences. Les Murray dealt with the DPs sympathetically in a 1977 poem entitled 'Immigrant Voyage', describing 'physicians nailing crates [and] attorneys cleaning trams' who would have to deal with taunts of 'wog, reffo, Commo Nazi' before becoming 'the misemployed, the unadaptable, those marked by the Abyss'. Flanagan's bleak 1997 novel, *The Sound of One Hand Clapping*, inspired by personal contacts among DP workers in Tasmania, follows a Slovenian DP and his daughter, whose DP mother committed suicide. Flanagan depicted DP workers as 'drunk and violent men' who had trouble talking about the past. Flanagan also characterised the displaced persons as victims: 'After all that trauma … to be given the job of building dams in the hope that Tasmania would become the Ruhr Valley of Australia seemed spectacularly ironic, strangely funny and enormously sad.' Interestingly, both Murphy and Flanagan focus on tragic themes in writing about DPs, a cultural theme since the 1980s. In 2005, playwrights Helen Howard and Michael Futcher, with Janis Balodis as dramaturg, wrote *The Drowning Bride*, based on a friend's journey unravelling her Latvian grandfather's dark past. Recently, playwright Julie Johnston has also commemorated the story of her husband's Polish grandparents with *Displaced* (2016), highlighting intergenerational family issues as well as the role of memory in a long life.[16]

By the 1990s, ordinary DPs had begun to write memoirs; in some cases the transcriptions of interviews by family members worked into books. Memoirs, as opposed to autobiographical novels, gained impetus as a literary form from a multicultural ethos that encouraged migrants to 'share their life experiences with everybody else'. These memoirs, usually self-published, are of variable quality. Some have been made to fit into national narratives of multiculturalism. Take for instance the friendship between Lithuanian-born DP Elena Jonaitis and Australian-born writer Amy Witting. Jonaitis published *Elena's Journey* in 1997 with help from Witting who wrote the foreword. Witting also used the story as source material for her 1998 novel, *Maria's War*. Witting described her attraction to Elena's autobiography: 'It is a story of dispossession, endurance, love and survival.' Elena's story, she said, echoing Corkhill, 'is *essentially Australian*, tracing the path followed by many of our present citizens and many of our ancestors' (my emphasis).[17]

This policy of multicultural inclusion has, of course, had its problems. An emphasis on the migrant as part of a wider Australian multicultural community has often been at the expense of individual and family stories, as well as particular national groups in migrant stories, which has led Sneja Gunew, daughter of a Bulgarian DP, to pose the question: 'Who are we writing for? Ourselves, or, rather, are we writing ourselves into being as subjects within the multicultural history of Australia?' Ukrainian DP Ludmilla Forsyth has similarly asked: 'To what extent do we expect migrant writing to be concerned with being displaced, disoriented, alienated, exiled? And for how long? And who is the migrant in Australia?' Privileging the Australian part of a migrant's life story in a sense domesticates and assimilates the 'exotic' migrant into a multicultural national project, where nation is firmly set above individual or non-Australian group interests.[18]

Perhaps it is easier for visual artists to sidestep nationalist themes. An exhibition 'Displaced Persons' by Anne Zahalka and Sue Saxon was held in Refugee Week 2006 to commemorate the journey of the artists' fathers to Australia from Eastern Europe in 1950. Twenty white handkerchiefs – 'cloths that are traditionally used to wipe away tears and to wave farewell' – contained montages of documents, maps, postcards, photographs and mementoes as well as embroidered words which highlighted the 'complexities and ironies of all migrant journeys to new lands'. Artist Anton Veenstra, whose mother was a Slovenian DP, has woven tapestries based on family photographs of his family at Scheyville and Cowra migrant centres; his work locates the migrant experience firmly in a context of assimilation, exploitation and marginalisation. Painter Nina Keri, meanwhile, explores the 'matriarchal, generational stories' of her Ukrainian grandmother's life, with an emphasis on the intimate.[19]

National commemoration

Multiculturalism also created a more receptive environment for the commemoration of migrant sites. The importance of the largest and longest-lived migrant holding centre at Bonegilla was ignored until the 1980s when it was hailed by migrants and community leaders as a founding place of multicultural identity: Australia's 'Ellis Island'.

Historian Glenda Sluga's history of Bonegilla challenged official versions of assimilation in its title – *Bonegilla: A Place of No Hope*. She points out how migrants with their European accents took over the very name of the place, changing the pronunciation from Bone-gilla to Bon-e-gilla. Sluga's observation influenced the ABC's Standing Committee on Spoken English which advises '/bohn-GIL-uh/ is the pronunciation for Bonegilla, the town and Army base, but when referring to the migrant hostel, the name should be pronounced [bon-uh-GIL-uh] because that's how the migrants pronounce the name'.[20]

Sluga saw that the original migrant camps could become the focus of a 'migrant dreaming', or foundation myth, for displaced persons and other migrants in Australia. Bonegilla migrant camp, she posited, could be memorialised to become: 'an antidote to the rootlessness of the exile, driven by the experience to give migrants back an understanding of their history, of which they had been ignorant carriers and victims, but about which they are now teaching themselves'. Wanda Skowronska, a child of Polish and Latvian DPs, has enthusiastically reiterated this theme in a number of published works, arguing that 'Bonegilla has become, in a mysterious way, a symbol of the hopeful journey, that physical and spiritual template so indelibly at the heart of Australian history.'[21]

In the early 1980s the army demolished most of the buildings and tried to sell off the rest of the site. This provoked former migrant residents and allies, including a former officer of the Department of Immigration, to initiate a campaign to transform Bonegilla into a commemorative site. Czech DP and academic Michael Cigler, a founding member of the Bonegilla Immigration Museum Committee, explained that the commemorative fervour leading up to the 1988 Bicentennial year was an important factor when a 'few local enthusiasts' proposed that Bonegilla 'should be highlighted for posterity'. Historian Catherine Panich, convinced the physical remnants of the migrant camps were important, complained of much that 'has been irrevocably lost to posterity through carelessness, a lack of official interest, ignorance and deliberate destruction'. Several ideas were proposed. Cigler suggested turning the site into an immigration museum. Wodonga Councillor Valentina Gillard, a second-generation Ukrainian DP, supported plans for a migrant studies library and school. Also mooted was hostel accommodation for 'young people of migrant background' and even a 'sister city' type arrangement with the Ellis Island Committee in the United States. Louis Maroya, President of the Bonegilla

Immigration Museum Committee, argued that Bonegilla should become a 'living plaque' to a vision of successful multiculturalism.[22]

Despite some Commonwealth Government support for a museum, the committee's bid for Bicentennial funding failed. However, due to the committee's advocacy, Bonegilla was placed on the Register of the National Estate (RNE) in 1990, saving the last remaining 28 huts from demolition. In 1995 the Australian Broadcasting Corporation produced *Bordertown*, a ten-hour drama series loosely based on Bonegilla that characterised the displaced persons and other postwar migrants as 'a straggly bunch of leftovers who talked funny'. More 'magic realist' soap drama than cultural or political commentary, the series nevertheless affirmed that 'Bonegilla' was a national story.[23]

The army finally relinquished the site in the late 1990s when it was placed on the Victorian Heritage List for reasons of significance to both migration and army history. In 2007, when the RNE was closed, local historian Bruce Pennay successfully nominated Bonegilla to the National Heritage List of sites of outstanding significance to the nation. The government's Australian Heritage Database set out the reasoning behind the decision:

> The site is significant to the whole nation as a host society. It invites exploration of the mixed community responses to newcomers, prompting examination and explanation of the expressions of feelings such as wariness, hostility, compassion, neighbourliness and indifference associated with 'taking in strangers'.

The national heritage listing was accompanied by placing a two-metre plinth at Bonegilla that declared it was 'a symbol of postwar migration which transformed Australia's economy, society and culture'. Bonegilla now displays a plethora of commemorative artworks and activities, dubbed 'The Bonegilla Migrant Experience'. Albury–Wodonga Region Parklands, the body that oversees the site, aims to tell the story of the migrant centre 'within the context of migration history and the movement towards multiculturalism', to assess and celebrate the 'contribution of migrants to Australia', and to foster 'artistic endeavours related to migration'. Bonegilla is now widely referred to as the 'birthplace of Australian multiculturalism'.[24]

Nationality-specific histories and exhibitions, usually incorporating oral testimony, both at Bonegilla and elsewhere, are now commonplace. Sometimes these accounts, captured in oral testimony and visitor comments, can be simplistic and somewhat anachronistic celebrations of multiculturalism. Sluga presciently noted in 1988 that the 'idea of Bonegilla' could be 'co-opted into the realm of immigration myth', and it has been. State agencies have used Bonegilla to construct their own images of a 'successful immigration program', and, later, a successful multicultural society, while some migrant groups and cultural workers have sought to include it in a national narrative of multiculturalism. More recently, historian Sara Wills has suggested further reimagining the site, arguing that Bonegilla (and other migrant sites) offer a 'prehistory' of contemporary refugee detention centres, a place to 'reconfigure the nation's pain and shame' in relation to Australia's treatment of all refugees.[25]

In setting out a main tenet of 'migrant dreaming', or community (re)creation, Sluga also critiqued such an approach, suggesting it might conceal more than it reveals: 'Sketched out as a particular shared experience of geographical displacement, the "migrant dreaming" encapsulates, contains and engulfs even greater distances, distances of class, gender and ethnicity, as well as of diverse individual pasts and divergent futures.' Pennay has analysed over 300 visitor comment books relating to Bonegilla and notes that themes of loss and harshness dominate:

> Many felt it important to record their father's trade, perhaps because of the indignity involved in Australia's not recognising overseas qualifications. Just as many told of the family upset when the father was forced by work to separate from the family unit. A common recollection was mother crying. One wrote of the confusing hurt of having her name Anglicised. The memories jotted down on a visit to the exhibition suggest that migrant memories carry strong feelings centred on self and on the impact on the fortunes of the family unit.

For contemporary visitors, says Pennay, 'above all else, Bonegilla is about family history'.[26]

While Bonegilla has been framed as the birthplace of Australian multiculturalism, for displaced persons and other migrants 'Boney-bloody-gilla' (as one respondent dubbed it) is more historically specific – a staging post in their personal migration experience. In this sense, Bonegilla is not a symbol of collectivity and nation-building, but a site that attracts individual memories which together reveal complex themes of transnational identities, intergenerational conflict, historical agency and identity, war trauma and mental illness, unmitigated sorrow as well as familial happiness. For displaced persons and their offspring, the liminal spaces of Bonegilla may contain lots of disparate and personal experience, while still being a temporary space which has little importance in their own history. It is not a fixed national story.[27]

Writing for the diaspora

Displaced persons were, of course, not just harbingers of a multicultural Australia. We have seen how through a sense of diaspora some desperately held on to the past, using language and memory, as well as propounding anti-communist politics. The few displaced persons who wrote in English, for instance, were not usually writing for an Australian audience but an international diasporic audience. Marketing to a diasporic audience still occurs in both English and native languages. Ukrainian DP Bohdan self-published two books in Ukrainian, *Ukrainians in Australia* and a biography of his father, and 'sent quite a few around to Canada and France, university, and then people, and most of it went to the library in Kiev ... to distribute it among the libraries in Ukraine'. Similarly, diasporic commemorations (histories, celebrations, reunions) are usually nationality-specific and have no place for other ethnicities.

Sociologist Ronald Taft, working in the 1950s, found that Baltic DPs were prepared to spend the rest of their lives in Australia, but their hearts belonged to their native country. Poles also expressed low satisfaction with life in Australia, and the desire to return home if political conditions changed. In fact, when the Soviet Union disbanded in 1991, some displaced persons and their children did return. Lithuania changed its citizenship requirements to allow the grandchildren of displaced persons citizenship, Croatia actively sought repatriates among the displaced, and former DPs became active in politics in Estonia, Latvia and Lithuania. DP Valdas Adamkus relocated from the United States to become President of Lithuania in 1998. Other DPs were recognised by newly free governments for their anti-communist activities in exile.[28]

Second-generation displaced person Anita 'returned' to Latvia in 2009, working as an art and English teacher while continuing the traditional weaving she had learned from her mother, Anna. Anna's primary weaving loom is displayed at the Immigration Museum in Melbourne, while her second loom, commissioned in the Fischbach DP camp in Germany and brought to Australia by another Latvian weaver, was donated to the Latvians Abroad – Museum and Research Centre in Riga. Anita returned to Australia in 2014, but the loom stayed in Riga, a symbol of the reconciliation work being carried out in Latvia between former displaced persons like Anita, and the majority, who stayed under a communist government.[29]

Of course, for most displaced persons the dissolution of the Soviet Union came too late – age prevented them from starting over. Latvian artist Gunta Parups died in Australia in 1994. But she had always described herself as an exile and wanted her ashes to be returned to Riga.

Asylum seekers and refugees

In 2010, historian Klaus Neumann pointed out that Australian historiography lacked sustained research into immigration and refugee topics and called for academics to add an 'informed historical perspective' to the debate on asylum seekers. Australian politicians of all persuasions, for instance, generally claim an unproblematic, welcoming tradition towards migrants and refugees; Prime Minister Malcolm Turnbull has described Australia as 'the most successful and harmonious multicultural nation in the world'. Arthur Calwell, speaking in 1953, began this trend by stating unequivocally that 'the Australian people have given an example to the world in their friendly reception to the new settlers'. Pointing to this (ahistorical) memory of humanitarian hospitality, contemporary conservative pundits contrast earlier migrant and refugee cohorts with twenty-first century 'boat people', who are portrayed as refugee 'queue-jumpers'. As historian Peter Gatrell has observed, unfortunately 'the field of refugee studies is notable for the absence of history'.[30]

The histories contained in this book speak to themes that are, and will remain, relevant to the many postwar migrant groups in Australia, and Australians generally. There is, for example, continuing controversy about distinguishing 'humanitarian refugees' from 'economic migrants'; the manner in which 'asylum seekers' are temporarily housed in Australia; and the settlement processes to be carried out after granting refugee status. Australia still lacks any standing means to investigate war crime allegations in new arrivals. The issues of assimilation and integration, as well as the place for diaspora in an ostensibly multicultural Australia, continue with new iterations.

The displaced persons, the first mass non-British migration to Australia, included refugees, victims of Nazi and Soviet policy, fascist war criminals, passionate anti-communists, and ordinary people who chose to leave Europe behind for the New World. Most importantly, DPs did not always fall into neat categories: they were individuals, with sometimes complex and ambiguous identities. Some found a haven in Australia, working and raising families in peace. Others became involved in domestic politics, including multicultural policy. Others still refused to move on from a sense of ethnic essentialism and nationalist struggle.

This book showcases these various experiences in a history which can sometimes seem negative (and of course, things were not perfect). Displaced Persons were subject to prejudice and parochialism both during the migrant selection process and upon their arrival in Australia; under the work contract, families were separated and DPs were given the worst jobs, with little subsequent opportunity for professional advancement. Despite its shortcomings, though, the postwar immigration scheme under Arthur Calwell and Ben Chifley was visionary and, ultimately, successful. The decision to select displaced persons and bring them to Australia as a source of labour and population made an immense contribution to national growth and the national character. The scheme also offered a new home to people who had been without one, for years.

The world is currently in the midst of the biggest refugee crisis since the postwar period. In contemporary

Australia, politicians highlight a need for skilled migrant labour and the 457 visa, developed to encourage temporary skilled migration, is constantly in the news. Yet politicians simultaneously demonise asylum seekers, ignoring their potential to contribute to modern Australia. The government has banned refugee boats and instituted offshore detention. Some people seeking asylum in Australia have been housed in Nissen and Quonset huts on Manus Island in Papua New Guinea. In a neat irony, the same huts, previously shipped from the former US Base on Manus to Australian reception and training centres for postwar displaced persons, are now feted as heritage items used to celebrate the birth of a multicultural Australia. Perhaps the most surprising aspect of the postwar displaced persons scheme was the extraordinary political will that overcame a number of hurdles, including entrenched public attitudes, in order to make use of a refugee crisis for national gain. Is there something we can learn from this when today's refugee policies seem so uncompromising?

Notes

Abbreviations

ANU	Australian National University
CIAC	Commonwealth Immigration Advisory Council
GDC	Gale Digital Collection
IRO	International Refugee Organization
NAA	National Archives of Australia
NA (UK)	National Archives (United Kingdom)
NBAC	Noel Butlin Archives Centre, Australian National University
NLA	National Library of Australia
SHAEF	Supreme Headquarters Allied Expeditionary Forces
SLQ	State Library of Queensland

Introduction

1   Mark Wyman, *DPs: Europe's Displaced Persons, 1945–1951* (New York: Cornell University Press, 1998), 18; War Office: Central Mediterranean Forces, (British Element): War Diaries, Second World War, Italy, 1945, Brigades, 36 Infantry Brigade: HQ, Cossacks, 1st May, 1945 – 31st May 1945, NA (UK), WO 170/4461.

2   Samuel J Newland, *Cossacks in the German Army 1941–1945*, Cass Series on Politics and Military Affairs in the Twentieth Century, Book 4 (Routledge, 1991), 170–174; Shane O'Rourke, *The Cossacks* (Manchester: Manchester University Press, 2007), 277; Fr Michael A Protopopov, *'We Can Swallow Them Alive ...': A Journey from Cross of St George to Golgotha* (Melbourne, 2000), 238; Anton Schleha, *Surviving Lienz* (Innsbruck: Innsbruck University Golf Publishers, 2009), 26; Cossacks, WO 170/4461; Nikolai Tolstoy, *Victims of Yalta* (London: Hodder and Stoughton, 1977), 151; Nadia Stakhanova, Natasha Stakhanova & Vera Stakhanova with

Charles Cherry, *Separated at Stavropol: A Russian Family's Memoir of Wartime Flight* (North Carolina: McFarland & Company, 2005), 143.

3   War Office, Evacuation of Cossack and Caucasian Forces from 36 Inf Bde Area, May – June 1945, Lt Col. Comd. 36 Inf Bde, 3 July 45, Cossacks and Caucasians, WO 204/10449, NA (UK); Martin Gilbert, *A History of the Twentieth Century, Volume One: 1900–1933* (London: Harper Collins Publishers, 1997), 736–737.

4   War Office, Letter from Tatiana Tiashelnikov, Camp Kellerberg Austria Karnten to Mr Tufton Beamish [Major], 30 June 1947, Extracts by Ministry of Defence, WO 204/10449; Cossacks, War Office WO 204/10450.

5   Lt Col. Comd. 36 Inf Bde, WO 204/10449; Cossacks War Diaries, 1st June, 1945 – 30th June, 1945, WO 170/4461; Schleha, *Surviving Lienz*, 27.

6   'Ivan', Migrant Selection Documents for Displaced Persons who travelled to Australia per *Anna Salen* departing Naples, Italy, 22 May 1949, 425–427, A11937, NAA.

7   Michael Alex Protopopov, 'The Russian Orthodox Presence in Australia: The History of a Church told from recently opened archives and previously unpublished sources', Doctor of Philosophy thesis, Australian Catholic University, 2005, 131, 191.

1   Deserving victims

1   Laure Humbert, 'French Politics of Relief and International Aid: France, UNRRA and the Rescue of European Displaced Persons in Postwar Germany, 1945–47', *Journal of Contemporary History*, 51:3 (2016), 606.

2   FJ Massey, National General Secretary of the YMCA, cited in 'Millions Homeless and Without Hope in Shattered Europe', *Mercury* (Hobart), 3 June 1946.

3   Interview with Jan Dworak, 1998, Polish Australians Oral History Project, TRC3796, NLA; Joseph Karlik, interviewed by Whitehorse Historical Society, 24 October 2006.

4   Anna Holian, *Between National Socialism and Soviet Communism: Displaced Persons in Postwar Germany* (Ann Arbor: University of Michigan Press, 2011), 47.

5   Tony Kushner, *Remembering Refugees: Then and Now* (Manchester: Manchester University Press, 2006), 7; Adm. Memo No. 39 (1 January 1944), SHAEF, Refugees and displaced persons in the Mediterranean Theatre: administration and movement: policy and correspondence, War Office: Allied Forces, Mediterranean Theatre: Military Headquarters Papers, Second World War, WO 204/2869, Post-War Europe Series I: Refugees, Exile and Resettlement, 1945–1950, Gale Digital Collections, 18; SHAEF planning directive: refugees and displaced persons (DPs), 3 June 1944, Prisoners of War/Displaced Persons Division: Registered Files (PWDP and other Series), Control Office for Germany and Austria and Foreign Office, Foreign Office (FO) 1052/10, Post-War Europe Series I: Refugees, Exile and Resettlement, 1945–1950, Gale Digital Collections.

6   G Daniel Cohen, 'The West and the Displaced, 1945–1951: The Postwar Roots of Political Refugees', PhD thesis, Department of History/Institute of French Studies, New York University, January 2000, 45.
7   Mark Spoerer & Jochen Fleischhacker, 'Forced Labourers in Nazi Germany: Categories, Numbers and Survivors', *Journal of Interdisciplinary History*, 22:2 (Autumn 2002), 171; Mark Wyman, *DPs: Europe's Displaced Persons, 1945–1951* (New York: Cornell University Press, 1998), 22; David Cesarani, *Justice Delayed: How Britain Became a Refuge for Nazi War Criminals* (London, 2001 [1992]), 35; Malcolm J Proudfoot, *European Refugees 1939–52: A Study in Forced Population Movement* (London, 1957), 79, 81; SHAEF planning directive: refugees and displaced persons (DPs), 3 June 1944, Prisoners of War/Displaced Persons Division: Registered Files (PWDP and other Series), Control Office for Germany and Austria and Foreign Office, Foreign Office (FO) 1052/10, Post-War Europe Series I: Refugees, Exile and Resettlement, 1945–1950, Gale Digital Collections; Louise W Holborn, *The International Refugee Organisation: A specialised agency of the United Nations, its history and work, 1946–1952* (London: Oxford University Press, 1956), 395. On forced labourer conditions see, for example, Paul Longley Arthur, 'Reclaiming the Past: Nadia's Story', *Life Writing*, 11:4 (2014), 459–476.
8   Jan-Hinnerk Antons, 'Displaced Persons in Postwar Germany: Parallel Societies in a Hostile Environment', *Journal of Contemporary History*, 49 (2014), 104; Filip Slaveski, *The Soviet Occupation of Germany: Hunger, Mass Violence, and the Struggle for Peace, 1945–1947* (Cambridge: Cambridge University Press, 2013), 18, 89; Tara Zahra, 'Prisoners of the Postwar: Expellees, Displaced Persons, and Jews in Austria after World War II', *Austrian History Yearbook*, 41 (2010), 204; Kathryn Hulme, *The Wild Place* (NY: Cardinal, 1960 [1953]), 18; Rieko Karatani, 'How History Separated Refugee and Migrant Regimes: In Search of their Institutional Origins', *International Journal of Refugee Law*, 17:3 (2005), 520; Yury Boshyk, 'Repatriation and Resistance: Ukrainian Refugees and Displaced Persons in Occupied Germany and Austria, 1945–48', in Anna C Bramwell (ed.), *Refugees in the Age of Total War* (London, Unwin Hyman, 1988), 202; Michael R Marrus, *The Unwanted: European Refugees from the First World War Through the Cold War* (Philadelphia: Temple University Press, 1985 [2002]), 300; Leonard Dinnerstein, *America and the Survivors of the Holocaust* (NY: Columbia University Press, 1982), 16; Walter Dushnyck & William J Gibbons, *Refugees are People: The Plight of Europe's Displaced Persons* (New York: American Press, 1947), 12; Peter Gatrell, 'Population Displacement in the Baltic Region in the Twentieth Century: From "Refugee Studies" to Refugee History', *Journal of Baltic Studies*, 38:1 (2007), 46.
9   Arieh Kovachi, 'The Politics of Displaced Persons in Postwar Europe, 1945–1950', *Postwar Europe: Refugees, Exiles and Resettlement, 1945–1950*, 2; Future of Inter-Governmental Committee, 5 September 1945, Foreign Office: Political Departments: General Correspondence from 1906–1967, FO 371/51138–0008, Post-War Europe Series I: Refugees,

Exile and Resettlement, 1945–1950, Gale Digital Collections; ML Kovacs, Immigration and Assimilation: An Outline Account of the IRO Immigrants in Australia, MA thesis, Department of History, University of Melbourne, 1955, 182–183; HG Brooks, 'Displaced Persons Volume 1', MS 8128, National Library of Australia (NLA), 4, 7.

10 G Daniel Cohen, 'Between Relief and Politics: Refugee Humanitarianism in Occupied Germany 1945–1946', *Journal of Contemporary History*, 43:3 (2008), 437, 439; Jessica Reinisch, 'Preparing for a new World Order: UNRRA and the International Management of Refugees', Post-War Europe Series I: Refugees, Exile and Resettlement, 1945–1950, Gale Digital Collections, 4, 5; Jessica Reinisch, '"We Shall Rebuild Anew a Powerful Nation": UNRRA, Internationalism and National Reconstruction in Poland', *Journal of Contemporary History*, 43:3 (2008), 452; Sharif Gemie & Laure Humbert, 'Comment: Writing History in the Aftermath of "Relief": Some Comments on "Relief in the Aftermath of War"' (Special Issue of *Journal of Contemporary History* July 2008), *Journal of Contemporary History*, 44:2 (2009), 316.

11 *Agreement for United Nations Relief and Rehabilitation Administration*, 9 November 1943, <www.ibiblio.org/pha/policy/1943/431109a.html>; Dinnerstein, *America and the Survivors of the Holocaust*, 17; Cohen, 'Between Relief and Politics', 439; Notes on 'G' Activities of 21 Army Group during Post-Surrender Period, War Office WO 205/139, NA (UK), in Carol Mather, *Aftermath of War: Everyone Must Go Home* (London: 1992), 16.

12 Letter from Helen Ferber, Paris, 26 May 1947, Papers of Helen Ferber, 1937–2005, MS Acc06.027, NLA, Canberra; VL Borin, *The Uprooted Survive: A Tale of Two Continents* (London: William Heinemann, 1959), 100.

13 ML Kovacs and AJ Cropley, *Immigrants and Society: Alienation and Assimilation* (Sydney: 1975), 85; Hulme, *The Wild Place*, 70; Sheila Fitzpatrick, 'UNRRA's South-West Pacific Area Office (SWPA), from UNRRA archive in New York', Australian Historical Association Conference (2014), (unpublished).

14 Cohen, 'Between Relief and Politics', 439; Jessica Reinisch, '"Auntie UNRRA" at the Crossroads', *Past and Present*, Supplement 8 (2013), 79.

15 Francesca M Wilson, *Aftermath: France, Germany, Austria, Yugoslavia, 1945 and 1946* (London: Penguin Books, 1947), 83; Cohen, 'The Politics of Recognition', 136; Hulme, *The Wild Place*, 116.

16 Janco, 'Unwilling', 433; Carol Mather, *Aftermath of War: Everyone Must Go Home* (London: Brassey's UK, 1992), 19; Mark Elliott, *Pawns of Yalta: Soviet Refugees and America's Role in their Repatriation* (Champaign: University of Illinois Press, 1982), 173; Wolfgang Jacobmeyer, 'The Displaced Persons Problem: Repatriation and Resettlement', in Johannes Dieter-Steinert and Inge Weber-Newth (eds), *European Immigrants in Britain, 1933–1950* (Munich: Saur, 2003), 140.

17 Anne Kuhlmann-Smirnov, 'The Resettlement of Soviet-Russian Displaced Persons and the Politics of "Fidelity"', Arizona State University, Place of Refuge Panel Series, (unpublished), 9; 1st May, 1945 – 31st May, 1945, Cossacks War Diaries 1945 HQ 36 Inf. BDE, WO 170/4461, NA (UK).

Notes to pages 24–31

18 Kuhlmann-Smirnov, 'The Resettlement', 7, 9; VL Borin, *The Uprooted Survive: A Tale of Two Continents* (London, 1959), 128–129; Cohen, 'Between Relief and Politics' 444; Kim Salomon, *Refugees in the Cold War: Toward a New International Refugee Regime in the Early Postwar Era* (Lund: 1991), 73; Agnes E Karlik, interviewed by Whitehorse Historical Society, 10 October 2006.
19 Kuhlmann-Smirnov, 'The Resettlement', 2.
20 Walter Lebedew, interviewed by Rob Linn for the Sport Oral History Project, OH ORAL TRC 5900/69, NLA.
21 Károly Zentai, Migrant Selection Documents for Displaced Persons who travelled to Australia per *Fairsea* departing Naples, Italy, 7 February 1950, R145–R149, A12014, NAA; Ruth Balint, 'Australia, Hungary and the case of Károly Zentai', *Inside Story*, 29 April 2009, <insidestory.org.au/australia-hungary-and-the-case-of-kroly-zentai>.
22 HR Hall, 'Some UNRRA-lated Tales', October 1945, Harold Rex Hall, Papers, 1945–1947, MS4626, NLA; Boshyk, 'Repatriation and Resistance', 363.
23 Ivan Bahryany, 'Why I Do Not Want to Go "Home"', *Ukrainian Weekly*, 17 February 1947, 3, <ukrweekly.com/archive/1947/The_Ukrainian_Weekly_1947-07.pdf>; Tanya Matthews, 'Refugees from Soviet Tyranny Tell Their Stories', *Sydney Morning Herald*, 13 June 1950.
24 Laszlo Makay, interviewed by Ann-Mari Jordens, 2008, OH-VN4318388, NLA; Stanislaw Harasymow, interviewed by Paul Sendziuk, 2009, Stalin's Poles Oral History Project, TRC 6175/7, NLA.
25 Boshyk, 'Repatriation and Resistance', 378, n. 23; Interview with Jan Dworak, Polish Australians Oral History Project, TRC3796, NLA.
26 Reinisch, '"We Shall Rebuild Anew a Powerful Nation"', 468; Dushnyck & Gibbons, *Refugees are People*, 30, 49; Mather, *Aftermath of War*, 19; Genovait/e/ Kazokas, *Lithuanian Artists in Australia: 1950–1990* (Melbourne: Europe–Australia Institute, 2003), 10; Boshyk, 'Repatriation and Resistance', 202.
27 Mark Elliott, 'The Soviet Repatriation Campaign', in Wsevolod W Isajiw, Yury Boshyk & Roman Senkus, *The Refugee Experience: Ukrainian Displaced Persons after World War II* (Edmonton: Canadian Institute of Ukrainian Studies Press, University of Alberta, 1992), 344.
28 Boshyk, 'Repatriation and Resistance', 378, n. 23; Ale Liubinas, *Aviete and After* (Melbourne: Fosbee Pty Ltd, 1998), 9; Anatolij Mirosznyk, *How Do You Like Australia?* (Sydney, 2009), 77; Wyman, *DPs*, 83; Antin Danyliuk, *My Recollections: A Journey from the Village of Shprakhy to Australia* (Melbourne: Bayda Books, 1995), 7.
29 Ihor Stebelsky, 'Ukrainian Population Migration after WWII', in Isajiw, Boshyk & Senkus, *The Refugee Experience*, 26; Patricia Meehan, *A Strange Enemy People: Germans under the British, 1945–50* (London: Peter Owen, 2001), 57; Antons, 'Displaced Persons in Postwar Germany', 96; Ihor V Zielyk, 'The DP Camp as a Social System', in Isajiw, Boshyk & Senkus, 464.
30 Victoria Valchev-Zabukovec, 'Immigration Stories', Immigration Place Australia; Boshyk, 'Repatriation and Resistance', 370.

31 Harold Hall, undated, Harold Rex Hall Papers, 1945–1947, MS4626, NLA.
32 Egon F Kunz, 'The Refugee Experience: Being a Refugee', *Refugees: The Challenge of the Future*, Academy of the Social Science of Australia, Fourth Academy Symposium, 3–4 November 1980, Proceedings, 123; Marian J Rubchak, 'Dancing with the Bones: A Comparative Study of Two Ukrainian Exile Societies', *Diaspora: A Journal of Transnational Studies*, 2 (1993), 360.
33 Rubchak, 'Dancing with the Bones', 360; Kavita Datla, 'Displacement Camps: Sites of Ethnic Renewal and Nationalism', (unpublished); Dan Diner, in Cohen, 'The Politics of Recognition', 129; G Daniel Cohen, 'Remembering Postwar Displaced Persons: From Omission to Resurrection', in Mareike Konig & Rainer Ohliger, *Enlarging European Memory: Migration Movements in Historical Perspective* (Ostfildern, Germany: Jan Thorbecke Verlag, 2006), 93–94, 337; Laura Hilton, 'Cultural Nationalism in Exile: The Case of Polish and Latvian Displaced Persons', *The Historian*, 71:2 (2009), 282.
34 Vasyl Markus, 'Political Parties in the DP Camps', in Isawjiw, Boshyk & Senkus, 119; Holian, *Between National Socialism and Soviet Communism*, 85–88; Sheila Fitzpatrick, '"Determined to Get On": Some Displaced Persons on the Way to a Future', *History Australia* (2015), 3; Gatrell, 'Population Displacement', 52.
35 Peter Gatrell, *The Making of the Modern Refugee* (Oxford: Oxford University Press, 2013), 98.
36 Gatrell, 'Population Displacement', 54; Peter Gatrell, 'Introduction: World Wars and Population Displacement in Europe in the Twentieth Century', *Contemporary European History*, 16:4 (2007), 423.
37 Eduard Bakis, 'DP Apathy', in HBM Murphy, *Flight and Resettlement* (Paris: United Nations Educational, Scientific and Cultural Organization, 1955), 76; Gatrell, 'Introduction', 421–422; Welfare Division: Report on Psychological Problems of Displaced Persons, 1945 (1 June 1945), JRU Co-operation with Other Relief Organisations: United Nations Relief and Rehabilitation Administration (UNRRA), HAS-4/3, Post-War Europe Series I: Refugees, Exile and Resettlement, 1945–1950, Gale Digital Collections.
38 Reinisch, '"We Shall Rebuild Anew a Powerful Nation"', 472; Hilton, 'Cultural Nationalism in Exile', 288, 290.
39 Ariela Kochavi, 'The Politics of Displaced Persons in Postwar Europe, 1945–1950', Post-War Europe Series I: Refugees, Exile and Resettlement, 1945–1950, Gale Digital Collections, 3; Sandor Berger, *An Appendix to An Appendix of Prose, A Supplement to A Supplement of 'I Protest': The Letters and Articles of Sandor Berger, Australia, 1964–1968* (Sydney, 1968), 307; Victoria Zabukovec, *The Second Landing* (Kangaroo Island: Penneshaw, 1993), 289; Jiri Kolaja, 'A Sociological Note on the Czechoslovak Anti-Communist Refugee', *American Journal of Sociology*, 58:3 (November 1952), 289.
40 Lubomyr Luciuk, *Searching for Place: Ukrainian Displaced Persons* (Toronto: 2000), 143; Tadeusz Borowski, in Holian, *Between National Socialism*

and Soviet Communism, 1; Suzanne D Rutland, 'Sanctuary for Whom? Jewish Victims and Nazi Perpetrators in Postwar Australian Migrant Camps', Conference Paper, 'Beyond Camps and Forced Labour', Second International Multidisciplinary Conference at the Imperial War Museum, London, 11–13 January 2006 (unpublished), 12.

41 Agnes E Karlik, interviewed by Whitehorse Historical Society, 10 October 2006; Hulme, *The Wild Place*, 113; George Fischer, 'The New Soviet Emigration', *Russian Review*, 8:1 (January 1949), 8.

42 Cohen, 'The West and the Displaced', 7.

43 Laura Hilton, 'How Anti-Communist Are You? An Examination of the Treatment of Polish and Latvian DPs in the US Occupation Zone of Germany', paper for the American Association for the Advancement of Slavic Studies, 16–19 November 2006, Washington DC, 6; Theresa Kurk McGinley, 'Embattled Polonia: Polish Americans and World War Two', *East European Quarterly*, 37:3 (2003), 5; Gerard Daniel Cohen, 'The Politics of Recognition: Jewish Refugees in Relief Policies and Human Rights Debates, 1945–1950', *Immigrants and Minorities*, 24:2 (2006), 131; George Ginsburgs, 'The Soviet Union and the Problem of Refugees and Displaced Persons, 1917–1956', *The American Journal of International Law*, 51:2 (April 1957), 358.

44 Andrew Paul Janco, 'Unwilling: The One-Word Revolution in Refugee Status, 1940–51', *Contemporary European History*, 23:3 (2014), 430–431; Elliott, 'The Soviet Repatriation Campaign', 343.

45 Elliott, 'The Soviet Repatriation Campaign', 343.

46 Definition of Term 'Refugee' and 'Displaced Person' (9 April 1946), Foreign Office: Political Departments: General Correspondence from 1906–1972, Foreign Office FO 371/57705–0007, Post-War Europe Series I: Refugees, Exile and Resettlement, 1945–1950, Gale Digital Collections; HG Brooks (Department of Immigration), 'Displaced Persons Volume 1', (unpublished manuscript), Papers (1933–1977) of Harland Gordon Brooks, 1920–1985, MS 8128, NLA, 3–4.

47 Office of the United Nations Commissioner for Refugees, *Constitution of the International Refugee Organization*, 15 December 1946, United Nations Treaty Series, 18, 3, <www.refworld.org/docid/3ae6b37810.html>; Cohen, 'The West and the Displaced', 28–29.

48 Louise W Holborn, *The International Refugee Organization: A specialized agency of the United Nations, its history and work, 1946–1952* (London: Oxford University Press, 1956), 206; Cohen, 'The West and the Displaced', 90, 94; Rutland, 'Sanctuary for Whom?', 23–24; Cesarani, *Justice Delayed*, 4, 40, 52.

49 Karatani, 'How History Separated Refugee and Migrant Regimes', 529; Sunil Amrith & Glenda Sluga, 'New Histories of the United Nations', *Journal of World History*, 19:3 (2008), 2; Marrus, *The Unwanted*, 342; Cohen, 'The West and the Displaced', 106–107, 265.

50 Klaus Neumann, *Refuge Australia: Australia's Humanitarian Record* (Sydney: UNSW Press, 2004), 12, 84; Sonia Tascón, 'Refugees and the Coloniality of Power: Border-Crossers of Postcolonial Whiteness', in

Aileen Moreton-Robinson (ed.), *Whitening Race: Essays in Social and Cultural Criticism* (Canberra: Aboriginal Studies Press, 2004), 245.

51 Cohen, 'The West and the Displaced', 2, 18, 112, 158; Rutland, 'Sanctuary for Whom?', 25; Susan L Carruthers & Carl Bon Tempo, 'The United States and Refugees, Comments', Place of Refuge Panel Series, Arizona State University, (unpublished), 2; Cohen, 'The Politics of Recognition', 127; Marrus, *The Unwanted*, 352; Salomon, *Refugees in the Cold War*, 65, 85.

52 Kovacs, 'Immigration and Assimilation', 188–189; Wilson, *Aftermath*, 152.

53 Kuhlmann-Smirnov, 'The Resettlement', 1.

54 Hulme, *The Wild Place*, 143, 175; Gemie and Humbert, 'Comment: Writing History in the Aftermath of "Relief": Some Comments on "Relief in the Aftermath of War"', 314.

55 Wendy Lowenstein & Morag Loh, *The Immigrants* (Melbourne: Penguin, 1991), 82.

56 Cohen, 'The West and the Displaced', 206; Elizabeth White, 'Reconstruction in the Immediate Aftermath of War: A Comparative Study of Europe, 1945–50', Workshop Report, Birkbeck College, <www.balzan.bbk.ac.uk/page24.html>; Silvia Salvatici, 'English Government and European Women Refugees after World War II', History/Gender/Migration Conference, Paris, March 2006, <barthes.ens.fr/clio/dos/genre/com/salvatici.pdf>, 7; Cesarani, *Justice Delayed*, 74; Haim Genizi, *America's Fair Share: The Admission and Resettlement of Displaced Persons, 1945–1952* (Detroit: Wayne State University Press, 1993), 23; Humbert, 'French Politics of Relief and International Aid', 630.

57 Hilton, 'Cultural Nationalism in Exile', 313, 316; Letter from Harry Leslie Daumont to Director, Current Affairs Bulletin, Commonwealth Office of Education, dated 21 November 1948, Daumont, Harry Leslie – Admission under D.P. Scheme – View on Assimilation of Migrants, Department of Immigration, Central Office, Correspondence Files, 1949/3/487, A434, NAA.

58 Letter from Robert C Doty, Director of Public Information, IRO, dated 20 June 1949, Immigration – Displaced Persons – General, Department of Information, Central Office, Correspondence Files, 021.134, CP815/1, NAA; Christiane Harzig, 'Book Review: Zwischen Fremde und Fremde: Displaced Persons in Australien, den USA, und Kanada, 1946–1952 (Between strangers and strangers: Displaced persons in Australia, the USA, and Canada, 1946–1952), by Henriette von Holleuffer (Osnabrück, 2001) in German, *The Journal of American History*, 90:1 (2004); V Irinin, 'Slave Labour of Displaced Persons in the Capitalistic Countries' and IRO, 'The Facts About Refugees', IRO, Geneva, 15 September 1948, IRO 1947–1977, Department of Immigration, Central Office, Correspondence Files, IRO, 1962/67355, A446, NAA; Cohen, 'The West and the Displaced', 51.

59 Constitution of the IRO, 15 December 1946, Office of the United Nations Commissioner for Refugees, *United Nations, Treaty Series*, 18, 3; Elizabeth White, 'Reconstruction in the Immediate Aftermath of War:

A Comparative Study of Europe, 1945–50', Workshop Report, Birkbeck College (2006); Daniel G Cohen, 'Regeneration through Labor: Vocational Training and the Reintegration of Déportés and Refugees, 1945–1950', *Proceedings of the Annual Meeting of the Western Society for French History, Selected Papers of the Annual Meeting*, 32 (2005), 380; Humbert, 'French Politics of Relief and International Aid', 629, 631.

60   Kuhlmann-Smirnov, 'The Resettlement', 304; Letter from the Australian Military Mission, Köln, to the Director General of Health, Canberra, 28 December 1949, Policy and Procedure in regard to Migrants and Applicants, for Landing Permits, Medical – Displaced Persons, A445, 200/1/5, NAA; Marrus, *The Unwanted*, 352; L Eitinger, 'Mental Diseases Among Refugees in Norway After World War II', in Charles Zwingmann & Maria Pfister-Ammende (eds), *Uprooting and After ...* (Berlin: 1973), 193, 203; Luciuk, *Searching for Place*, 139; Kay & Miles, *Refugees or Migrant Workers?*, 64; Hulme, *The Wild Place*, 144; Andrew Markus, 'Labour and Immigration 1946–9: The Displaced Persons Program', *Labour History*, 47 (1984), 81; Holian, *Between National Socialism and Soviet Communism*, 4; Angelika Königseder & Juliane Wetzel, 'Displaced Persons, 1945–1950: The social and cultural perspective', Post-War Europe Series I: Refugees, Exile and Resettlement, 1945–1950, Gale Digital Collections, 9; Stone, 'Introduction', 3; Datla, 'Displacement Camps: Sites of Ethnic Renewal and Nationalism'; Zahra, 'Prisoners of the Postwar', 211; Gatrell, 'Introduction', 419.

61   Markus, 'Labour and Immigration', 81.

62   Egon F Kunz, interviewed by Peter Biskup, March–April 1988, TRC 2262, NLA.

63   Helen Simanowskyj (Garan), 'Seedorf (Germany), 1948', in Vasilios Vasilas (ed.), *In Search of Hope and Home*, 188; Bohdan Mykytiuk, interviewed by Rob Willis, 21 October 2004, Oral TRC 5373/21–23, NLA; Fitzpatrick, 'Determined to Get On', 14; Stanislaw Gotowicz, *Bittersweet Bread* (London: Minerva Press, 1998), 76.

2   'Chifley liked them blond'

1   AA Calwell, *Be Just and Fear Not* (Melbourne: Lloyd O'Neill in assoc. with Rigby, 1972), 103.

2   Frank Clune, *All Roads Lead to Rome: A Pilgrimage to an Eternal City, and a Look Around War-torn Europe* (Sydney: Angus & Robertson, 1950), viii, 40, 220, 231, 268.

3   Stuart Macintyre, *Australia's Boldest Experiment: War and Reconstruction in the 1940s* (Sydney: NewSouth Publishing, 2015), 13; Brian Murphy, *The Other Australia: Experiences of Migration* (Cambridge & Melbourne: Cambridge University Press, 1993), 88; Jerzy Zubrzycki, 'Arthur Calwell and the Origin of Postwar Immigration', address given to the Migration Division Seminar, Department of Immigration and Ethnic Affairs, Canberra, 6 October 1994, <www.multiculturalaustralia.edu.au/doc/zubrzycki_1.pdf>; Glenda Sluga, 'Bonegilla Reception and Training Centre, 1947–1971', MA thesis (University of Melbourne, 1985), 11, n. 4;

Suzanne Rutland, *Edge of the Diaspora: two centuries of Jewish settlement in Australia* (Sydney: Collins, 1988), 226.

4   Josef Sestokas, *Welcome to Little Europe: Displaced Persons and the North Camp* (Sale: Little Chicken Publishing, 2010), 51; Janis Wilton & Richard Bosworth, *Old Worlds and New Australia: The Postwar Migrant Experience* (Melbourne: Penguin, 1984), 21; Zubrzycki, 'Arthur Calwell', 3; Graeme Freudenberg, 'Calwell, Arthur Augustus (1896–1973)', Australian Dictionary of Biography, National Centre of Biography, ANU, <adb.anu.edu.au/biography/calwell-arthur-augustus-9667>.

5   Rt Hon. Arthur Calwell, interviewed by Mel Pratt, 25–28 May 1971, Oral TRC 121/7, NLA; Gwenda Tavan, 'Leadership, Arthur Calwell and the Postwar Immigration Program', *Australian Journal of History and Politics* 58:2 (June 2012), 210; Arthur A Calwell, *How Many Australians Tomorrow?* (Melbourne: Reed & Harris, 1945); Andrew Markus & Margaret Taft, 'Postwar Immigration and Assimilation: A Reconceptualisation', *Australian Historical Studies*, 46:2 (2015), 234–251.

6   A Calwell, *Australia, House of Representatives, Debates*, 15 October 1947, 762; Calwell's discussion with Addison, London, 1 July 1947, Department of Foreign Affairs and Trade, Australian Government, <dfat.gov.au/about-us/publications/historical-documents/Pages/volume-12/280-calwells-discussion-with-addison.aspx>; Press Release, 9 July 1947, Cabled from Bremen, Australian News and Information Bureau, Displaced Persons – Policy General (including Accommodation at Chermside Military Camp, contains details about aliens' and refugees' treatment in Queensland), 1947–54, Department of Immigration, Queensland Branch, Case files, 1949/1493, J25, NAA; 'Migrant Pool: Britain's Shortage of Labour', *West Australian*, 12 January 1949; Letter from Migration Services, Social Activities Division, 15 September 1947, Department of Immigration, Central Office, Correspondence Files, IRO, 1962/67355, IRO 1947–1977, A446 1962/67355, NAA; *Daily Mirror* (London), 15 August 1947.

7   Cabinet Agendum No. 6950, Cabinet Secretary/Secretariat, Curtin, Forde and Chifley Ministries – folders of Cabinet minutes and agenda, Australian Participation in the IRO and Post-UNRRA Relief, A2700 695D, NAA.

8   Film Australia's Immigration DVD: Interview with Jerzy Zubrzycki, Questions by Paul Byrnes and Penelope McDonald (2004), unpublished, 2; John Lack & Jacqueline Templeton, *The Bold Experiment: A Documentary History of Australian Immigration Since 1945* (Melbourne: Oxford University Press, 1995), 21.

9   Andrew Markus, 'Labour and Immigration 1946–9: The Displaced Persons Program', *Labour History*, 47 (1984), 77; Agendum No. 6950, 12 May 1947, Minutes of the Full Cabinet, with index – 16 January 1947 to 9 November 1949 – Chifley Ministry, A2703, Volume 4, NAA; Agendum No. 6950, Department of the Treasury and Department of External Affairs, and Memorandum for HV Evatt, Minister for External Affairs, 12 May 1947, Australian participation in the IRO and Post-UNRRA relief, Cabinet Office, A2700, 695D, NAA; *Australia, House*

of *Representatives, Debates,* 28 November 1947, 2922; Monthly Digest: No. 1, 10 February 1947, Inter-Governmental Committee On Refugees, 1944–51, JCRA General: Liaison, The Henriques Collection, Wiener Library, Archives Unbound.

10 Markus, 'Labour and Immigration', 77–78; Charles Price, Australia and Refugees 1921–1976, Report for the National Population Council's Refugee Review, The Australian Immigration Research Centre, Canberra, 1990, 18; Klaus Neumann, *Refuge Australia: Australia's Humanitarian Record* (Sydney: UNSW Press, 2004), 29.

11 Jock Collins, *Migrant Hands in a Distant Land: Australia's Postwar Immigration* (Sydney: Pluto Press Australia, 1988), 54; John Hirst, 'Political Courage: Some Australian Examples', *The Monthly*, 25 (July 2007); Despatches from Australian Military Mission, Berlin, Number 32/1947 (dated 10 April 1947) to Number 48/1947 (dated 30 September 1947), Department of Defence [III], Central Office, 37/301/337 Attachment 17, NAA; Sestokas, *Welcome to Little Europe*, 84; Tavan, 'Leadership', 209; Noel Lamidey, *Partial Success: My Years as a Public Servant* (Sydney: NW Lamidey, 1970), 35.

12 Sir Robert Jackson of UNRRA, interview by ABC Radio National (1986), Soundcloud: Siobhan McHugh, <soundcloud.com/siobhan-uow/sir-robert-jackson-of-unrra>; 'Chifley's Hundreds of Thousands – Europe hasn't enough migrants to go around', *Daily Telegraph*, 18 June 1947; Joy Damousi, '"We are Human Beings, and have a Past": The "Adjustment" of Migrants and the Australian Assimilation Policies of the 1950s', *Australian Journal of Politics and History*, 59:4 (2013), 501.

13 Collins, 54; Neumann, *Refuge Australia*, 29–30; *Morning Bulletin* (Rockhampton), 5 July 1947; 'Minister will Seek Immigrant Ships Overseas', 19 June 1947, Publicity undertaken by the Department of Information for Department of Immigration, Department of Immigration, Central Office, A436, 1947/5/2588, NAA.

14 Cablegram Calwell to Chifley, 30 June 1947, Department of Foreign Affairs and Trade, Australian Government, <dfat.gov.au/about-us/publications/historical-documents/Pages/volume-12/279-calwell-to-chifley.aspx>; Calwell Press Release, 8 July 1947 & 9 July 1947, Cabled from Bremen, Australian News and Information Bureau, Displaced Persons – Policy General (Chermside); Calwell Press Release, 18 July 1947 & 22 July 1947, Cabled from Berlin, Australian News and Information Bureau, Displaced Persons – Policy General (including Accommodation at Chermside Military Camp, contains details about aliens' and refugees' treatment in Queensland), 1947–54, Department of Immigration, Queensland Branch, Case files, 1949/1493, J25, NAA; Meeting of Executive Committee and General Council Geneva, 18th October – 26th October, 1951, IRO 1947–1977, IRO, Department of Immigration, Central Office, Correspondence Files, A446 1962/67355, NAA; Telegram from Army Melbourne to Army Berlin, 12 May 1950, George Vincent Greenhalgh, 1903–, Papers, 1947–1956, MS 8863, NLA.

15 Egon Kunz, *Displaced Persons: Calwell's New Australians* (Sydney: ANU Press, 1988), 35.
16 George Kiddle, interviewed by Ann-Mari Jordens, Chief Migration Officers' Oral History Project, 2008, Oral TRC 5930/5, NLA; HG Brooks, 'Displaced Persons Volume 1: 1947', (unpublished manuscript), Papers (1933–1977) of Harland Gordon Brooks, 1920–1985, MS 8128, NLA.
17 'The flow had to begin somehow', *Mercury* (Hobart), 26 July 1947; Calwell interviewed by Pratt.
18 Markus, 'Labour and Immigration', 78; Calwell Press Release, 15 July 1947, Cabled from Paris, Australian News and Information Bureau, Displaced Persons – Policy General (including Accommodation at Chermside Military Camp, contains details about aliens' and refugees' treatment in Queensland), 1947–54, Department of Immigration, Queensland Branch, Case files, 1949/1493, J25, NAA.
19 IRO Press Release dated 23 July 1947, Immigration – Displaced Persons – General, IRO [IRO] Agreement, Department of Information, Central Office, Correspondence Files, CP 815/1, 021.114, NAA; United States Department of State, Foreign Relations of the United States, 1948, vol. VI, *The Far East and Australasia*, 3, <digicoll.library.wisc.edu/cgi-bin/FRUS/FRUS-idx?type=turn&entity=FRUS.FRUS1948v06.p0017&id=FRUS. FRUS1948v06&isize=M>; Calwell Press Release, 15 July 1947, Cabled from Paris & 18 July 1947, Cabled from Berlin, Australian News and Information Bureau, Displaced Persons – Policy General (including Accommodation at Chermside Military Camp, contains details about aliens' and refugees' treatment in Queensland), 1947–54, Department of Immigration, Queensland Branch, Case files, 1949/1493, J25, NAA; (PC) IRO Agreement with Australia dated 21 July 1947, 2, and IRO Press Release, 21 July 1947, Immigration – Displaced Persons – General, IRO Agreement, 1947–1948, Department of Information, Central Office, Correspondence Files, 021.114, CP 815/1, NAA.
20 Calwell, *Australia, House of Representatives, Debates*, 3 October 1947, 483; Lack & Templeton, 21–22.
21 Letter from Hugh J Murphy, Information Publicity Officer to Secretary, Department of Immigration, 16 March 1949, Publicity – Displaced Persons, Correspondence Files, Department of Immigration, Central Office, 1949/7/926, A438, NAA; Ruth Balint, 'Industry and Sunshine: Australia as home in the displaced persons' camps of postwar Europe', *History Australia* 11:1 (April 2014), 103; Ann Mihkelson, *Three Suitcases and a Three-Year-Old* (East Roseville, NSW: Kangaroo Press, 1999), 43.
22 Calwell, Australia, House of Representatives, *Debates*, 3 October 1947, 483; Immigration – Displaced Persons – General, Correspondence Files, Department of Immigration, Central Office, 021.134 Attachment CP815/1, NAA; 'Radio drive to get Balts here', *Argus*, 23 September 1948; Justine Greenwood, 'The Migrant Follows the Tourist: Australian Immigration Publicity after the Second World War', *History Australia*, 11:3 (December 2014), 88–89.

Notes to pages 61–63

23 IRO, 'The Facts About Refugees', 15 September 1948, 24, IRO – International Refugee Organization, 1947–1977, Department of Immigration, Central Office, A446, 1962/67355, NAA; Suzanne Rutland, 'The History of Australian Jewry, 1945–1960', PhD thesis, University of Sydney, 1990, 6; Marilyn Lake & Henry Reynolds, *Drawing the Global Colour Line: White Men's Countries and the Question of Racial Equality* (Melbourne: Melbourne University Press, 2008), 339, 343, 352.

24 Suzanne Rutland, 'Subtle Exclusions: Postwar Jewish Emigration to Australia and the impact of the IRO Scheme', *The Journal of Holocaust Education*, 10:1 (2001), 62; Sluga, 'Bonegilla Reception and Training Centre', 22, n. 5; Clune, *All Roads Lead to Rome*, 40.

25 Kunz, *Displaced Persons*, 17; Memorandum, Department of the Interior, 11 May 1939, Admission of Jews Policy Part 3, Department of Immigration, Correspondence Files, 235/5/4, A445, NAA; Conference on Displaced Persons, 18 July, with British Control Commission Officials in Berlin, Minister's Visit to Europe – Report on, 1947, Department of Immigration, Central Office, Correspondence Files, 1949/7/1067, A438, NAA; Markus, 'Labour and Immigration', 80; Suzanne Rutland & Sol Encel, 'No room at the inn: American responses to Australian immigration policies, 1946–1954', *Patterns of Prejudice*, 43:5 (2009), 513; Rutland, 'Subtle Exclusions', 56–57.

26 Immigrants for Australia, Berlin Dispatch No. 46/47, 26 June 1947, from Australian Military Mission, Berlin to Department of Defence and Department of External Affairs, Despatches from Australian Military Mission, Berlin – (New Series) – Number 32/1947 (dated 10 April 1947) to Number 48/1947 (dated 30 September 1947), Department of Defence [III] Central Office, 37301/337 Attachment 17, A816, NAA.

27 (PC)IRO Agreement with Australia dated 21 July 1947, 2, and IRO Press Release dated 23 July 1947, and Australian Department of Information Press Release dated 13 October 1947, Immigration – Displaced Persons – General, IRO Agreement; Calwell Press Release, 18 July 1947, Cabled from Berlin, Australian News and Information Bureau, Displaced Persons – Policy General (including Accommodation at Chermside Military Camp, contains details about aliens' and refugees' treatment in Queensland), 1947–54, Department of Immigration, Queensland Branch, Case files, 1949/1493, J25, NAA; Markus, 'Labour and Immigration', 80; Arthur Calwell quote cited by Helen Ferber, an Australian working with the (PC)IRO. Ferber described Calwell's delegation as discussing with her 'DP immigrants for Australia, whom they were off to select'. Helen Ferber, letter dated 21 July 1947, Letters from Paris and Geneva March 1947–November 1947, Papers of Helen Ferber, MS 9740, NLA.

28 Clune, *All Roads Lead to Rome*, 178; Letter from M Stewart, Senior Medical Officer, Australian Military Mission, to Head, Australian Military Mission, 18 June 1946, Medical – Displaced Persons. Policy and Procedure in regard to Migrants and Applicants, for Landing Permits, 200/1/5, A445, NAA; Letter from Dr Cameron, Australian MO with the Selection Committee in Germany, to Dr Walker, Bonegilla, 1949,

Medical – Displaced Persons. Policy and Procedure in regard to Migrants and Applicants, for Landing Permits, Correspondence Files, Department of Immigration, Central Office, 200/1/5, A445, NAA.

29 Mark Wyman, *DPs: Europe's Displaced Persons, 1945–1951* (New York: Cornell University Press, 1998), 191; Barbara E Bryan, 'Recalcitrant Women? The Effects of Immigration Policies on Displaced Persons Women 1948–1952', MA thesis, Griffith University, 1996, 15; Minutes of Conference held at Lancaster House, 18 July 1947, Employment of Displaced Persons (DPs) in Australia, FO 1052/417, NA (UK); Calwell, *Be Just and Fear Not*, 103; ML Kovacs, 'Immigration and Assimilation: An Outline Account of the IRO Immigrants in Australia', MA thesis, University of Melbourne, 1955, 193; Lack & Templeton, 11; Kiddle interviewed by Jordens.

30 Rutland, 'Subtle Exclusions', 57; George Kiddle, 'The first party of displaced persons – November 1947', *Post Migration*, no. 100 (Aug 1995), 16; Neumann, *Refuge Australia*, 32.

31 Press Statement by the Minister for Immigration, the Honourable Arthur A Calwell, dated 7 November 1947, Displaced Persons – Policy General (including Accommodation at Chermside Military Camp, contains details about aliens' and refugees' treatment in Queensland), 1947–54, Department of Immigration, Queensland Branch, Case files, 1949/1493, J25, NAA; Adam Wells (Executive Producer), 'Immigration Nation' (SBS TV: 2011).

32 Rutland, 'Subtle Exclusions', 57; Suzanne D Rutland, 'Sanctuary for Whom? Jewish Victims and Nazi Perpetrators in Postwar Australian Migrant Camps', Conference Paper, 'Beyond Camps and Forced Labour', Second International Multidisciplinary Conference at the Imperial War Museum, London, 11–13 January 2006', (unpublished), 28.

33 Rutland, *Edge of the Diaspora*, 407; Bruce Pennay, 'Selling Immigration', *Context*, National Trust of Australia (NSW), Sydney (June 2007), 6; Rutland, 'Subtle Exclusions', 58.

34 Rutland, 'Sanctuary for Whom?'; Cohen, 'The West and the Displaced', 2; AC Menzies, *Review of Material relating to the Entry of Suspected War Criminals into Australia*, (Canberra The Review, 1986).

35 Helen Ferber, letter dated 21 July 1947, Letters from Paris and Geneva March 1947–November 1947, Papers of Helen Ferber, MS 9740, NLA; Suzanne Rutland, 'The History of Australian Jewry', 7.

36 Mather, *Aftermath of War*, 191; Rutland, 'Sanctuary for Whom?', 24–25; Kiddle interviewed by Jordens; Interview with Dr George Klim, Polish Australians Oral History Project, TRC 3498, NLA.

37 Kiddle, 'The First Party of Displaced Persons', 16; Minutes of Conference held at Cologne, 17–18 December 1948, Papers of George Vincent Greenhalgh, 1903–, 1947–1956, MS 8863, NLA; Mark Aarons, *Sanctuary: Nazi Fugitives in Australia* (Port Melbourne, Vic: William Heinemann Australia, 1989), 110; Markus, 'Labour and Immigration', 80.

38 Kiddle interviewed by Jordens.

39 Cablegram Calwell to Chifley, London, 18 July 1947, Department of Foreign Affairs and Trade, Australian Government, <dfat.gov.au/about-

us/publications/historical-documents/Pages/volume-12/282-calwell-to-chifley.aspx>; David Horner, *The Spy Catchers: The Official History of ASIO 1949–1963* (Sydney: Allen & Unwin, 2014), 250; Memorandum from Brigadier FG Galleghan to Secretary to Immigration, 11 August 1949, Article in *Washington Post* – 10 August 1949 – 'Australia puts United States Displaced Persons Mission to Shame', Department of Immigration, Central Office, 1949/3/8754, A434, NAA; Memorandum to the Director, Military Intelligence, Army Headquarters, Melbourne, from THE Heyes, Secretary of the Department of Immigration, 17 August 1950, Admission of Poles [Polish displaced persons] from East Africa [also reports of migrant selection missions to Middle East, Greece, East Africa], Department of Immigration, Central Office, 255/1/4, A445, NAA; Kiddle interviewed by Jordens; Rutland, 'Sanctuary for Whom?', 25; Jane Cadzow, 'Another Time, Another Place', *Good Weekend Magazine*, *Sydney Morning Herald*, 14 June 2008, 27; Aarons, *Sanctuary*, xxv, 35, 46; Cesarani, *Justice Delayed*, 182; MM Alagich, 'Croatians', in James Jupp (ed.), *The Australian People: An Encyclopedia of the Nation, Its People and Their Origins* (Sydney: Angus & Robertson, 1988), 337; 'False Reports of Nazis Here', *Sunday Telegraph*, 1 April 1951; Harry Martin, *Angels and Arrogant Gods: Migration Officers and Migrants Reminisce 1945–85* (Commonwealth of Australia, 1989), 19.

40 Philip Mendes, 'Jews, Nazis and Communists Down Under: The Jewish Council's Controversial Campaign Against German Immigration', *Australian Historical Studies*, 33:119 (April 2002), 78–79.

41 Mendes, 88; Károly Zentai, Migrant Selection Documents for Displaced Persons who travelled to Australia per *Fairsea* departing Naples, Italy, 7 February 1950, R145–R149, A12014, NAA; Balint, 'Australia, Hungary and the case of Károly Zentai'; 'Ivan', Migrant Selection Documents for Displaced Persons who travelled to Australia per *Anna Salen* departing Naples, Italy, 22 May 1949, 425–427, A11937, NAA.

42 Calwell Press Release, 18 July 1947, Cabled from Berlin, Australian News and Information Bureau, and *Courier-Mail* (Brisbane), 26 September 1947, Displaced Persons – Policy General (including Accommodation at Chermside Military Camp, contains details about aliens' and refugees' treatment in Queensland), 1947–54, Department of Immigration, Queensland Branch, Case files, 1949/1493, J25, NAA; Bruce Pennay, *The Young at Bonegilla: Receiving Young Immigrants at Bonegilla Reception and Training Centre, 1947–71* (Wodonga: Parklands Albury–Wodonga, 2010), 1; Holborn, *The International Refugee Organization*, 393; Script of interview broadcast over United Nation Radio on 10 October 1949, Publicity – Displaced Persons, Department of Immigration, Central Office, Correspondence Files, 1949/7/926, A438, NAA; Neumann, *Refuge Australia*, 32–33; Telegram from Army Melbourne to Amber Berlin, 12 May 1950, Papers of George Vincent Greenhalgh, 1903–, 1947–1956, MS 8863, NLA.

43 Letter from JN Wheatley to A/D Department of Health, IRO Lemgo, 25 August 1949, and Letter from R Taylor, Zone Resettlement Officer

for Assistant Director, Chief, Re-Establishment of A/D Health to JN Wheatley, 8 October 1949, Resettlement and Employment of Displaced Persons (DPs), Foreign Office FO 1052/229, NA (UK).

44 Egon Kunz born 11 March 1922, 110, Migrant Selection Documents for Displaced Persons who travelled to Australia per *General Stewart* departing Naples, Italy, 24 June 1949, Department of Immigration, Central Office, A11939, NAA.

45 Egon F Kunz, 'The Genesis of the Postwar Immigration Programme and the Evolution of the Tied-Labour Displaced Persons Scheme', *Ethnic Studies* (Melbourne) 1:1 (1977), 39; 'D.P. Migrants for Australia', *Courier-Mail* (Brisbane), 26 September 1947; Interview with HC (Nugget) Coombs, Formerly of the Department of Postwar Reconstruction, 1982, <www.multiculturalaustralia.edu.au/library/media/Audio/id/372>; Stanislav Gotowicz, Interviewed by Barry York, 8 April 2001, TRC 4716, NLA; Ramunus Tarvydas, *From Amber Coast to Apple Isle: Fifty Years of Baltic Immigrants in Tasmania, 1948–1998* (Hobart: Baltic Semicentennial Commemoration Activities Organising Committee, 1997), 18; Mirosznyk, *How Do You Like Australia?*, 96.

46 Letter from Calwell to Dr Andrew, Australian Military Mission, dated 2 September 1949, Medical – Displaced Persons; Medical Selection of European Displaced Persons as 'New Australians': A Guide for Medical Officers, 12, Medical – Displaced Persons. Policy and Procedure in regard to Migrants and Applicants, for Landing Permits, Department of Immigration, Central Office, Correspondence Files, 200/1/5, A445, NAA; Borin, *The Uprooted Survive*, 129.

47 Memorandum of AJ Metcalfe, Director-General of Health, dated 1 February 1949; Medical Selection of European Displaced Persons as 'New Australians': A Guide for Medical Officers, 19, Medical – Displaced Persons. Policy and Procedure in regard to Migrants and Applicants, for Landing Permits, Department of Immigration, Central Office, Correspondence Files, 200/1/5, A445, NAA; Wendy Lowenstein & Morag Loh, *The Immigrants* (Melbourne: Penguin, 1991), 81; Ale Liubinas, *Aviete and After* (Melbourne: Fosbee Pty Ltd, 1998), 261, 274; *Advertiser*, 5 May 1949.

48 Rutland, 'Sanctuary for Whom?', 23; Kunz, *Displaced Persons*, 47; Neumann, *Refuge Australia*, 33; Letter from M Stewart, Senior Medical Officer, Australian Military Mission, to Head, Australian Military Mission, 18 June 1946, and Letter from HG Andrew, Senior Medical Officer, Australian Military Mission, to Director General of Health, Canberra, dated 28 December 1949, Medical – Displaced Persons; Minutes of Conference held at Cologne, 7–18 December 1948, Papers of George Vincent Greenhalgh, 1903–, 1947–1956, MS 8863, NLA; Letter from THE Heyes, Secretary, Department of Immigration to Immigration Publicity Officer, Department of Information, Report on Visit to Australia by IRO Representative dated January 1949, Immigration – DPs – General, Department of Information, Central Office, Correspondence Files, CP 815/1, 021.134, NAA; 'Andriy and Nina', Migrant Selection Documents

for Displaced Persons who travelled to Australia per *Skaugum* departing Naples, Italy, 31 August 1949, 1169–1173, A11746, NAA.
49 Ruth Balint, '"To Reunite the Dispersed Family": War, Displacement and Migration in the Tracing Files in the Australian Red Cross', *History Australia*, 12:2 (2015), 129–130.
50 Letter from Victor E Lederer, Australian Military Mission, Austria, to GV Greenhalgh, Chief Migration Officer, Australian Military Mission, Cologne, 14 September 1949, Papers of George Vincent Greenhalgh, 1903–, 1947–1956, MS 8863, NLA.
51 Kunz, *Displaced Persons*, 43; Clune, *All Roads Lead to Rome*, 269.

3 'A hot Siberia'

1 *Argus*, 22 March 1949.
2 Egon Kunz, *Displaced Persons: Calwell's New Australians* (Sydney: ANU Press, 1988), 242.
3 Stuart Macintyre, *Australia's Boldest Experiment: War and Reconstruction in the 1940s* (Sydney: NewSouth Publishing, 2015), 124.
4 Macintyre, *Australia's Boldest Experiment*, 177.
5 Kunz, *Displaced Persons*, 38–39, 139; Carolyn Holbrook, 'The Transformation of Labor Party Immigration Policy, 1901–1945', *Journal of Australian Studies* (December 2016).
6 Charles Price, Australia and Refugees 1921–1976, Report for the National Population Council's Refugee Review, Australian Immigration Research Centre, Canberra, 1990, 20.
7 Susan Hesch, 'Australian Immigration Policy: Displaced Persons, Contracts and Camps', Honours thesis, History Department, University of Adelaide, 1985, 44; TAG Hungerford, interviewed by Hazel de Berg, 31 May 1965, Oral TRC 1/99, NLA; Bruce Pennay, 'First Impressions', *So Much Sky: Bonegilla Reception and Training Centre, 1947–71*, <www.migrationheritage.nsw.gov.au/exhibitions/somuchsky/firstimpressions.html>.
8 Report on Visit to Australia by IRO Representative dated January 1949, Immigration – DPs – General, Department of Information, Central Office, Correspondence Files, 021.134, CP 815/1, NAA; HBM Murphy, 'The Assimilation of Refugee Immigrants in Australia', *Population Studies*, 5:3 (March 1952), 182; Bianka Vidonja Balazategui, *Gentlemen of the Flashing Blade*, Series: Studies in North Queensland History (Townsville: James Cook University, 1990), 18.
9 Circular from THE Heyes, Department of Immigration c. October 1948, Accommodation and Placement in Employment of Family Units Arriving under the Displaced Persons (DP) Scheme Procedure, Department of Immigration, Western Australian Branch, Correspondence Files, 1948/H/2935, PP6/1, NAA; Wanda Skowronska, *To Bonegilla from Somewhere* (Ballarat: Connor Court Publishing, 2013), 8; Wendy Lowenstein & Morag Loh, *The Immigrants* (Melbourne: Penguin, 1991), 82.
10 Eerik Purje, 'Greta (New South Wales), 1948', in Vasilios Vasilas (ed.), *Across Lands and Oceans … to Freedom: Stories and Photographs from the*

Estonian Journey to Australia & New Zealand, vol. II (Sydney: 2015), 273; Luda Popenhagen, *Australian Lithuanians* (Sydney: NewSouth Publishing, 2012), 49; Glenda Sluga, *Bonegilla: A Place of No Hope* (Melbourne: University of Melbourne, 1988); Leopoldine Mimovich, 'A Chip in Time: The Tale of Leopoldine Mimovich', in Will Davies & Andres Dal Bosco (eds), *Tales from a Suitcase* (Melbourne: Lothian Books, 2001), 43; Phillip Knightley, *Australia: A Biography of a Nation* (London: Vintage, 2001), 219.

11 Hesch, 'Australian Immigration Policy', 40; Letter from JE Walsh, Regional Administrative Officer, Perth WA, DLNS to the Director, Hostels – Employment of DPs – Pregnant Women, Migrant Workers' Accommodation Division, Alexandria, 17 November 1949, Migrant Workers' Accommodation Division, Central Office, Department of Labour and National Service, Correspondence Files, 100/5/5, SP446/1, NAA.

12 Karen Agutter, 'Displaced Persons and the "Continuum of Mobility" in the South Australian Hostel System', in Margrette Kleinig & Eric Richards, *On the Wing: Mobility Before and After Emigration to Australia*, Visible Immigrants: Seven (Adelaide: Flinders University and the Migration Museum of South Australia, 2012), 147.

13 Halina Netzil (1920–), interviewed by Donna Kleiss, 1991–1992, Migrant Women Oral History, OH24–0005, SLQ.

14 'Married Migrants are unhappy living hundreds of miles apart – migrants are in despair', *Sun* (Sydney), 27 January 1950; Bruce Pennay assisted by Jayne Persian, *Receiving Europe's Displaced: Bonegilla Reception and Training Centre, 1947–53* (Wodonga: Parklands Albury–Wodonga, 2010), 17; Popenhagen, *Australian Lithuanians*, 66.

15 Inese Petersons (1947–), interviewed by Allison Murchie, 2002, South Australians Acting for Change: Welcoming Refugees Oral History Project, OH 636/2, SLSA; 'Irma' (1919–), interviewed by Karobi Mukherjee, 1989, Lives of Older Women of Non-English Speaking Background and their Adaption to and Contribution to Life in South Australia, OH 18/15, SLSA.

16 Antoni Suryak, interviewed by Barry York, 2001, Polish Australians Oral History Project, Oral TRC 4766/1, NLA.

17 Pennay & Persian, *Receiving Europe's Displaced*, 15; Josef Sestokas, *Welcome to Little Europe: Displaced Persons and the North Camp* (Sale: Little Chicken Publishing, 2010), 174; 'Children Flying to Aust.', *News* (Adelaide), 2 December 1949.

18 Halina Netzil interview, 1991–1992; Notes on Discussion between Expert Advisers and the Social Welfare Committee of the Immigration Advisory Council, held on Friday, 1 February 1952, CIAC, Committee on Social Welfare, 140/5/6, A445, NAA; Edith Tórókfalvy, *Letters of Heartache and Hope* (Hastings, Vic: 1995), 116; Murphy, 'The Assimilation of Refugee Immigrants in Australia', 185.

19 Andrew Markus & Eileen Sims, *Fourteen Lives – Paths to a Multicultural Community*, Monash Publications in History: 16 (Melbourne: Monash University, 1993), 23; John Murphy, *Imagining the Fifties: Private*

Sentiment and Political Culture in Menzies' Australia (Sydney: Pluto Press, 2000), 160; Ramunus Tarvydas, *From Amber Coast to Apple Isle: Fifty Years of Baltic Immigrants in Tasmania, 1948–1998* (Hobart: Baltic Semicentennial Commemoration Activities Organising Committee, 1997), 13.

20 Lindsay Ronald Smith, 'A Study of European Immigration to Australia, 1942–1949', MA thesis, University of Queensland, 1970, 403; Kunz, *Displaced Persons*, 167; Pennay & Persian, *Receiving Europe's Displaced*, 16; Anna Curtis (1942–) & Zofia McCormack (1943–), interviewed by Donna Kleiss, 1991, Migrant Women Oral History, OH24–0002, SLQ.

21 Letter from A/Director, Northam Reception and Training Centre, to Commonwealth Migration Officer for WA, 18 July 1950. Approved Institutions transfer of Displaced Persons, minors, Department of Immigration, Western Australian Branch, 1950/H/4191, NAA; Anna Curtis (1942–) & Zofia McCormack (1943–), interviewed by Donna Kleiss, 1991, Migrant Women Oral History, OH24–0002, SLQ.

22 Minutes of Conference held at Cologne, 7–18 December 1948, Papers of George Vincent Greenhalgh, 1903–, 1947–1956, MS 8863, NLA; Karen Agutter, 'Fated to be Orphans: The Consequences of Australia's Postwar Resettlement Policy on Refugee Children', *Children Australia*, 41:3 (2016), 225–229.

23 Notes on Discussion between Expert Advisers and the Social Welfare Committee of the Immigration Advisory Council, held on Friday, 1 February 1952, CIAC, Committee on Social Welfare, 140/5/6, A445, NAA; Karen Agutter, 'Fated to be Orphans: The Consequences of Australia's Postwar Resettlement Policy on Refugee Children', *Children Australia*, 41:3 (2016), 227, 230; Pennay, *Benalla*, 5, 19, 28.

24 'Near Riot at Migrant Camp, 5 Hurt', *Canberra Times*, 13 June 1950; Hesch, 'Australian Immigration Policy', 44–45; Elisabeth Edwards, *Half a World Away: Postwar Migration to the Orange District, 1948–1965* (Orange: Orange City Council, 2007), 50–51.

25 Details of the Scheme Under Which Displaced Persons May Emigrate to Australia, Publicity – Displaced Persons, Department of Immigration, Central Office, Correspondence Files, 949/7/926, A438, NAA; Lucy Daugalis, 'The Immigrant Experience – Joys and Hardship', *Ethnic Communities Council of South Australia Newsletter*, 2 (1989), 27; 'Olga Iszczyszyn (Alexandra)', Immigration Place Australia, <immigrationplace.com.au/story/olga-iszczyszyn-alexandra>.

26 Kunz, *Displaced Persons*, 178; Zabukovec, *The Second Landing*, 307.

27 *Australia, House of Representatives, Debates*, 3 October 1947, 482 and 15 October 1947, 767; Kunz, *Displaced Persons*, 178.

28 *Sydney Morning Herald*, 7 April 1948; Calwell, *Be Just and Fear Not*, 104.

29 Kunz, *Displaced Persons*, 141–142.

30 Kunz, *Displaced Persons*, 169; Jupp, *Arrivals and Departures*, 46.

31 Considerations to Govern the Employment of Displaced Persons During the Two Years after their Arrival in Australia, undated, Displaced Persons Employment Opportunities Policy Part 1 (1947–1948), Department of

Immigration, Central Office, Correspondence Files, 179/9/3, A445, NAA; Zabukovec, *The Second Landing*, 283; James Jupp, *Exile or Refuge? The Settlement of Refugee, Humanitarian and Displaced Immigrants* (Canberra: Australian Government Publishing Service, 1994), 34–35; Arthur Calwell, Letter to the Federated Ironworkers' Association, 20 June 1949, <www.multiculturalaustralia.edu.au/library/media/Document/id/42>.

32 Visitor Book, Displaced Persons, Gallery, Migration Museum (South Australia), 2006.

33 Paul Öpik, 'Ingham (Australia), 1948' in Vasilas (ed.), *Across Lands and Oceans*, 218.

34 Discussions with Officers of the Commonwealth Employment Service on placement of Displaced Persons in Employment, 13 January 1948. Displaced Persons Employment Opportunities Policy Part 1, 1947–1948, Department of Immigration, Central Office, A445, 179/9/3, NAA; 'Migrant Pool: Britain's Shortage of Labour', *West Australian*, 12 January 1949; Alexander Mountain, *I Protest [In a hundred thousand words ...]: The (150) Letters and Articles [to the Press, Etc.] of 'Sandor Berger'*, *Australia, 1954–1961* (Sydney: Sandor Berger, 1962), 38.

35 'Balts Complain About Camp', *News* (Adelaide), 15 January 1948; Sestokas, *Little Europe*, 97.

36 Sestokas, *Little Europe*, 157; Clark, 'South Australia and the Displaced Persons Programme 1947–1952', 57; Letter from SJ Dempsey, Department of Immigration to the Acting Secretary, 3 January 1951, Displaced Persons Employment Policy Part 3, Department of Immigration, Central Office, Correspondence Files, 179/9/5, A445, NAA.

37 Bryan, 'Recalcitrant Women?', 51; 'Balt Problems', Report of Miss H Dobson from Ingham, Queensland, dated 12 August 1948, Reports by Social Workers, Displaced Persons, Employment Division [III], Department of Labour and National Service, Correspondence Files, 1948/23/4096, B550, NAA; Ale Liubinas, *Under Eucalypts: Stories of Migrant Struggles* (Melbourne: Fosbee Pty Ltd, 2001), 9.

38 Egon Kunz, *The Intruders: Refugee Doctors in Australia* (Canberra: ANU Press, 1975), 21.

39 RT Appleyard, 'Displaced Persons in Western Australia: Their Industrial Location and Geographical Distribution: 1948–1954', in *University Studies in History and Economics* (University of Western Australia), II: 3 (1955), 71; EF Kunz, Demographer, 1970–1980, AWV 253, NBAC; DPs with Professional or Technical Qualifications, Regional Director Form Letter, Department of Labour and National Service, Central Office, Policy, Procedure and Property Files, T35522, SP193/1, NAA; Kunz, *Displaced Persons*, 153.

40 Kunz, *The Intruders*, 27, 53, 130.

41 Kunz, *The Intruders*, 57, 90.

42 Kay Dreyfus, *Silences and Secrets: The Australian Experience of the Weintraub Syncopators*, (Melbourne: Monash University Publishing, 2013).

43 Fitzpatrick, 'Determined to Get On', 120; 'Adelaide Plans to Help Migrants', *Advertiser*, 25 January 1950; 'Displaced Persons with

Professional and Technical Qualifications', 1 November 1949, W Funnell, Director to the Regional Director, Employment Division, Sydney, Circular CES 25, DPs with Professional or Technical Qualifications, Department of Labour and National Service, Central Office, Policy Procedure, T35522, SP193/1, NAA; AA Calwell, 'The Why and How of Postwar Immigration', *Conference Proceedings, 19th Summer School of the Australian Institute of Political Science*, Canberra ACT, 24–26 January 1953 (London: Angus & Robertson, 1953), 15.

44 Kunz, *Displaced Persons*, 179, 144.

45 Zabukovec, *The Second Landing*, 323–324.

46 Egon F Kunz, interviewed by Peter Biskup, March–April 1988, TRC 2262, NLA.

47 Telegram from Immigration, Canberra to Passports, Perth, received 23 January 1951, Displaced Persons Employment Policy Part 3, Department of Immigration, Central Office, Correspondence Files, 179/9/5, A445, NAA; TAG Hungerford, *Riverslake* (Sydney: Angus & Robertson, 1953), 33.

48 'Moscow's Crocodile Tears for DPs', *Sydney Morning Herald*, 21 June 1949; Hungerford, *Riverslake*, 7; Kunz, *Displaced Persons*, 147.

49 Section III, Work of the Section – Major Problems Handled, Index to Report, Social Welfare Section (1949–51), CIAC, Committee on Social Welfare, 140/5/6, A445, NAA.

50 Tarvydas, *From Amber Coast to Apple Isle*, 90; Stanislav Gotowicz, interviewed by Barry York, 8 April 2001, TRC 4716, NLA; Ann Tündern Smith, *FifthFleet.net*, <www.fifthfleet.net/index.html>; Ann Tündern-Smith, 'Agnes Tündern, A First Transporter', in Vasilas (ed.), *Across Lands and Oceans*, 262; Ilma Kalar, 'Zeehan (Tasmania), 1949', in Vasilas (ed.), *Across Lands and Oceans*, 289.

51 Netzil interview, 1991–1992; Donald Horne, *The Lucky Country* (Melbourne: Penguin, 1971), 85.

52 Letter from AL Nutt to the Minister of Immigration, 18 February 1949, Displaced Persons in Queensland Brickyards and Repatriation Hospitals – Refusing to Work and Leaving Employment Without Authority, A434, 1949/3/5831; Kunz, *Displaced Persons*, 177; Bryan, 'Recalcitrant Women?', 71; Sestokas, *Little Europe*, 112, 119.

53 Appendix 'A', Letter from J Cliffe, Commonwealth Migration Officer, to the Department of Immigration, 23 February 1949, Displaced Persons in Queensland Brickyards and Repatriation Hospitals – Refusing to Work and Leaving Employment Without Authority, A434, 1949/3/5831, NAA; *Sunday Mail* (Brisbane), 4 July 1948.

54 Letter from J Cliffe, 23 February 1949; Memorandum to the Secretary, Department of Immigration, dated 23 February 1949, Displaced Persons – Policy General (including Accommodation at Chermside Military Camp, contains details about aliens' and refugees' treatment in Queensland), 1947–54, Department of Immigration, Queensland Branch, Case files, 1949/1493, J25, NAA; Murphy, 'The Assimilation of Refugee Immigrants in Australia', 183; Maximilian Brändle, *Refugee Destination Queensland*

(Brisbane: Multicultural Writers and Arts Friendship Society (Qld), 1999), 121.
55 Memorandum of GAM Edson, Commonwealth Migration Officer for SA, dated 27 April 1951, Part 1, Former Displaced Persons. List of Absconders (All States Except WA), 1951–1952, Department of Immigration, Western Australian Branch, Correspondence Files, 1949/H/4010, PP 6/1, NAA; Murphy, 'The Assimilation of Refugee Immigrants in Australia', 182.
56 Appleyard, 'Displaced Persons in Western Australia', 84; Letter from J Cliffe, 23 February 1949; 'Balts to the Bush', *Clay Products Journal of Australia*, April 1950, 13; 'Thousand Migrants Have Broken Work Contracts', *Sydney Morning Herald*, 7 March 1951.
57 Letter from J Cliffe, 23 February 1949.
58 'Migrants Breaking Contracts', *Barrier Miner*, 19 March 1951; Markus & Taft, 'Postwar Immigration and Assimilation', 243, 249; Jordens, *From Alien to Citizen*, 184.
59 Kunz, *Displaced Persons*, 149; Sean Brawley, 'Finding home in white Australia: The O'Keefe deportation case of 1949', *History Australia*, 11:1 (April 2014), 137; 'Deportations' and Letter from THE Heyes to Acting Chief of the UNIRO in Australia and New Zealand dated 18 July 1951, EF Kunz (personal papers), 1970–1980, AWV 253, NBAC; *Herald* (Melbourne), 15 May 1950; 'Thousand Migrants Have Broken Work Contracts', *Sydney Morning Herald*, 7 March 1951; Memorandum A/g. Sen. Migration Officer, undated, Displaced Persons Employment Policy Part 3, Department of Immigration, Central Office, Correspondence Files, 179/9/5, A445, NAA; Markus & Taft, 'Postwar Immigration and Assimilation', 249.
60 Letter from F Tice, Social Worker, to Senior Social Worker, Department of Immigration, 28 May 1952, Social Worker's Report, Bonegilla Reception & Training Centre, Victoria (1949–1952), Department of Immigration, Central Office, Correspondence Files, Class 6 (Aliens Registration), 1949/6/381, A437, NAA; Letter from Heyes to General Lloyd, Chief of the UNIRO in Australia and New Zealand dated 24 April 1950, Kunz (personal papers), 1970–1980, AWV 253, NBAC.
61 Letter from Heyes to General Lloyd, 14 March 1950; Kunz, *Displaced Persons*, 178; Tarvydas, *From Amber Coast to Apple Isle*, 30; Brawley, 'Finding home in White Australia', 142.
62 Balint, 'Industry & Sunshine', 110; Kunz, *Displaced Persons*, 180; Lesleyanne Hawthorne, *Making It In Australia* (Melbourne: Edward Arnold, 1988), 80; Kuzma Ivanov – [arrived Fremantle 3 March 1950 per *Fairsea*] Application for Release from Period of Exemption, PP9/2, 1952/62/6222, NAA.
63 Peter Beilharz, Trevor Hogan & Sheila Shaver, *The Martin Presence: Jean Martin and the Making of the Social Sciences in Australia* (Sydney: NewSouth Publishing, 2015), 93, 95; Jean I Martin, *Refugee Settlers: A Study of Displaced Persons in Australia* (Canberra: ANU, 1965), 76; Erika Boas, '"Leading Dual Lives": Lithuanian Displaced Persons in Tasmania',

BA Honours thesis, University of Tasmania, 1999, 35, n. 105; *Age*, 18 August 1950.

4 'New Australians'

1 Dr Egon F Kunz, interviewed by Dr Peter Biskup, March/April 1988, TRC 2262, NLA.
2 Summary of Statement made by the Rt Hon. Arthur Calwell at the meeting of the Preparatory Commission for the IRO, 22 July 1947, DPs to Australia, FO 945/474, NA (UK); Josef Sestokas, *Welcome to Little Europe: Displaced Persons and the North Camp* (Sale: Little Chicken Publishing, 2010), 149; 'Labor's Big Dinner to Prime Minister', *Australian Worker*, Sydney, 2 November 1949.
3 *Australia, House of Representatives, Debates*, 28 November 1947, 2928; Anna Haebich, *Spinning the Dream: Assimilation in Australia 1950–1979* (Fremantle: Fremantle Press, 2008), 11; Richard White, 'The Australian Way of Life', *Historical Studies*, 18:73 (1979), 530.
4 Bruce Pennay, *The Young at Bonegilla: Receiving Young Immigrants at Bonegilla Reception and Training Centre, 1947–71* (Wodonga: Parklands Albury–Wodonga, 2010), 1; *Sydney Sun*, 17 August 1949; Letter from Heyes to the Defence Secretariat, 26 July 1949, Reception – Arrival of Fifty-Thousandth Displaced Person [Kalnins, Maira; Richard; Zenta; Inaru], A434, 1949/3/16409, NAA.
5 Egon Kunz, *Displaced Persons: Calwell's New Australians* (Sydney: ANU Press, 1988), 16; 'Displaced Persons' Plight in Germany "Desperate"', *Mercury* (Hobart), 21 July 1947; 'Publicity Memorandum of Immigration Publicity Officer', and Hugh J Murphy, 'Publicity Needs in Australia for IRO and the Displaced Persons Migrants', Immigration – Displaced Persons – General, 021.134, CP815/1, NAA; Kamini Badhu & Julie Fairclough, 'Migrants in Australian Society: A Comparison of the 1950s and 1970s', Advanced Diploma in Teaching Thesis, Flinders University, 1975, 8; Lindsay Ronald Smith, 'A Study of European Immigration to Australia, 1942–1949', MA thesis, University of Queensland, 1970, 230.
6 'Publicity Needs in Australia for IRO and the Displaced Persons Migrants', Immigration – Displaced Persons – General, 021.134, CP815/1, NAA; Newspaper article (unidentified), 25 January 1949 and 'Australia's New Citizens: These people are trying to forget', *Brisbane Mail*, 2 July 1948, Displaced Persons – Policy General (including Accommodation at Chermside Military Camp, contains details about aliens' and refugees' treatment in Queensland), 1947–54, 1949/1493, J25, NAA.
7 Brian Murphy, *The Other Australia: Experiences of Migration* (Cambridge & Melbourne: Cambridge University Press, 1993), 137; Haebich, *Spinning the Dream*, 125.
8 R Maslyn Williams, Director, *Mike and Stefani* (Department of Immigration: 1952); Paul Byrnes & Penelope McDonald, Film Australia, 'Film Australia's Immigration' (2004), unpublished; Haebich, *Spinning the Dream*, 127–128; Emma Greenwood, 'No Migrants Here: Migrant Absence Within Australian Migrant Publicity', *Antithesis*, 7:2 (1995), 113.

9   ML Kovacs, 'Immigration and Assimilation: An Outline Account of the IRO Immigrants in Australia', MA thesis, University of Melbourne, 1955, 91; Gwenda Tavan, '"Good Neighbours": Community organisations, migrant assimilation and Australian society and culture, 1950–1961', *Australian Historical Studies*, 28:109 (October 1997), 83.
10 *Australia, House of Representatives, Debates*, 28 November 1947, 2921; AA Calwell, *Be Just and Fear Not* (Melbourne: Lloyd O'Neill in assoc. with Rigby, 1972), 103; *Border Morning Mail*, 9 December 1947; Bruce Pennay, 'Picturing Assimilation in Postwar Australia', *Australian Historical Studies*, 44:1 (2013), 138; Stella Lees & Julie Senyard, *The 1950s ... how Australia became a modern society, and everyone got a house and car* (Melbourne: Hyland House Publishing, 1987), 108.
11 Lees & Senyard, *The 1950s*, 108–109; Kunz, *Displaced Persons*, 144.
12 *Australian Women's Weekly*, 3 January 1948; Hulme, *The Wild Place*, 188–189; Lees & Senyard, *The 1950s*, 105, 109.
13 *Daily Telegraph* (Sydney), 17 June 1949; *Argus* (Melbourne) 11 August 1949; Kovacs, 'Immigration and Assimilation', 96–98.
14 Catherine Panich, *Sanctuary?: Remembering Postwar Immigration* (Sydney: Allen & Unwin, 1988), 162; EF Kunz, 'Postwar Non-British Immigration', in James Jupp (ed.), *The Australian People: An Encylopedia of the Nation, Its People and Their Origins* (Sydney: Angus & Robertson, 1988), 101; Henriette Von Holleuffer, 'After 1945: Surviving as Survivors? The Tyranny of History, The Blessing of Distance and the Idea of "Corporate Identity" in the Resettlement Campaigns of Australia and the USA', in Johannes-Dieter Steinert & Inge Weber-Newth (eds), *Beyond Camps and Forced Labour: Current International Research on Survivors of Nazi Persecution: Proceedings of the First International Multidisciplinary Conference at the Imperial War Museum*, London, 29–31 January 2003 (Secolo Verlag, Osnabrük Germany, 2005), 140; Lesa Morgan, 'Remember the Peasantry: A study of genocide, famine, and the Stalinist Holodomor in Ukraine, 1932–33, as it was remembered by postwar immigrants in Western Australia who experienced it', PhD thesis, University of Notre Dame, Fremantle, 2009, 237; Haebich, *Spinning the Dream*, 178.
15 Von Holleuffer, 'After 1945: Surviving as Survivors?', 140; Barbara E Bryan, 'Recalcitrant Women? The Effects of Immigration Policies on Displaced Persons Women 1948–1952', MA thesis, Griffith University, 1996, 32; Janis Wilton & Richard Bosworth, *Old Worlds and New Australia: The Postwar Migrant Experience* (Melbourne: Penguin, 1984), 150; Joy Damousi, *Memory and Migration in the Shadow of War: Australia's Greek Immigrants after World War II and the Greek Civil War* (Cambridge: Cambridge University Press, 2015), 58.
16 Damousi, *Memory and Migration in the Shadow of War*, 58.
17 Ann-Mari Jordens, *Alien to Citizen: Settling Migrants in Australia, 1945–75* (Sydney: Allen & Unwin, 1997), 78; Mark Edele & Sheila Fitzpatrick, 'Displaced Persons: From the Soviet Union to Australia in the wake of the Second World War', *History Australia*, 12:2 (August 2015), 12; Wilton & Bosworth, *Old Worlds and New Australians*, 7.

18 HBM Murphy, 'The Assimilation of Refugee Immigrants in Australia', *Population Studies*, 5:3 (March 1952), 196; Lees & Senyard, *The 1950s*, 107–108; James Jupp, *Immigration* (Melbourne: Oxford University Press, 1998), 157; Andrew Markus & Margaret Taft, 'Postwar Immigration and Assimilation: A Reconceptualisation', *Australian Historical Studies*, 46:2 (2015), 244, 246, 248.

19 Bruce Pennay, *Calwell's Beautiful Balts: Displaced Persons at Bonegilla* (Wodonga: Parklands Albury–Wodonga, 2007), 8.

20 Tavan, 'Good Neighbours', 78; HBM Murphy, *Flight and Resettlement* (Paris: UNESCO, 1955), xxi; Richard Boyer, 'The Australian Good Neighbour Movement – Past and Present' in *Australian Citizenship Convention* (Sydney: Conpress Printing, 1957), 2.

21 Kovacs, 'Immigration and Assimilation', 48; M Greenhalgh, 'Migrant Mothers – How we can help them', English Classes for Migrant Women in Canberra Play Centres, 1953–1955, 174/8/24, A445, NAA; Elisabeth Edwards, *Half a World Away: Postwar Migration to the Orange District, 1948–1965* (Orange: Orange City Council, 2007), 108.

22 Kovacs, 'Immigration and Assimilation', 347; Damousi, *Memory and Migration in the Shadow of War*, 55; Murphy, *The Other Australia*, 137.

23 Ruth Arndt, 'Contact Work in Ainslie', and M Greenhalgh, 'Migrant Mothers – How we can help them', English Classes for Migrant Women in Canberra Play Centres, 1953–1955, 174/8/24, A445, NAA.

24 John Murphy, *Imagining the Fifties: Private Sentiment and Political Culture in Menzies' Australia* (Sydney: Pluto Press, 2000), 163; Murphy, *Flight and Resettlement*, xxi; Tavan, 'Good Neighbours', 79.

25 James Jupp, *Arrivals and Departures* (Melbourne: Lansdowne Press, 1966), 9; Tavan, 'Good Neighbours', 79; Bryan, 'Recalcitrant Women?', 38.

26 Tavan, 'Good Neighbours', 81; Boyer, 'The Australian Good Neighbour Movement', 9.

27 Tavan, 'Good Neighbours', 81, 84; Murphy, *The Other Australia*, 143; Leszek Szymański, *Living with the Weird Mob* (Los Angeles: Trident International Book Publishers, 1973), 54.

28 'Contract Period May Be Cut for Displaced Persons', *Canberra Times*, 29 March 1949; Murphy, 'The Assimilation of Refugee Immigrants in Australia', 199; Wilton & Bosworth, *Old Worlds and New Australia*, 9; John Lack & Jacqueline Templeton, *The Bold Experiment: A Documentary History of Australian Immigration Since 1945* (Melbourne: Oxford University Press, 1995), 10; Murphy, *Imagining the Fifties*, 159; Karen Agutter, 'Displaced Persons and the "Continuum of Mobility" in the South Australian Hostel System', in Margrette Kleinig & Eric Richards, *On the Wing: Mobility Before and After Emigration to Australia*, Visible Immigrants: Seven (Adelaide: Flinders University and the Migration Museum of South Australia, 2012), 150.

29 Vasilios Vasilas (ed.), *In Search of Hope and Home: Stories and Photographs from the Ukrainian Journey to Australia* (Sydney: 2015), 274; *Sunshine Advocate*, 6 October 1950.

30 Andrew Jakubowicz, 'Text Commentary – Building an Industrial Nation',

A Multicultural History of Australia, <www.multiculturalaustralia.edu.
au/library/media/Timeline-Commentary/id/8.Postwar-reconstruction->;
Jean I Martin, *Refugee Settlers: A Study of Displaced Persons in Australia*
(Canberra: ANU, 1965), 40.
31 Stanislaw Gotowicz, *Bittersweet Bread* (London: Minerva Press, 1998), 289.
32 Ramunus Tarvydas, *From Amber Coast to Apple Isle: Fifty Years of Baltic Immigrants in Tasmania, 1948–1998* (Hobart: Baltic Semicentennial Commemoration Activities Organising Committee, 1997), 13; ML Kovacs & AJ Cropley, *Immigrants and Society: Alienation and Assimilation* (Sydney: McGraw-Hill Book Company, 1975), 110; Edith Törökfalvy, *Letters of Heartache and Hope* (Melbourne: 1995), 156; Martin, *Refugee Settlers*, 380.
33 Jordens, *Alien to Citizen*, 123; Notes on Discussion between Expert Advisers and the Social Welfare Committee of the Immigration Advisory Council, held on Friday, 1 February 1952, CIAC, Committee on Social Welfare, 140/5/6, A445, NAA; Kovacs, 'Immigration and Assimilation', 246, 350, 431; Pennay, *Calwell's Beautiful Balts*, 8; 'Our Migrants Are Being Neglected', *Brisbane Mail*, 2 July 1948; Sherry Morris, *Uranquinty Remembers: A Migrant Experience 1948–1952* (Wagga Wagga: Active Print, 2001), 112; Markus & Taft, 'Postwar Immigration and Assimilation', 244.
34 Delaney Michael Skerrett, 'History and Memory in the "Return" of the Descendants of Latvian and Estonian Refugees to the Baltic: A Survey', *Journal of Baltic Studies* 39:1 (2008), 42; Kolaja, 'A Sociological Note on the Czechoslovak Anti-Communist Refugee', 289.
35 Marko Pavlyshyn, 'The Dislocated Muse: Ukrainian Poetry in Australia, 1948–1985', *Canadian Slavonic Papers*, 28:2 (1986), 187, 190.
36 Balint, 'To Reunite the Dispersed Family', 139–140.
37 Siobhan McHugh, *The Snowy: The People Behind the Power* (Sydney: Angus & Robertson, 1995), 173; 'Without Women', *Australasian Post*, 5 February 1953.
38 VL Borin, 'Australian Bachelors of Misery', *Quadrant* 5:3 (1961), 4–7; Letter from VL Borin to Hon. Harold Holt, Treasurer, dated 12 February 1960 [Personal Papers of Prime Minister Holt] Miscellaneous Correspondence, 47, Correspondence Files, The Rt Hon. Harold Edward Holt CH, PC, M2606, NAA.
39 'Too Many Lost Weekends', *Advocate* (Burnie), 12 May 1951.
40 Morris, *Uranquinty Remembers*, 100; Jordens, *Alien to Citizen*, 148; Murphy, 'The Assimilation of Refugee Immigrants in Australia', 201; 'Suicide of Ill Migrant: "Examination hopeless", says doctor', *Argus*, 10 December 1949; Uranquinty Social Worker's Report dated August – December 1950, Procedure – Social Work – Records and Reports, 1950/7/478, Department of Immigration, Central Office, Correspondence Files, A438, NAA.
41 *Truth*, 10 August 1958; Haebich, *Spinning the Dream*, 178; *Age*, 27 March 1950; Mark Dapin, 'Tales from the Underground', *Good Weekend Magazine*, *Sydney Morning Herald*, 18 October 2008.
42 Helena Walsh, *Reaching for the Moon: A Migrant's Story from War-torn*

Latvia to Australia (Sydney: Kangaroo Press Pty Ltd, 1996), 212; Section III, Work of the Section – Major Problems Handled, Index to Report, Social Welfare Section (1949–51), CIAC, Committee on Social Welfare, 140/5/6, A445, NAA; Liubinas, *Under Eucalypts*, 9, 111.

43 Martin, *Refugee Settlers*, 27; Damousi, *Memory and Migration in the Shadow of War*, 46; Murphy, 'The Assimilation of Refugee Immigrants in Australia', 190; HBM Murphy, *Flight and Resettlement*, 92.
44 Walsh, *Reaching for the Moon*, 190.
45 Mihkelson, *Three Suitcases and a Three-Year-Old*, 84, 106.
46 Cecile Kunrathy, *Impudent Foreigner* (Sydney: Edward & Shaw, 1963), 138; Diane Armstrong, *Mosaic: A Chronicle of Five Generations* (Sydney: Random House, 1998), 421; Ludmilla Forsyth, 'On the Slippery Margins', in Robert Pascoe (ed.), *Alienation and Exile: Writings of Migration* (Melbourne: Footprint Australian Writers, The Footscray Foundation for Australian Studies, 1990), 1–2; Martin, *Refugee Settlers*, 51, 73, 74.
47 Damousi, *Memory and Migration in the Shadow of War*, 56; 'Rail Strike over New Australians', *Newcastle Sun*, 21 February 1950; Martin, *Refugee Settlers*, 15.
48 'Bernard Pilecki', Immigration Place Australia,<immigrationplace.com.au/story/bernard-pilecki/>; Grazina Pranauskas, 'National and Cultural Identity in Diaspora: A Study of Australian–Lithuanians', MA thesis, Deakin University, 2003, 46; William Dick, *A Bunch of Ratbags* (London, Collins: 1965), 66.
49 Martin, *Refugee Settlers*, 7; Paul Kraus, *The Not So Fabulous Fifties: Images of a Migrant Childhood* (Sydney: Kangaroo Press Ltd, 1985), 54; Questionnaire Responses, 'Clubs, Ethnic', Kunz, AWV 253, NBAC.
50 Kovacs & Cropley, *Immigrants and Society*, 108, 110.
51 Walsh, *Reaching for the Moon*, 186, 220.
52 Mountain, *I Protest*, 225; Markus & Taft, 'Postwar Immigration and Assimilation', 240; Questionnaire Responses, 'Clubs, Ethnic', Kunz, AWV 253, NBAC.
53 Jean I Martin, *The Migrant Presence: Australian Responses 1947–1977*, Research Report for the National Population Inquiry, Studies in Society, 2, series ed. Colin Bell (Sydney: George Allen & Unwin, 1978), 78; Edward Bakis, 'The So-Called DP Apathy in Germany's DP Camps', *Transactions of the Kansas Academy of Science*, 55:1 (March 1952), 85; Gatrell, 'Population Displacement in the Baltic Region in the 20th Century', 44; Gatrell, 'Introduction: World Wars and Population Displacement in Europe in the Twentieth Century', 423.
54 Notes on Discussion between Expert Advisers and the Social Welfare Committee of the Immigration Advisory Council, held on Friday, 1 February 1952, and Section III, Work of the Section – Major Problems Handled, Index to Report, Social Welfare Section (1949–51), CIAC, Committee on Social Welfare, 140/5/6, A445, NAA.
55 Murphy, 'The Assimilation of Refugee Immigrants in Australia', 179–180, 182, 202; HBM Murphy, 'Assimilating the Displaced Person', *Australian Quarterly*, 24:1 (March 1952), 58.

56 HBM Murphy, 'Migration, Culture and Mental Health', *Psychological Medicine*, 7:4 (1977), 677.
57 J Hamnet, 'Marginality and Mental Health: The Price of Failure to Adjust', *Australian Journal of Social Issues*, 2 (1965), 19; Jerzy Krupinski, Alan Stoller and Lesley Wallace, 'Psychiatric Disorders in East European Refugees Now in Australia', *Social Science and Medicine*, 7 (1973), 34, 37, 46, 47; A Stoller & J Krupinski, 'Immigration to Australia: Mental Health Aspects', in Charles Zwingmann & Maria Pfister-Ammende (eds), *Uprooting and After...* (Berlin: Springer-Verlag, 1973), 265; J Krupinski, 'Sociological Aspects of Mental Ill-Health in Migrants', *Social Science & Medicine*, 1 (1967), 268.
58 Murphy, 'The Assimilation of Refugee Immigrants in Australia', 203.
59 Martin, *Refugee Settlers*, 5, 32, 36, 90.
60 Jerzy Zubrzycki, *Settlers of the Latrobe Valley: a sociological study of immigrants in the brown coal industry in Australia* (Canberra: ANU, 1964), 87.
61 Jean Craig, 'The Social Impact of New Australians', *Conference Proceedings: 19th Summer School of the Australian Institute of Political Science*, Canberra ACT, 24–26 January 1953 (London: Angus & Robertson, 1953), 67; Martin, *The Migrant Presence*, 207.

5   Inside the Cold War

1 'Migrants Still Fight Russia', *Sun-Herald*, 2 May 1954.
2 Dr George Klim interviewed by Barry York, 1996, Polish Australians Oral History Project, Oral TRC 3498, NLA.
3 'The Census Will Tell Us What Our Migrants Do', *Sunday Telegraph*, 20 June 1954.
4 Dr George Klim interviewed by Barry York, 1996.
5 Kazimierz Sosnowski interviewed by Paul Sendziuk, 2009, Stalin's Poles Oral History Project, Oral TRC 6175/10, NLA.
6 Bohdan Mykytiuk interviewed by Rob Willis, 21 October 2004, Rob Willis Folklore Collection, TRC 5373/21–23, NLA; Michael Protopopov, 'The Russian Orthodox Presence in Australia: The history of a church told from recently opened archives and previously unpublished sources', PhD thesis, Australian Catholic University, 2006, 125; Anna Curtis (1942–) & Zofia McCormack (1943–) interviewed by Donna Kleiss, 1991, Migrant Women Oral History, OH24–0002, SLQ; Mark Edele & Sheila Fitzpatrick, 'Displaced Persons: From the Soviet Union to Australia in the wake of the Second World War', *History Australia*, 12:2 (2015), 12; Halina Netzil (1920–) interviewed by Donna Kleiss, 1991–1992, Migrant Women Oral History, OH24–0005, SLQ; Miriam Gilson & Jerzy Zubrzycki, *The Foreign-Language Press in Australia: 1848–1964* (Canberra: ANU Press, 1967), 116; Peter Beilharz, Trevor Hogan & Sheila Shaver, *The Martin Presence: Jean Martin and the Making of the Social Sciences in Australia* (Sydney: NewSouth Publishing, 2015), 95.
7 Andrew Markus & Eileen Sims, *Fourteen Lives – Paths to a Multicultural Community*, Monash Publications in History: 16 (Melbourne: Monash University, 1993), 112.

8   Gilson & Zubrzycki, *The Foreign-Language Press in Australia*, 26–27; Jean Craig, 'The Social Impact of New Australians', *Conference Proceedings*, 19th Summer School of the Australian Institute of Political Science, Canberra ACT, 24–26 January 1953 (London: Angus & Robertson, 1953), 22; ML Kovacs, 'Immigration and Assimilation: An Outline Account of the IRO Immigrants in Australia', MA thesis, University of Melbourne, 1955, 320.

9   Sonia Mycak, 'The Role of Networks in Australian Multicultural Literature: Postwar "New Australians" as an Empirical Case Study', *Sun Yat-sen Journal of Humanities*, 17 (Winter 2003), 19; Sonia Mycak, 'Multicultural Literature', in Craig Munroe & Robyn Sheahan (eds), *Paper Empires: A History of the Book in Australia 1946–2005* (Brisbane: UQP, 2006) 275; Marko Pavlyshyn, 'Culture and the émigré Consciousness: Ukrainian Theatre in Australia 1948–1989', *Australasian Drama Studies*, 20 (1992), 65; Katarzyna Kwapisz Williams, 'Beyond Stories of Victimhood: Narrating Experiences of Displacement', *Life Writing*, 11:4 (2014), 447; Dmytro Chub (Dmytro Nytczenko), *So This Is Australia: The Adventures of a Ukrainian Migrant in Australia* (Melbourne: Bayda Books, 1980), 7–8; Pavlyshyn, 'Aspects of Ukrainian Literature in Australia', in Jacques Delaruelle, Alexandra Karakostas-Sêdá & Anna Ward (eds), *Writing in Multicultural Australia 1984: An Overview*, Papers presented at the Multicultural Writers' Weekends in Sydney, 13–14 October 1984 and in Melbourne, 27–28 October 1984 (Sydney: Australia Council for the Literature Board, 1985), 71–72.

10 Barry York, *Michael Cigler: A Czech–Australian Story, from displacement to diversity*, Studies in Australian Ethnic History Series, No. 11 (Canberra: Centre for Immigration & Multicultural Studies, Research School of Social Sciences, ANU, 1996), 10–11, 81; Michael Cigler, *The Czechs in Australia*, Australian Ethnic Heritage Series, ed. Michael Cigler (Melbourne: Australasian Educa Press, 1983), 73.

11 Markus & Sims, *Fourteen Lives*, 100.

12 Kovacs, 'Immigration and Assimilation', 413, 318.

13 Peter Beilharz, 'Miss Craig Goes to Chicago (Jean Martin finds Australian Sociology)', The Australian Sociological Association, Conference Publication Proceedings, 1–4 December 2009, <www.tasa.org.au/wp-content/uploads/2015/03/Beilharz-Peter.pdf>, 3; Jean Martin, *Community and Identity: Refugee Groups in Adelaide* (Canberra: ANU Press, 1972), 10.

14 Lyn Richards, 'Displaced Politics: Refugee Migrants in the Australian Political Context' (Paper No. 45), *La Trobe Sociology Papers*, Department of Sociology, School of Social Sciences (Melbourne: La Trobe University, May 1978), 1; Halina Netzil (1920–), interviewed by Donna Kleiss, 1991–1992.

15 Suzanne D Rutland, 'Sanctuary for Whom? Jewish Victims and Nazi Perpetrators in Postwar Australian Migrant Camps', Conference Paper, 'Beyond Camps and Forced Labour', Second International Multidisciplinary Conference at the Imperial War Museum, London,

11–13 January 2006 (unpublished), 15–16; Mark Aarons, *Sanctuary: Nazi Fugitives in Australia* (Melbourne: William Heinemann Australia, 1989), 98; Phillip Knightley, *Australia: A Biography of a Nation* (London: Vintage, 2001), 219; 'Hitler statue taken from migrant', *News* (Adelaide), 17 January 1951.
16   Aarons, *Sanctuary*, 96.
17   Rutland, 'Sanctuary for Whom?', 26.
18   Aarons, *Sanctuary*, 129, 139; Rutland, 'Sanctuary for Whom?', 17; Kovacs, 'Immigration and Assimilation', 289.
19   John Radzilowski, 'Introduction: Ethnic Anti-Communism in the United States', in Ieva Zake (ed.), *Anti-Communist Minorities in the US: Political Activism of Ethnic Refugees* (Palgrave Macmillan US, 2009), 18.
20   Cigler, *The Czechs in Australia*, 87; Protopopov, 'A History of the Russian Orthodox Presence in Australia', 118; Gilson & Zubrzycki, *The Foreign-Language Press in Australia*, 30; John Radzilowski, 'Introduction', 18; Antin Danyliuk, *My Recollections: A Journey from the Village of Shprakhy to Australia* (Melbourne: Bayda Books, 1995), 9; Richards, 'Displaced Politics', 8–9.
21   Val Colic-Peisker, *Split Lives: Croatian Australian Stories* (Fremantle: Fremantle Arts Centre Press, 2004), 62; Aarons, *Sanctuary*, 138.
22   Mark Wyman, *DPs: Europe's Displaced Persons, 1945–1951* (New York: Cornell University Press, 1998), 157; John Hughes, *The Idea of Home: Autobiographical Essays* (Sydney: Giramondo Publishing Company, 2004), 24; Mark Wyman, 'On the Trail of Displaced Persons', *Spectrum*, 6 (1994), 20; Jiri Kolaja, 'A Sociological Note on the Czechoslovak Anti-Communist Refugee', *American Journal of Sociology*, 58:3 (November 1952), 291.
23   Bohdan Mykytiuk interviewed by Rob Willis, 21 October 2004; Danielle Drozdzewski, 'A Place called "Bielany": Negotiating a Diasporic Polish Place in Sydney', *Social & Cultural Geography*, 8:6 (2007), 861; Suzanna Prushynsky interviewed by Rob Willis and Graham Seal, 26 October 2004, Rob Willis Folklore Collection, Oral TRC 5373/33–34, NLA; Gilson & Zubrzycki, *The Foreign-Language Press in Australia*, 116.
24   Andra Kins, 'Gunta Parups: A Latvian in Australia', *Artlink*, 11:1–2 (Autumn-Winter 1991), 90; Andra Kins, *Coming and Going: A Family Quest* (Fremantle: Fremantle Arts Centre Press, 2004), 151, 96, 106, 92, 120.
25   Jan Lencznarowicz, 'Polish Displaced Persons in Australia After World War II', in Olavi Koivunkangas & Charles Westin (eds), *Scandinavian and European Migration to Australia and New Zealand: Proceedings of the conference held in Stockholm, Sweden, and Turku, Finland, June 9–11, 1998* by Migration Studies C 13, CEIFO Publications, 81, (Turku, Finland: Institute of Migration, 1999), 216.
26   Marko Pavlyshyn, 'Culture and the émigré Consciousness', 57–58.
27   Radzilowski, 'Introduction', 3; Anna Mazurkiewicz, '"The Voice of the Silenced Peoples": The Assembly of Captive European Nations', in Zake (ed.), *Anti-Communist Minorities in the U.S.*, 168.

28 Martin Nekola, 'For the Freedom of Captive European Nations: East-European Exiles in the Cold War', *Historical Research*, 87:238 (November 2014), 724; Mazurkiewicz, 'The Voice of the Silenced Peoples', 169, 171–172; John Foster Leich, 'Great Expectations: The National Councils in Exile, 1950–60', *Polish Review*, 35:3/4 (1990), 185; Martin, *Community and Identity*, 70; Anna Holian, 'Anticommunism in the Streets: Refugee Politics in Cold War Germany', *Journal of Contemporary History*, 45 (2010), 149; Richards, 'Displaced Politics', 13; Paul Babie, 'Ukrainian Catholics in Australia: Past, Present and Future', *Journal of the Australian Catholic Historical Society*, 28 (2007), 41.
29 Aarons, *Sanctuary*, 82, 57.
30 Martin, *Community and Identity*, 14; Sheila Fitzpatrick, 'The Other Face of Repatriation: Persuading displaced persons (DPs) to return after the Second World War', (unpublished manuscript, 2015), 12.
31 Fitzpatrick, 'The Other Face of Repatriation', 17, 21.
32 'Migrants Still Fight Russia', *Sun-Herald*, 2 May 1954; Anatole Konovets, 'The role and function of conflicts in the life of the Russian community in Sydney', Diploma of Sociology thesis, UNSW, (1968), 37.
33 Dr George Klim interviewed by Barry York, 1996.
34 Kovacs, 'Immigration and Assimilation', 290; 'Hermit Leaves Cave After Wife's Death', *Canberra Times*, 13 February 1979; Balint, 'To Reunite the Dispersed Family', 136–137.
35 Kovacs, 'Immigration and Assimilation', 400; 'Migrants Still Fight Russia', *Sun-Herald*, 2 May 1954; 'Migrants Remember Reds' Victims', *Canberra Times*, 21 June 1954.
36 'New Australians Celebrate Decision', *Age*, 21 April 1954.
37 'Suspected Informer Condemned by Other Latvians', *Examiner* (Launceston, Tas.), 21 October 1954; Protopopov, 'A History of the Russian Orthodox Presence in Australia', 164.
38 'Labor to Enrol New Australians', *Age*, 8 April 1950; *Clay Products Journal of Australia*, August 1948; Letter from Regional Director (Victoria), Builders Labourers Federation, 7 December 1949, Displaced Persons – industrial relations – building trades – Plumbers Union, Builders Labourers' Federation, Building Trades Federation, Building Workers Industrial Union, MP17221/1, 1949/23/2621, NAA.
39 Josef Sestokas, *Welcome to Little Europe: Displaced Persons and the North Camp* (Sale: Little Chicken Publishing, 2010), 113–114.
40 Sestokas, *Little Europe*, 168–169; 'False Reports of Nazis Here', *Sunday Telegraph*, 1 April 1951; Paul Kraus, *The Not So Fabulous Fifties: Images of a Migrant Childhood* (Sydney: Kangaroo Press Ltd, 1985), 54.
41 Richards, 'Displaced Politics', 4; Drew Cottle & Angela Keys, 'Douglas Evelyn Darby, MP: Anti-Communist Internationalist in the Antipodes', *Labour History*, 89 (2005), 96.
42 Cottle & Keys, 'Douglas Evelyn Darby, MP', 91–92; Lachlan Clohesy, 'Anti-Communism Undermined: The Uncomfortable Alliances of WC Wentworth', in Melanie Noland (ed.), *Labour History and Its People: The 12th Biennial National Labour History Conference* (Canberra: Australian

Society for the Study of Labour History, 2011), 328, 330; Doris LeRoy, 'Worker for Peace from behind the Iron Curtain', <labourhistorymelbourne. org/worker-for-peace-from-behind-the-iron-curtain>; Aarons, *Sanctuary*, 80.
43 Gilson & Zubrzycki, *The Foreign-Language Press in Australia*, 89.
44 Richards, 'Displaced Politics', 7–8, 11–15; I McAllister, 'Political Attitudes and Electoral Behaviour', in James Jupp (ed.), *The Australian People: An Encylopedia of the Nation, Its People and Their Origins* (Sydney: Angus & Robertson, 1988), 920.
45 Gilson & Zubrzycki, *The Foreign-Language Press in Australia*, 90–92; 'Warns on New Citizens Council', *Canberra Times*, 12 February 1960; 'New Australians Refused Renewal of ALP Tickets', *Canberra Times*, 23 January 1960.
46 Martin, 'Forms of Recognition', 190, 192.
47 Jan Pakulski, 'Polish Migrants in Hobart: A Study of Community Formation', in Roland Sussex and Jerzy Zubrzycki (eds), *Polish People and Culture in Australia* (Canberra: Department of Demography, Institute of Advanced Studies, ANU, 1985), 91.
48 Stephen Holt, 'Nothing if not a Survivor: Vladimir Lezak Borin', *NLA News*, XI:10 (2001); Vladimir Borin-Lezar [sic]: Czech, 1940–1941, Security Service KV 2/2482, NA (UK).
49 Vladimir Borin-Lezar, Security Service KV 2/2482, NA (UK).
50 Vladimir Borin-Lezar, Security Service KV 2/2483, NA (UK).
51 Graham Macklin, *Very Deeply Dyed in Black: Sir Oswald Mosley and the Resurrection of British Fascism after 1945* (London: IB Tauris, 2007), 177; Vladimir Borin-Lezar, Security Service KV 2/2486 & KV 2/2484, NA (UK).
52 Memorandum of Andre D Koson, 66th CIC Detachment, Region V, Regensburg, 6 January 1950, <www.cia.gov/library/readingroom/docs/PRCHALA,%20LEV_0051.pdf>.
53 Rod Shearing, 'A Czech in the Woods' (2012), <rodshearing.wordpress.com/a-czech-in-the-woods/>.
54 Gilson & Zubryzcki, *The Foreign-Language Press in Australia*; Richards, 'Displaced Politics', 8–11.
55 Doris LeRoy, 'Worker for Peace from behind the Iron Curtain', in Phillip Deery & Julie Kimber (eds), *Proceedings of the 14th Biennial Labour History Conference* (Melbourne: Australian Society for the Study of Labour History, 2015), 72–73.
56 Telegram to Lewis, Canberra from Devlin, Melbourne, 21 November 1956, Debor, Ian [formerly Lezak, Vladimir], also known as Borin, 1957/10070, Department of Immigration, Queensland Branch, J25, NAA.
57 Shearing, 'A Czech in the Woods'; Miscellaneous Correspondence [Personal Papers of Prime Minister Holt], 47, Correspondence Files, The Rt Hon. Harold Edward HOLT CH, PC, M2606, NAA.
58 VL Borin, *The Uprooted Survive: A Tale of Two Continents* (London: Heinemann, 1959).
59 'World Citizen', *Times* (Canberra), 8 June 1962; Shearing, 'A Czech in the Woods'; 'Vladimir Ležák-Borin', *Music Open*, <www.musicopen.cz/index.php/osobnosti/3608-kdyz-se-slim-howard-stane-evergreenem>.

60 'World Citizen', *Times* (Canberra), 8 June 1962.
61 Martin, *Community and Identity*, 33, 46; Konovets, 'The Role and Function of Conflicts in the Life of the Russian Community in Sydney', 112.

Conclusion: Memory and multiculturalism

1   Bruce Pennay, 'Block 19 Bonegilla Visitor Book Entries', (unpublished).
2   Bruce Pennay, *The Young at Bonegilla: Receiving Young Immigrants at Bonegilla Reception and Training Centre, 1947–71* (Wodonga: Parklands Albury–Wodonga, 2010), 22.
3   James Jupp, *Immigration* (Melbourne: Oxford University Press, 1998), 107.
4   Sara Wills, 'Losing the Right to Country: The Memory of Loss and the Loss of Memory in Claiming the Nation as Space (Or being Cruel to be Kind in the Multicultural Asylum)', *New Formations*, 51 (2004), 52; Jupp, *Immigration*, 109.
5   Jean Martin, *Community and Identity: Refugee Groups in Adelaide* (Canberra: ANU Press, 1972), 76–77; ML Kovacs & AJ Cropley, *Immigrants and Society: Alienation and Assimilation* (Sydney: McGraw-Hill Book Company, 1975), preface; Peter Beilharz, 'Miss Craig Goes to Chicago (Jean Martin finds Australian sociology)', *TASA Conference Proceedings* (Canberra: ANU, 2009), 3.
6   Jock Collins, *Migrant Hands in a Distant Land: Australia's Postwar Immigration* (Sydney: Pluto Press Australia, 1988), 231; Martin, *Community and Identity*, 128; J Zubrzycki, 'Multicultural Australia', in James Jupp (ed.), *The Australian People: An Encylopedia of the Nation, Its People and Their Origins* (Sydney: Angus & Robertson, 1988), 129; Sheila Shaver, 'A Public Sociology for the Mainstream: Jean Martin's sociology for nation-building', *TASA Conference Proceedings*, 2009, 7.
7   J Zubrzycki, 'Multicultural Australia', 129; Mark Lopez, *The Origins of Multiculturalism in Australian Politics 1945–1975* (Melbourne: Melbourne University Press, 2000), 55; Shaver, 'A Public Sociology for the Mainstream', 7, 9.
8   NLA, Oral TRC 2569, interview with Professor Jerzy Zubrzycki (1920–2009) interviewed by Peter Biskup, 1990; Janis Wilton & Richard Bosworth, *Old Worlds and New Australia: The Postwar Migrant Experience* (Melbourne: Penguin, 1984), 21; Ann-Mari Jordens, *Alien to Citizen: Settling Migrants in Australia, 1945–75* (Sydney: Allen & Unwin, 1997), 22, 23; Lopez, *The Origins of Multiculturalism*, 55, 98.
9   Davide Però & John Solomos, 'Introduction: Migrant Politics and Mobilisation: Exclusion, Engagements, Incorporation', *Ethnic and Racial Studies*, 33:1 (2010), 4.
10 Brian Murphy, *The Other Australia: Experiences of Migration* (Cambridge & Melbourne: Cambridge University Press, 1993), 198; Zubrzycki, 'Multicultural Australia', 130.
11 Murphy, *The Other Australia*, 198; Wills, 'Losing the Right to Country', 61.
12 Stepan Kerkyasharian, 'Death of a Multicultural Giant', Community

Relations Commission, (unpublished); Murphy, *The Other Australia*, 228; Jupp, *Immigration*, 140; Bill Jegorow, 'The Rock on Which We Stand', *Infocus* (Ethnic Communities' Council of NSW), 18:4 (1995), 10, <www.multiculturalaustralia.edu.au/doc/jegorow_1.pdf>.

13 Annette Robyn Corkhill, *The Immigrant Experience in Australian Literature* (Melbourne: Academia Press, 1985), 11.

14 Loló Houbein, *Ethnic Writings in English from Australia: A Bibliography* (Adelaide: Australian Literary Studies, Department of English Language and Literature, University of Adelaide, 1984); Alexandra Karakostas-Sêdá, *Creative Writing in Languages other than English in Australia, 1945–1987* (Melbourne: Monash University Library, 1988); Corkhill, *The Immigrant Experience*, 11.

15 Sneja Gunew, Loló Houbein, Alexandra Karakostas-Sêdá & Jan Mahyuddin (eds), *A Bibliography of Australian Multicultural Writers* (Geelong, Vic: Centre for Studies in Literary Education, Humanities, Deakin University, 1992), 147; Peter Skrzynecki, <www.peterskrzynecki.com/HSC.htm>; Raimond Gaita, *Romulus: My Father* (Melbourne: Text Publishing, 1998); Janis Balodis, *The Ghosts Trilogy* (Sydney: Currency Press, 1997); John Hughes, *The Idea of Home: Autobiographical Essays* (Sydney: Giramondo Publishing Company, 2004); Sophia Turkiewicz (Director), *Silver City* (Limelight Productions: 1984); Sophia Turkiewicz (Director), *Once My Mother* (Screen Australia and Change Focus Media: 2014); Peter Skrzynecki, 'Translated into Polish', *Old/New World* (Brisbane: UQP, 2007), 292–293; Victoria Zabukovec, *The Second Landing* (Kangaroo Island: Penneshaw, 1993).

16 Barry York, 'Migrant Tales', *NLA News* (May 2007), <www.nla.gov.au/pub/nlanews/2007/may07/story-4.pdf>), 16, 18; Les Murray, 'Immigrant Voyage', <www.poetrylibrary.edu.au/poets/murray-les/immigrant-voyage-0617020>; Richard Flanagan, *The Sound of One Hand Clapping* (Sydney: Vintage Books, 1997); Murray Waldren, 'Many Hands Clapping', *Weekend Australian*, 1997; Julie Johnston, *Displaced* (2016), (unpublished).

17 Sonia Mycak, 'The Role of Networks in Australian Multicultural Literature: Postwar "New Australians" as an Empirical Case Study', *Sun Yat-sen Journal of Humanities*, 17 (Winter 2003), 27; Amy Witting, 'Foreword', in Elena Jonaitis, *Elena's Journey* (Melbourne: Text Publishing, 1997), vii.

18 Sneja Gunew, 'Multicultural Writers', in Jacques Delaruelle, Alexandara Karakostas-Sêdá & Anna Ward (eds), *Writing in Multicultural Australia 1984: An Overview*, Papers presented at the Multicultural Writers' Weekends in Sydney, 13–14 October 1984 and in Melbourne, 27–28 October 1984 (Sydney: Australia Council for the Literature Board, 1985), 18; Ludmilla Forsyth, 'On the Slippery Margins', in Robert Pascoe (ed.), *Alienation and Exile: Writings of Migration* (Melbourne: Footprint Australian Writers, The Footscray Foundation for Australian Studies, 1990), 4; Klaus Neumann, 'Swinburne University historian on migrants' writings: Memoirs tell a new story', *Sydney Morning Herald*, 10 May 2016; Brigitta Olubas, 'The Nostalgia of Others: The Construction of the White

Migrant', in Peter Drexler & Andrea Kinsky-Ehritt (eds), *Identities and Minorities: Postcolonial Readings* (Berlin: Trafo, 2003), 150, 155.

19 Australian National Maritime Museum, 'Displaced Persons' and 'Refugee Week 2006', (unpublished); Anton Veenstra, 'The Imagined Homeland: The Slovene-Australian Diaspora, A Narrative in Woven Tapestry' (Sydney: Anton Veenstra, 2003); Nina Keri, 'Displaced', <tasmanianartsguide.com.au/whats-on/exhibitions/displaced>.

20 Glenda Sluga, 'The Migrant Dreaming', *Journal of Intercultural Studies*, 8:2 (1987), 42; Bruce Pennay, *So Much Sky: Bonegilla Reception and Training Centre, 1947–1971* (Migration Heritage Centre, 2008).

21 Glenda Sluga, *Bonegilla: A Place of No Hope* (Melbourne: University of Melbourne, 1988), 133; Glenda Sluga, 'Bonegilla and Migrant Dreaming' in Kate Darian-Smith & Paula Hamilton (eds), *Memory and History in Twentieth-Century Australia* (Oxford: Oxford University Press, 1994), 207; Wanda Skowronska, 'Journey to Bonegilla: A child of refugees looks back on a journey that ended happily', *Annals Australasia* (August 2004), 14.

22 Papers of Michael Cigler, MS 8235, NLA; Catherine Panich, *Sanctuary?: Remembering Postwar Immigration* (Sydney: Allen & Unwin Australia Pty Ltd, 1988), 188–189.

23 Bruce Pennay, *The Army at Bonegilla: 1940–71* (Wodonga, Vic: Parklands Albury–Wodonga, 2007), 19; Bruce Pennay, 'Remembering Bonegilla: The Construction of a Public Memory Place at Block 19', *Public History Review*, 16 (2009), 43; 'Bordertown', Knapman Wyld Television (1995); ABCTV Publicity, 'Bordertown', <www.multiculturalaustralia.edu.au/doc/abctv_1.pdf>.

24 Heritage Victoria, 'Block 19 Bonegilla', *Inherit* 14 (July 2002), 10; Department of the Environment, Water, Heritage and the Arts, Australian Heritage Database, 'Bonegilla Migrant Camp – Block 19', <www.environment.gov.au/heritage/places/national/bonegilla/index.html>; NSW Migration Heritage Centre Newsflash Email (20 October 2010).

25 Pennay, 'Framing Bonegilla for the Tourist Gaze', 3; Sluga, 'Bonegilla and Migrant Dreaming', 207.

26 Jayne Persian, 'Bonegilla: A Failed Narrative', *History Australia*, 9:1 (April 2012), 64–83; Jayne Persian, 'Displaced Persons (1947–1952) in Australia: Memory in Autobiography', in Paul Arthur (ed.), *Australian Identity and Culture: Transnational Perspectives in Life Writing* (Anthem Press: London, 2017); Paul Ashton, 'The Birthplace of Australian Multiculturalism? Retrospective Commemoration, Participatory Memorialisation and Official Heritage', *International Journal of Heritage Studies*, 15:5 (2009), 391; Bruce Pennay, 'Framing Bonegilla for the Tourist Gaze', *Albury & District Historical Bulletin* (October 2004), 3; Bruce Pennay, 'Remembering Benalla Migrant Camp', *The History of the Family* (pending).

27 Sluga, 'The Migrant Dreaming', 40, 41.

28 Ronald Taft, *From Stranger to Citizen: A Survey of Studies of Immigrant Assimilation in Western Australia* (Perth: University of Western Australia Press, 1965), 36, 52, 61; Mark Wyman, *DPs: Europe's Displaced Persons,*

1945–1951 (New York: Cornell University Press, 1998),9–11; Malgorzata Klatt, *The Poles & Australia* (Melbourne: Australian Scholarly Publishing, 2014), 42–43.

29   Karen Schamberger, 'Weaving a Family and a Nation Through Two Latvian Looms', Conference Paper, Global Histories of Refugees in the 20th and 21st Centuries, University of Melbourne, 6–8 October 2016.

30   *West Australian*, 11 August 1949, cited in Joy Damousi, *Memory and Migration in the Shadow of War: Australia's Greek Immigrants after World War II and the Greek Civil War* (Cambridge: Cambridge University Press, 2015), 62; 'Former Quonset Huts', Victorian Heritage Database Report; <vhd.heritagecouncil.vic.gov.au/places/64260/download-report>; Hostel Stories: Finsbury/Pennington, Migration Museum SA, <migration.history.sa.gov.au/content/finsbury-pennington>; Peter Gatrell, 'Population Displacement in the Baltic Region in the Twentieth Century: From "Refugee Studies" to Refugee History', *Journal of Baltic Studies*, 38:1 (2007), 45.

Acknowledgments

This book was written some years after the end of my PhD thesis on which it is based. My thanks must go to those who supported me not only during the writing of the thesis, but as I sometimes floundered in postdoctoral uncertainty.

Unconditional support from loved ones is much appreciated. My thanks in this regard to Libby and Wally Persian, Ann Whiteside, Kylie Freeman, and, above all, my wonderful husband, Chris Persian. And to my own little DP descendants: Anna, Sascha and Luka.

The idea of writing this book was given a firm prod when Sheila Fitzpatrick generously offered me a postdoctoral position to examine Soviet-origin DPs. Her encouragement has been vital. My thanks also to Ruth Balint, for everything.

My sincere thanks to Phillipa McGuinness at NewSouth Publishing, and freelance copyeditor Victoria Chance; the School of Arts and Communication at the University of Southern Queensland; my doctoral supervisor, Glenda Sluga, and SOPHI at the University of Sydney; the Australian Historical Association for mentoring assistance in the form of an AHA–Copyright Agency Limited (CAL)

Postgraduate Travel and Writing Bursary; Australian Policy and History for a CAL Cultural Fund Early Career Grant; the Museum of Australian Democracy for a Fellowship on Calwell; members of the Illawarra Migration Heritage Project; and staff at Bonegilla Block 19, Fisher Library at the University of Sydney, the International Tracing Service (Bad Arolsen), the Migration Museum of South Australia, the National Archives (UK), the National Australian Archives, the National Library of Australia, the Noel Butlin Archives at the Australian National University, the State Library of New South Wales, and the State Library of South Australia. I also thank *History Australia* and the *Australian Journal of Politics and History* for permission to use parts of articles already published.

Grateful thanks for various kindnesses to Karen Agutter, Michelle Arrow, Martin Braach-Maksvytis, Georgine Clarsen, Sharon Crozier-De Rosa, Mark Edele, Hannah Forsyth, the late John Hirst, Carolyn Holbrook, Marilyn Lake, Kelly Lawler, Humphrey McQueen, Andrew Markus, Kate Matthew, Glenn Mitchell, Bruce Pennay, Nick and Teressa Persian, Suzanne Rutland and John Shoebridge. Also to those who commented on draft chapters: Jess Carniel, Robert Carr, Martin Crotty, Alexandra Dellios, Rebecca Fleming, Justine Greenwood, Naomi Parry, Evan Smith and Richard White.

Thank you also (and especially) to those who agreed to be interviewed for this project.

Index

A
ACTU (Australian Council of Trade Unions) 53, 78, 172
Adam (pseudonym) 10, 86, 135
Adamkus, Valdas 199
Adelaide 155
Adult Migrant Education Scheme 130
age criteria for selecting DPs 64, 70
Albania 161–162
Albury–Wodonga Region Parklands 196
alcoholism 134–137, 144
Alexander, Field Marshal Harold 2
American Relief Administration 18
Ana Salen (ship) 7
Andriy (pseudonym) 10, 73, 91, 150
Anita (pseudonym) 199
Anna's loom 199
Anti-Bolshevik Bloc of Nations 32, 66, 162, 169
anti-communism 41, 66–75, 131, 146, 148, 157, 159–167, 168–169, 170 *see also* Cold War
anti-Semitism 156–157 *see also* Jewish DPs
Anug (pseudonym) 154
Argentina 6, 43
Arndt, Ruth 125
Arved (pseudonym) 11, 14
Asian refugees 53
ASIO 157, 169, 178
Assembly of Captive European Nations 162
assimilation 62–65, 110–111, 112, 119–120, 121, 122, 126, 138, 142, 144, 145–146
Australia *see also* immigration policies
   Australians as British subjects 121
   cost of resettling DPs 56, 90
   deportation of DPs 108–110
   secrecy over DPs 54–55
   selection rights over DPs 56–57
Australia Unlimited (slogan) 116
Australian Broadcasting Commission 123, 193, 195
Australian Citizenship Act 1948 121
Australian Council of Trade Unions 53, 78, 172
Australian Heritage Database 195–196
Australian Labor Party 53, 171–172
   1950s split 169, 170–171
Australian League of Rights 148, 178
Australian Medical Association 97
Australian Military Ministry in Germany 54, 60, 62, 65, 68
Australian National University 186
Australian Railways Union 139
Australian way of life (phrase) 113, 122
Australian Women's Weekly, The 118
Australijos Lietuvis 151–152
Austria 15–16, 36, 47, 65, 183

B
Bakaitis, Eugenia 82
Balodis, Janis 189, 191
Balt Cygnets 43
Baltic Council of Australia 161
Baltic DPs 45
   Balts as derogatory term 119
   as 'Beautiful Balts' 45–46
   countries of origin 58 *see also* Estonian DPs; Latvian DPs; Lithuanian DPs
   disparagement of 11
   as preferred migrants 61, 62–64, 74
Bana, Eric 189
Barsdell, Len 60
Bathurst (NSW) camp 78
Beazley, Kim 91

241

Becsulettel 158
Belarusian DPs 27, 39
Belgium 35, 43
Benalla (Vic) camp 89
Benes, Edvard 173–176
Berger, Moses 157
Berger, Sandor 141
BHP 85, 93, 94
Bialogusky, Michael 164
Bicentennial (1988) 194
Bielski, George 133
Bielski, Jerzy 165–166, 171–172
Bildusas, Statys 135
Birman, J 94
Blagi, Jewsygnij 109
Blue Hills (radio program) 117
Bohdan (pseudonym) 10, 48, 93, 198
Bonegilla
   DPs experiences of 77–82, 85–86, 113, 156
   national commemoration of 193–198
Bonegilla Immigration Museum Committee 194–195
border-hoppers 6, 36, 38
Borrie, WD 52, 186
Boudreau, Frank 18–19
boy scouts 159
Britain
   Allied occupation zones 17–18, 46
   British fascists 175
   British migrants 52–53, 119
   Cossacks and 2–4
   DPs as labour in 43, 45, 68–69
   IRO 39
   multicultural policy 187
   Yalta Agreement 3, 5, 22, 25
British Medical Association 97
Bulgaria 31, 161–162
Burlin, Lieutenant-General 8
business interests *see* private sector
Byelorussia 162

C
Calwell, Arthur 145, 150, 168, 200
   assimilation 112
   deportation of DPs 108, 109
   indentured labour program 91, 103, 104–105, 127, 129
   IRO agreement 76–78
   as Minister for Immigration 6
   as Minister for Information 113

New Australians, coins term 50, 118–119
populate or perish 51–58
professional lockout of DPs 99
Sapalis 100
security checks 67–69
selection of DPs 61–64
warns about impersonation methods 72
camps in Australia 77–89
   average length of stay 88–89
   camp commanders 80–81
   camp names, major and other 78–79
   DP employees of camp system 82
   family separation 83–87
   labour contract *see* indentured labour program
   reception 81
   unrest in 89
camps in Europe
   Australia recruits migrants from 59, 63–65
   as cauldrons 36–37
   Cossack's camp in Drau Valley 1–5, 13–14
   DP elites in 33–34
   DPs outside camp system 34
   handicapped DPs 47
   nationality-specific 31–32, 148–149, 151
   organisation 30–31
   UNRRA establishes 19
Canada
   DPs as labour in 43, 44
   DPs resettle in 6, 12, 110–111
   multicultural policy 187
   Nazi collaborators 37–38
Canberra 124–125
Catholic Social Studies Movement (the Movement) 170–171, 177
Central and Eastern European DPs 5–6, 12, 27–28, 61, 76
Central Intelligence Agency 161, 176
CES *see* Commonwealth Employment Service
Chifley, Ben 54, 55–56, 58, 62, 69, 73, 112
childbirth 85
children 73–74, 85, 87–88
Chile 183
China 18
Cigler, Michael 84
citizenship 121, 126, 139, 178
Citizenship Conventions 119, 123, 125–126
Clune, Frank 50–51, 61, 74–75

Index

Cold War 29, 37, 38, 41–42, 48 *see also* anti-communism
Commonwealth Employment Service 82–83, 92, 96, 109–110
Commonwealth Immigration Advisory Council 53–55, 79–80, 116, 168
Commonwealth Jubilee Year 115
Communist Party of Australia 168
Community and Identity: Refugee Groups in Adelaide (Martin) 155
Coober Pedy 136
Cooper, Kanty 44
Cossacks
 anti-communism 27
 camp in Drau Valley, Austria 1–5, 13–14
 Cossack Army 29, 69–70
 Cossack associations in Australia 8, 158
 Ivan and Nastasia's story *see* Ivan and Nastasia
 as *Kazachi Stan* 2
 surrender to British 2–4
Country Women's Association 123–124
Cowra (NSW) camp 89
Croatia 66, 158, 163, 199
Czechoslovakia 36, 161–162, 173–176, 183
Czechoslovakian DPs 6, 35, 64, 74, 176
 Czech Club (Melbourne) 153
 Czech factions 157–158

D

Dapin, Mark 136
Darby, Douglas Evelyn 169
Demchenko, Lydia 128–129
Democratic Labor Party 148, 169, 170–171, 177
Denmark 35
Department of External Affairs 98
Department of Immigration 6, 9, 117
 establishment 52
 family separation 87
 interpreters to 67
 language classes 130–131
 multiculturalism 186
 New Australians (term) 119
 organises camps in Australia 78
 promotes Australia to DPs 50–51, 59, 60
 recruits migrants from European camps 59, 63–65
 responsibility for work contracts 92, 96–97, 108
 selection variation 66
 supervision of foreign language press 121–122
 warned of impersonation methods 72–73
Department of Information 59, 60, 113, 115–116, 117
Department of Labour and National Service 92, 94, 96
Dezséry, András 93–94, 188
diasporas *see* nationalist diasporas
dictation test 108
Diner, Dan 33
Displaced Persons Act (US, 1948) 43–44
District Employment Officers 103–104
DLP *see* Democratic Labor Party
Downer, Alexander 178–179
DPs (displaced persons)
 as asylum seekers 42
 in Australia *see* DPs (displaced persons) in Australia
 border-hoppers 6, 36, 38
 category broadened 39
 definition intra-war 15–16
 difficulties of identification and classification 23
 employment by Allies 21
 as European Voluntary Workers 43
 as labour supply 42–49
 national breakdown 15–16
 national hierarchy 61
 negativity towards 17
 numbers 16, 42
 as people outside their national boundaries 15
 reasons for displacement 5–6
 reasons for inclusion as 15
 refugees vs. 15
 repatriation *see* repatriation of nationals
 resettlement *see* resettlement of nationals
 as 'surrendered personnel' 5
 term 5, 14, 15
 variation in experiences 16–17
DPs (displaced persons) in Australia
 animosity between 155
 becoming New Australians 112–127
 camp life *see* camps in Australia
 challenges and traumas 132–137
 citizenship 119
 complexity of stories 11–12, 14, 201
 diasporas *see* nationalist diasporas
 as labour supply *see* indentured labour program

medical examination 72–73
names for 119, 139–140
national breakdown 10–11, 56–57, 64–65, 74, 149 *see also* Baltic DPs
numbers 49, 59, 74, 76
post-contract life 127–132
processing 7–8, 74
psychological problems of 134–137, 142–146
reasons for settling 48
recruitment and selection 59–66
relationships with Australians 137–142
reports of Australia unfavourable 110–111
term officiallly banned 119
Dubcek, Alexander 148, 180
Dukas, Edward 90

E
Eastern European DPs 5–6, 12, 27–28, 61, 76
economic migrants 6, 42, 200
Edgar (pseudonym) 10, 11
Eisenhower, Dwight D 15, 37–38
Ergas, Dr 64
Estonian DPs 22, 25, 27, 162, 199 *see also* Baltic DPs
Ethnic Communities' Council of NSW 187
European Voluntary Workers 43
Evatt, Dr HV 54, 170
Evian Conference on Jewish refugees (1938) 18, 53
Executive Council of Australian Jewry 62, 69

F
false identity papers 6, 9, 23–25, 67
family groups 73
family reunion 73
family separation 70, 83–87
family tracing 132–133
fascism 17, 66, 156–157, 162–163, 167–168, 169, 175
Federated Ironworkers' Association of Australia 167–168, 172
films about DPs 115–116, 189, 195
Flanagan, Richard 190–191
foreign accents 122
foreign language press 121–122, 151–152, 158
France 17–18, 35, 39, 46
Franco 68

Frank (pseudonym) 10, 14, 106
Fridenbergs, Andrei 166
Full Employment in Australia (1945 White Paper) 52
Futcher, Michael 191

G
Gaita, Raimond 189
Galleghan, Brigadier FG 65, 70
gender criteria for selecting DPs 70
General Black (ship) 64
General Heintzelman (ship) 67, 72
German DPs 16, 39
    Australia selects 65
    Nazis as *see* Nazi collaborators; war criminals
German language as *lingua franca* 130
Germany
    Allied occupation zones 17–18
    DPs in 15–16, 17, 47
    invasion of Soviet Union 1–2
Gillard, Valentina 194
global exile groups 161
Good Neighbour Councils 124–126
Good Neighbour Movement 123–126, 137
Good Neighbour (newsletter) 123
Gordeev, Anatoly 163
Gorton, John 169
Gotowicz, Stanislav 71
Goulburn 129, 137
Grassby, Al 186–187
Great Depression (1930s) 76
Greece 10, 35, 183
Greta (NSW) camp 78
Grew, JC 161–162
Grigory (pseudonym) 165
Guide International Service 114
Gustav & Adele (pseudonyms) 11

H
Halas, Martin 165
Halina (pseudonym) 150, 155
handicapped DPs 47
Harkoff, Nikolai 166
Haylen, Les 53, 79–80
Heydon, Peter 186
Heyes, THE 65
Hitler, Adolf 65
Hodza, Milan 174
Holt, Harold 88, 98–99, 121, 134, 141–142, 168, 178–179

Index

Horner, Joyce 21
How Do You Like Australia? (Saks & Mirosznyk) 141
Howard, Helen 191
Hrelica, Rudolf 109–110
Hromadka, Dr Josef 177–178
Hungarian border-hoppers 36
Hungarian DPs 6, 25, 28, 48, 74, 158
Hungarian Jews 36
Hungary 69, 161–162, 183

I

immigration policies *see also* White Australia Policy
   assimilation 62–65, 110–111
   asylum seekers and refugees 42, 53, 200–202
   boat people (term) 200
   migrant return 186, 199
   migration agreements 183
   migration programs of 1950s and 1960s 183
   non-British mass migration 9–10, 51–58, 183
   offshore detention 202
   queue-jumpers (term) 200
   reasons for resettling DPs 6, 51, 52, 57–58
Immigration Restriction Act (1901) 108
indentured labour program 59
   as donkey work 93–96
   DP characterisation of 104
   DPs defy contract 105–111
   as dual labour market 129
   early release 127
   inflexibility of 103–105
   models for 76–77
   period 89–90
   policing 107–110
   professional lockout 96–105
   public opinion in Australia 114–115
   as punishment 105
   types of labour 74–75
   work camps 94–96
   work contract 91–93
industrial accidents 94
industrialisation 52, 116
industry sectors 92–93, 95
Institution of Engineers 98
integration 120, 145, 184–185
Intergovernmental Committee on Refugees 18, 42, 54

International Refugee Organization
   Australia as signatory 53, 54
   Australian agreement on DPs with 56–57, 62, 73, 76–77, 112
   cost of resettling DPs 43, 56, 90
   deportation of DPs 108, 110
   DPs and 5, 9
   DPs as asylum seekers 42
   DPs as labour 46
   draft constitution 40
   establishment 54
   false identity papers 24
   formed to replace UNRRA 39
   Medical Boards 97
   process of emigration 47
   Professional Medical Register 96
   review of UNRRA cases 40
   screening process 68
   success of scheme 47–48
   task of resettlement 42–43
   UNRRA and 6
IRO *see* International Refugee Organization
Iron Curtain nations 161–162
Israel 33, 43
Italy 10, 18, 77, 183
Ivan and Nastasia (pseudonyms)
   in Australia 7–8, 9–11, 28, 30
   in Cossack camp in Drau Valley 4–5, 13–14
   false identity papers 6
   family in Soviet Union 28
   family separation in Australia 83–84
   Ivan's alcoholism 135
   screening process 69–70
   Soviet repatriation attempts 30
Ivanov, Kuzma 110

J

Jakub (pseudonym) 10, 36, 48
Jan (pseudonym) 10, 14, 28, 160
Jewish DPs
   anti-Semitism 156–157
   Australia accepts 53
   Australia rejects 61–62, 65–66, 68
   camps in Europe 37, 47
   classified as refugees 41
   classified as stateless 22
   from Eastern Europe 36
   Israel and 33, 43
   names for 119
   negativity towards 17

rejected as labour 45
Joe (pseudonym) 158
Johnston, Julie 191
Jubilee Train 115
Julija (pseudonym) 10, 20, 32, 128
Jupp, James 186

K
Kalejs, Konrad 156
Kalnenas, Dr Kostas 98
Kalnins, Maria 113
Karl (pseudonym) 10, 94, 132, 135
Kasia (pseudonym) 10, 11, 101
Katherina (pseudonym) 9, 10, 11, 14, 27, 86, 132
Kohut, Zoia 132
Korean War 131
Kormos, V 171
Kozolowski, J 89

L
La Guardia, Fiorello 26
La Perouse 128–129
labour shortages 43, 97
labour supply, DPs as 42–49
labour supply, DPs in Australia *see* indentured labour program
Lachowicz, Andrew 119
land profiteering 128
language, English 130–131, 159
language, German as *lingua franca* 130
language preservation 159
Latvian DPs 162, 199 *see also* Baltic DPs
  Australia selects 62
  experience in Europe 20, 22, 25, 27, 37–38
  Melbourne community 166
  race and class issues 45
  resettlement 49
League of Nations 18–19, 27
Learning to be Australians 119–120
Leo (pseudonym) 10, 14, 66, 128
Ležák Borin, Vladímir 147–148, 173–180
Liberal Party 168–169, 172
Libuinas, Ale 30, 96
Lifanov, Nikolai 163
literature and the arts 141, 152–153, 188–193, 198–199
Lithuanian DPs 111, 162, 199 *see also* Baltic DPs
  camps in Europe 32

experience in Europe 20, 22, 25, 27
race and class issues 45–46
Locher, Dr Jan 176
Loescher, Gil 41
Lukas (pseudonym) 10, 102, 154
Lukic, Milorad 157, 158
Luxembourg 35, 45

M
McCollum, Robert S 38
Magyar Elet 158
Makay, Laszlo 82
Malta 183
Manus Island 202
Maroya, Louis 194–195
marriage 86, 118, 133–134
Marta (pseudonym) 10, 140
Martin, Jean 150–151, 186
Maslyn, Ron 59–60
Massey, JT 124, 126
medical doctors (DPs) 70–71, 96, 97–98, 100–101, 111
Megay, Laszlo 162, 169
mental hospital admissions 134–137
Menzies, Robert 116, 123, 168
Meredith, Gwen 117
MI5 174–175
Michael (pseudonym) 10, 31, 134, 154
Middleton, Dr PC 135
Milanov, Kajica 120
Mirosznyk, Anatolij 30, 72, 141
Monk, Albert 172
Morozow, Arkadi Alexandrovich 166–167
multiculturalism 10, 181, 184–187, 196
Murphy, Hugh 117
Murray, Les A 190–191
Musicians' Union 98–99
Muslim DPs 65

N
Nansen International Office 18, 27
Nastasia *see* Ivan and Nastasia
National Committee for a Free Europe 161
National Cossack Association of Australia 8
National Heritage List 195–196
nationalist diasporas 148–158, 198–199
  national mission of exiles 159–167
  national reconstruction 33–34
  national self-determination 32

Index

naturalisation *see* citizenship
Nazi collaborators 25, 28, 37–38, 66, 68–69, 156
Nazi memorabilia 156
The Netherlands 35, 43, 183, 187
Neumann, Klaus 200
New Australian Council 171, 172
New Australian (newsletter) 122–123
New Australians (term) 11, 50–51, 75, 118–119, 138–139
New Citizens' Council 171–172
New Guinea 91, 97
New Settlers' Association, Tasmania 178
New Settlers' League, Goulburn 129, 137
New Settlers' League, Orange 123
Nina (pseudonym) 10, 73
Noiman, Olga 163
Northam (WA) camp 78
Norway 35, 47

O

Office of the High Commissioner for Refugees Coming from Germany 18
Office of the League of Nations High Commissioner 18
Oksana (pseudonym) 10, 94, 101, 149
Onufriienko, Vasyl 132
The Overlanders (film) 60

P

Pacific Islander refugees 53
Pacific war 51
Parkes (NSW) camp 89
Parups, Andra 159–160
Parups, Gunta 159–160, 199
Patton Jr, General George S 17
Pawlowski, Stanislaw 109
PCIRO (Preparatory Commission of the International Refugee Organization) 56–58
peace movement 177–178
Petrov, Evdokia 166
Petrov, Vladimir 164
Petrov Affair 166
Pietroszys, Stefan and Genovefa 165
Pilecki, Bernard 140
pluralism *see* multiculturalism
Poland
    Anders army 29
    ceded (part) to Soviet Union 25
    DPs return 199
    Iron Curtain 161–162

Poles deported to gulag in Soviet Union 27
Polish ex-servicemen 77
Poznan uprising 171
refugees from 183
Ukraine divided into 24
UNRRA 18
Polish DPs
    Australia selects 62, 74
    experience in Europe 6, 22, 24–25, 28, 31, 39
    Newcastle community 164–165
    Polish associations 160
    race and class issues 45
    resettlement 48, 49
Polish Jews 36
Polish–American Congress 38
political refugees 6, 37, 42, 66–75, 113–114, 167–173
political voting patterns 172–173
populate or perish 52, 113
population of Australia 10, 76
postwar housing crisis 76–77, 78, 88
postwar reconstruction 51–52, 92
Prague Spring 148, 180
pregnancy 96
Preparatory Commission of the International Refugee Organization 56–58
press 56, 64, 103, 106, 117, 125, 136, 138
press, foreign language 121–122, 151–152, 158
Price, Charles 186
private sector 91–93, 95, 97
private sponsorship of DPs 102
professional associations 97, 98–99
professions and DPs
    education levels 71
    labour shortages 97
    lockout 96–105, 129–130
    loss of status 101
    medical doctors *see* medical doctors (DPs)
    as professional assistants 99
    qualifications 70–71, 74–75
propaganda materials 113, 115–118, 122–123
prostitution 86
pseudonyms 11
psychiatry 143
public opinion in Australia 61, 113–115, 122–123
    engagement with DPs 117–118, 137–142

prejudice against DPs 119, 137–138, 139–140
public service 97

R
race and class 10, 45–46, 62–65 *see also* White Australia Policy
Rafferty, Chips 60
Rajkovic, Mihailo 157, 158
Ralf (pseudonym) 10, 27
Rankin Affair 167–168
Red Cross 114
Red Cross Tracing Service 132–133
referendum (1951, on banning CPA) 168
refugees 15, 39–41, 200
refugee crisis 201–202
Register of the National Estate 195
repatriation of nationals
  from Dachau 22–23
  DP refusal to repatriate 21–22, 35–36
  forced 21–25, 30
  Soviet DP resistance 30
  UNRRA and 19, 31–32, 37
  voluntary 25
resettlement of nationals
  IRO task 42–43
  reclassification of DPs 39
  UN responsibility for 39, 40
Robert (pseudonym) 10
Romania 6, 36, 162–163
RSL (Returned and Services League) 56, 123–124
rural employment 94, 127–128
Russian DPs 24–25, 39, 74, 164 *see also* Soviet DPs
  Russian organisations 8, 158, 164
Russian Liberation (Vlasov) army 29

S
Saks, Jimmy 141
Sakurovs, Janis 141
Santamaria, BA 170–171, 177
Sapalis, Apalonia 99–100
Saxon, Sue 192
Scandinavian migrants 53
schizophrenia 143–144
security 67–68, 69
Serbia, Nazi puppet government of 156
Serbian Chetniks 66
sex 83
SHAEF *see* Supreme Headquarters, Allied Expeditionary Force
Skrzynecki, Peter 140
slave market 46
Smythe, Dr JS 71
Snowy (pseudonym) 151
Snowy Mountains Scheme 9, 86–87, 94–95, 133
social and political groups 149–150
social class and status 139, 154 *see also* race and class
social clubs 151
social workers 130
Southeast Asia 179
Soviet DPs 22–33 *see also* anti-communism; Russian DPs
  citizens at 1 September 1939 22
  Cossacks *see* Cossacks
  false identity papers 23–25
  reasons against returning 26–28
  reclassified 39
  resistance to repatriation 30
  UNRRA 38
Soviet Union *see also* anti-communism; Cold War
  Allied occupation zones 17–18
  anti-communism 36
  attempts to repatriate DPs 26, 29–30, 163–164
  Clune and 61
  DPs from *see* Soviet DPs
  DPs return after disbandment 199
  German invasion of 1–2
  IRO 39
  mass deportations 27
  military conflict between West and 48
  military opposition to 29
  occupation of Central and Eastern Europe 6
  peace movement and 177–178
  persecution of DPs 28–29
  Poland (part) ceded to 25
  Red Army in Eastern Europe 27–28
  Soviet agents as DPs 66, 163–164, 165
  Soviet Embassy in Canberra 163–167
  Ukraine divided into 24
  views of DPs as labour 46
  views of DPs in Australia 102–103
  Yalta Agreement 3, 5, 22
Spain 68, 183
Spry, Charles 157
Stalin, Josef 28, 132

Index

State Department (US) 161
State Rivers, Springvale, Victoria 86
stateless DPs 22
Stetsko, Jaroslav 169
Supreme Headquarters, Allied Expeditionary Force 15, 17, 21
Suschinsky, Eugene 108–109
Swan Boys' Home, Perth 87

T

Tanya (pseudonym) 10, 11, 85
Taylor, Ralph 123
Theodore (pseudonym) 9, 11
Todt Organisations 16
Tolstaya, Alexandra 24
Tolstoy, Leo 24
Tolstoy, Nikolai 2
Tolstoy Foundation 24
Torok, Laszlo 142
trade unions 53, 56, 91, 93, 96–97, 113–114, 167, 170–172
Trieste 183
Turkey 43, 183
Turkiewicz, Sophia 189
Turnbull, Malcolm 200

U

Ukraine 24, 27, 162
Ukrainian DPs
  Australia selects 63, 64, 74
  camps in Europe 31–32
  from Eastern and Western Ukraine 24, 25
  experience in Europe 9, 22, 26–27, 30, 39
  national mission of exiles 160
  resettlement 48–49
  as stateless 36
unemployment 76–77
United Kingdom *see* Britain
United Nations 54, 60–61
United Nations Convention Relating to the Status of Refugees (1951) 41
United Nations Relief and Rehabilitation Administration 6, 18–21, 62
  attitudes to DPs 34
  Australia as signatory 53
  discontinues assistance 35
  IRO formed to replace 39
  IRO review of cases 40
  psychology of DPs 34–35
  Soviet DPs 38
United States *see also* Cold War

Allied occupation zones 17–18, 21
American migrants 53
anti-communism 157
DPs as labour 43–44, 45
DPs resettle in 6, 12, 43, 68, 110–111
IRO 39
Ležák-Borin 179
Nazi collaborators 37–38
Yalta Agreement 3, 22, 25, 38
UNRRA *see* United Nations Relief and Rehabilitation Administration
Untaru, Constantin 162–163, 169
Uranquinty riot 89

V

Venezuela 7
Vera (Borin's daughter) 174, 176
Vera (pseudonym) 10, 11
Vietnam 183
Visvaldis 136–137
Vyshinskii, Andrei 29

W

war criminals 39, 68–69, 157, 158, 162, 167, 169, 200
War Workers Housing Trust 77
wartime manpower scheme 77
Wentworth, William Charles 169
West Germany 183
White, Thomas 91
White Australia Policy
  culture and 113
  deportation of Asians and Pacific Islanders 53
  government propaganda 116–117
  nation building and cultural diversity 187
  race and 10, 45–46, 52, 60–61
White Russians 164
Whitlam Labor Government 183, 186–187
Williams, Katarzyna Kwapisz 152
Wills, Sara 196
Witting, Amy 191
Wladimir (pseudonym) 10, 27, 101
women DPs
  camps in Australia 84–85
  shortage for single men 133–134
  widows, deserted wives and unmarried mothers 73, 87–88
  in work camps 96
Woodside (SA) camp 78
World Refugee Year (1959–60) 47

Y
Yallourn North
  as 'hot Siberia' 105
  Rankin Affair 167–168
Yalta Agreement 3, 5, 22, 25, 38
YMCA & YWCA 123–124
Yugoslavia 157, 183
Yugoslavian DPs 39, 44, 62, 64, 74, 158

Z
Zabukovec, Victoria 90, 100–101, 190
Zahalka, Anne 192
Zofia (pseudonym)

www.ingramcontent.com/pod-product-compliance
Lightning Source LLC
Chambersburg PA
CBHW031725230426
43669CB00007B/251